HARVARD
DIARY II

HARVARD DIARY II

ESSAYS ON THE SACRED AND THE SECULAR

ROBERT COLES

A Crossroad Book
The Crossroad Publishing Company
New York

1997

The Crossroad Publishing Company
370 Lexington Avenue, New York, NY 10017

Printed in the United States of America

ISBN 0-8245-1649-4
Library of Congress Catalog Card Number 96-72495

J. H. C.

Contents

Introduction

WITH THE APPEARANCE of this second volume of *Harvard Diary*, sixteen years will have passed since I began writing a monthly column with this book's title, and nine years since the first volume appeared. I had no idea, from the start, what specific subjects I would attend in those columns, nor had I any right to think I'd be given the time and the editorial permission to keep writing about what matters to me — novels and what we learn from them, moral and spiritual questions. Indeed, for a couple of years (from May 1992 to June 1994) I stopped writing the column, because I was struggling with enough low back pain (sciatica) to slow me down — and, maybe, make me cranky, not a good state of mind to inform essays meant to draw upon one's daily thoughts, worries, concerns. When my back improved, my mind also became less cramped — and I was most glad to be able to resume those monthly efforts to write down what seemed important to me, in hopes thereby of connecting with readers, as writers seek to do, but also, I must say, so that I myself would learn what I believe, what truly is of consequence to me.

I hope that last remark won't trouble those who come upon it! These days the social sciences, with their dense, elaborate, sometimes overwrought theoretical constructs, dominate our way of thinking about ourselves and others — a mix of psychological and sociological formulations as a lens through which we are to view the world around us. No wonder, then, my students write extended outlines of what they think, what they are hoping, trying to say before they dare start writing their actual papers. No wonder they want to explore this or that "methodology" before they commit themselves to a point of view: a self-consciousness dictated by a culture's imprint on our sense of how we ought to think — the notion that we ought to call upon ideological hypotheses and postulates, let them determine the direction of a presentation of ideas, speculations. God forbid that one sit at a desk and let one's mind wander and wonder; that one take seriously what William James called its "booming, buzzing confusion"; that one learn from what one has sensed, experienced, remembered; that one allow the head to settle into a train of thought, put it down on paper — then, lo, discover what seems significant to oneself. All that is, of course, rampant impressionism, unbridled subjectivity — hence thoroughly dubious, suspect.

I recall William Carlos Williams taking up this matter of the personal, the idiosyncratic, as against the so-called objective — the latter a major claim, naturally, of some psychologists, sociologists, with their eagerness to be connected to what gets called "science." He was mulling over the biggest subject — how we get to understand others — and he expressed himself this way: "I hope I wasn't ranting when I kept saying [in his greatest, longest poem, *Paterson*] 'no ideas but things.' I'll tell you, I have watched us get so full of ourselves in this century, and we're only half way through it [the year was 1953]. The more we call on abstractions, on ideas unconnected to something we've seen, someone we know, the more we surrender ourselves to those ideas, lose our experiencing self as the means by which we try to figure out what's going on, what's happening around us."

There was much more, an extended "rap" of sorts, which had me entranced, but at the same time (I was in medical school, learning all sorts of "ideas"!), anxious, even fearful. A poet's "wildness" may be provocative, suggestive — but as today's saying goes: give me the facts, man, the facts! Yet, he *was* giving me a huge "fact," indeed — I would gradually realize — he was letting me know of the hazards that a kind of culturally inflated and prized rationalism can present to us: the notion, for instance, that there is a "value-free" kind of analysis (or psychoanalysis) that requires no acknowledgment of one's own assumptions, one's adventures and encounters, as they constantly live in the mind, a private brew of sorts that gives more shape to what we take seriously, to how we think, and, yes, how we express ourselves, than (these days) we are wont to acknowledge. The "things" that Dr. Williams kept mentioning are the concrete instances that are forever ours to witness, to absorb as part of our life's continuing felt experience. Insofar as we won't let that kind of daily mental activity, human activity, come to bear on our expressed life, inform what we acknowledge to be our thoughts (in our declared statements, our school papers, our letters, not to mention our research proposals, our articles and books) then we are, well, maybe, blind to ourselves, let alone others, that "other" of the world's "things," with which Dr. Williams kept exhorting us to connect.

I fear the foregoing is a long, self-justifying windup to what follows in this book — a mind's discursive, even rambling expository efforts to comprehend various aspects of a late twentieth-century American life as it has been lived by a doctor, a teacher, a husband, a father, and, not least, a citizen who has had good reason to worry about the country to which he belongs, and which he was brought up to love, and does love, all our troubles and flaws not withstanding. In no time the reader will find quite apparent that concern and, at times, that alarm: the essays on our so-called underclass and, too, the essays on our nation's shifting social and cultural climate — the cheapness, the coarseness, and worse that increasingly impose themselves on us if we put on our television sets, go to the movies, and, yes, pick up our so-called "better," more influential magazines. From Hollywood to Washington to Manhattan the pursuit of celebrity and of notoriety is everywhere in evidence — a constant emphasis on movie stars and political stars and rock stars that contributes mightily, alas, to what the late Christopher Lasch called "a culture of narcissism." Nor, I worry, have our intellectuals, our professors and writers, been altogether removed from this scene, wherein whim and fancy become powerfully persuasive, only to yield to the next preoccupation, fad. A secular world fiercely intent on itself as the be-all and end-all, both, takes whomever and whatever it can lay its hands on, moment after moment, all grist for its idolatrous mill. Under such circumstances, actually, drugs become a peculiarly appropriate, if legally illicit (so far!), companion to this broader cultural climate — its highs, one after the other. The holy self, in general, gets exalted through a succession, a procession of such selves paraded before us on film, in photographs, in words of rave — and there are academic "stars" as well as the kind who sing songs, win elections, take part in talk-shows, sit-coms, movies, athletic events: the high of the worshiping fan, abuzz, if not wild, with enthusiastic (even orgiastic) commitment to this or that big shot, become a passing demigod, matched by the high of the drug-user, who learns physiologically a sensation that, again, has its psychological, cultural counterpart. The ups and downs of trends become trendiness as a way of life: clothes, food, travel, interests, and hobbies all summoned to give one a sense of belonging, of membership in a world, even as that world constantly shifts with respect to what is upheld, what is forsaken, even regarded with contempt.

I don't enjoy offering such an account of contemporary life in the United States. I know, too, that there is substantial resistance to this consumerist, materialist secular world — a yearning on the part of many of us for what used to be called "social ethics," the living out, daily, of certain values, such as respect for others, a thoughtfulness and kindness that has the flesh of deeds. Moreover, we hunger for a sanctioned inwardness, a chance to think privately and with others about what this life means and, again, how we ought to live it. Here religion ought to be our great refuge, and, too, the theater, and the books of the moral and social imagination which our poets, our writers of fiction, our essayists send our way. Yet, all too often, in our churches and synagogues the banalities, even the crudities of the secular world become triumphantly present, to no one's apparent embarrassment — the clergy as television celebrities, as self-conscious psychologists or sociologists, ever ready to stay "with it," mouth the pieties, the catch-words of the moment. No wonder mention of "sin" is almost a cause for embarrassment (certainly, for perplexity) in many of our religious circles and, of course, in the lecture halls and seminar rooms of our colleges and universities, where relativism and deconstructionist criticism make a mockery of any person's struggle to find a faith that persuades, convinces, and even a mockery of the attempts that particular novelists, or poets or short story writers have made to find meaning in life, and render it through words, through images, through narration that bespeaks of, well, the utter essence of their humanity: we are the creature of language, and through it a moral awareness that gives us a sense of the ought, the naught.

I try in the pages ahead to take up such matters, to discuss those legendary "seven sins" of yore as they continue, in disguised or unacknowledged ways, to exert themselves in our everyday lives. I try, as well, to keep learning from my students, from those whom I "interview" (speak with) in connection with my "research" (my attempt to learn about this world through the help of my fellow human beings, now called "informants," a word that is quite appropriate if taken literally, but a word sadly laden with abstractly patronizing connotations — a lower order of "them," who set up us big-deal "experts," we who tell the *real* score in our reports, papers, textbooks).

Most important to me are the novelists who, thank God, are still with us, to give us balance and proportion, not to mention the earned wisdom to which storytelling makes them privy. Many of the "entries" to which this "diary" (this series of essays written in a particular working setting, hence the place-name attached to the diary) deal with one or another piece of fiction as it has turned a reader's mind, got it reflectively going, stirred it to worry and hope, amused it wryly or alarmed it considerably. All the time I call upon Raymond Carver or Ralph Ellison or Shusaku Endo or Toni Morrison or Graham Greene in my teaching life, in my personal life, as I sort things out, try to estimate what truly counts, what matters little, no matter the press of opinion in its favor at the moment — and so, I would naturally turn to the work of those writers as I sat down to pen these columns, these expressions, I hope and pray, of someone's attempted inwardness as it seeks moral and spiritual direction, purpose.

Many of these essays originally appeared in the *New Oxford Review,* one or two in a different form than is presented here. I no longer write for that magazine, but I thank its editor, Dale Vree, for his constant encouragement. I've added two pieces of writing (on Endo's *Deep River* and on a biography by Edward Hopper) that appeared in the *New York Times* and the *Washington Post*, respectively, because I had marked them in my head for the column I then wrote for the *New Oxford Review* (also titled "Harvard Diary"), only to be asked to write on those subjects by the aforementioned other publications. I have also added, at the end of these pages, five essays that I wrote for this book—matter very much on my mind as I was preparing the manuscript for publication.

I thank Michael Leach for his warm editorial interest in these essays, for the rallying attentiveness he showed to these various efforts on my part to figure out what I believe and why. I also thank my colleagues, my students, my patients, and, not least, my family for all those men and women have taught me. It has been a privilege to be able to take leave of my ongoing life, as it were, to write these essays, and through that activity to be given pause about these last years of the second millennium, as they all too quickly present themselves for our witness, our engagement.

Children and Media Violence

F OR MANY YEARS I've tried to figure out what, if anything, happens to children when they watch television shows that are full of assaults, shootings, killing; or when they see movies of a similar nature; or when they watch rock videos or go to rock concerts that offer violent themes, not to mention violent language. I keep reading the social science journals on the subject, the pediatric ones, those put out for child psychiatrists. I go to meetings where the subject is discussed. Yet, I still find the entire question of the effect of media violence on the young a hard one to deal with — especially when I'm asked to come up with reasonably clear-cut conclusions.

For one thing, and this is very important, children vary enormously. Some lucky children are being brought up, even today, in homes where television is only a controlled presence in the entire family's life. Those same children aren't permitted, either, to go running to any old film that happens to be playing at the nearby movie house, nor do video cassettes pile up in their living rooms. The parents of such children may be religious, and determined for that reason to consider carefully what their children see, or they may be quite secular in many respects, yet offended by various television shows or movies, and anxious to keep them out of their children's sight for a mix of moral and psychological reasons.

Some parents often find it hard to decide what legal steps, if any, ought to be taken to deal with television shows or films which they clearly regard as undesirable for their children, if not potentially hurtful to them. As I go from home to home, talking with boys and girls, I find the dilemma of such parents interesting to hear, and often eloquently put. A mother, a father, ruminating about what a son or daughter ought or ought not to be watching and why, can manage to touch upon many of the ethical or constitutional conflicts the nation as a whole is struggling to comprehend, to resolve. When the speaker is a lawyer, much interested in the rights of the individual, but also the father of three children under twelve, the discussion can get quite intense as well as edifying: "We try to keep my kids away from most of television, but we don't want to turn a prohibition into a source of temptation. Our son's friends watch those Saturday morning cartoons, one after the other. They are such junk — and full of craziness

15

and violence, if you ask me. Even the ads — a brainwashing for the kids: buy sugar of all kinds, and eat it all day long! But we decided not to turn those programs into 'a federal case'; we told our son he can watch 'one or two.' I watch them with him, because I'm home then. He knows how I feel. Sometimes he'll watch two in a row; usually, he'll watch one, and then I can tell he's ready to quit. He'll give me a quick look, and I'll suggest we go downtown to do errands. He's quick to say yes!

"My nephew is fifteen, and he's seen lots of rock videos. We can get a lot of stuff on cable. My brother [a businessman] asks me what to do. I say: 'Tell him [the nephew] what your limits are, and why you're setting them.' But then I look at my son [who is ten] and ask what I'll be saying in a few years. Even now, he'll look at that cable stuff sometimes. Should we get rid of cable? Should we get rid of our VCR? Should we in the future tell our kids not to buy certain [rock music] tapes? I'm not in favor of 'censorship'; I'm not wanting to ban magazines and tapes and movies and videos, or to set up 'watch-dog committees.' We can take care of ourselves — in this family. There may be flak; it may be tough, at times — but we can manage. But I'll be in town and see kids — they're thirteen, fifteen, sixteen, maybe — flipping through those magazines [he mentioned *Penthouse* in another conversation] and playing those tapes, right out there on the streets, wearing the earphones, and I begin to waver. I get thoughts I'd never want to defend in a constitutional law class. I see albums like The Dead Kennedys or WASP, and I say to my brother: 'draw the line.' In our town there's an agreement: the drugstores don't sell *Playboy,* never mind other stuff. But kids go to Boston. They get what they want. They get people to buy booze and drugs for them; they get the magazines they want, and the videos and tapes. They flip on the TV, and even in the sit-coms, people are blowing other people up, the machine guns rat-tat-tatting away. And the flicks — *Rambo;* they must be making *Rambo Ten* by now. It's all crazy, and if you're a parent you wonder what it all means — what it'll do to your kids. That's the big question. What?"

My answer to him, frankly, would be: not all that much — because he and his wife are devoted, attentive parents, with ample means at their disposal to help engage their children in a wide range of activities and interests. This is a family that assembles for evening meals, goes to church on Sundays, goes skiing and ice-skating in winter, has a much used summer home, takes an annual vacation to one or another spot here or abroad. This is a family that will not abandon its children, when they are teenagers, to the streets, suburban or urban. Most important, this a family whose mother happens to be a high school teacher (and a Sunday school teacher, as well) and whose father knows when to stop working and go home in order — as he once wryly put it — "to start working again," as a parent who doesn't booze it up all the time, or snort coke, or in general behave in such a way that more than sets the stage for such influences as the rock group WASP, which stands for "We Are Sexual Perverts."

But not all families, obviously, can take on with any hope of success the kind of influences which worry even the father I just quoted. I visit children in homes where television is a parent of sorts — a box of sound and pictures which holds children in its commanding orbit for hour upon hour, day after day. The mother may be a teenager, and herself a constant watcher; or the mother may be at work, leaving older children to take care of younger ones — meaning, for all of them, long spells with soaps and sit-coms and cartoons and the endless rock video performances cable networks offer. If the family has a father, and he has a job, he comes home tired, and often as not himself takes to the television set — a formidable, hypnotic presence, indeed. In such homes the lawyer's question — what will such an exposure to media sex and violence mean? — becomes a real challenge. I sometimes sit in those homes, with those children, and wonder what does happen to them as they see people zapping other people in cartoons; as they see people gunning down other people on various television programs; as they listen to rock lyrics such as these, offered by The Motley Crue, which has a wide following: "I'll either break her face / Or take down her legs, / Get my ways at will. / Go for the throat, / Never let loose, / Going in for the kill."

I could fill pages with such lyrics, which millions of young Americans hear (on records), or both see and hear (on rock video cassettes or cable television). When Anna Freud was alive, in the early 1980s, I would show her such lyrics and tell her about some of the children I knew who listened to them. "Surely," she said once, aghast, "they don't really pay much attention to the words." She was hoping against hope that it was the music that really mattered to those youngsters — the wild orgiastic rhythms which bestirred them. She was convinced that anyone "reasonably normal," as she put it, would not want to pay significant heed to the madness and hate and meanness, the constant resort to images of murder, rape, and sexual perversity which those children were, in fact, seeing or hearing expressed in movies, on television, and on stereos. She mentioned "denial," one of the "mechanisms of defense" which she had studied closely in the course of a clinician's long life of work with children and adolescents.

But I had to point out that those children weren't in fact practicing "denial" — a refusal to let into their everyday consciousness a comprehension of the violence to which they were exposed, not to mention the "polymorphous (sexual) perversity," to use a phrase given us by Anna Freud's father. Again and again I have seen children wince, or look aghast, or smile ironically, or shake their heads, or look at one another with anxiety or fear, or a mix of curiosity and perplexity, as they have heard lyrics such as "I kill children, / I love to see them die. / I kill children, / I make their mothers cry." The big question, of course, is what happens to the minds of children who experience such a continual awareness — thousands of hours listening to junk lines or demented ones, thousands of hours observing blatant pornography and murders and rapes and outbursts of various kinds of sadism? Do they become violent, sexually disturbed, morally debased? Do they shrug off such media exposure — in a sense, proving Miss Freud in the long run correct? That is, do their lives not give ongoing daily (or even sporadic) evidence of being shaped and distorted by the above-mentioned looking and listening they do?

We read of a Michael Ryan, running amok in an English village, killing sixteen, wounding fourteen, doing so with a semi-automatic rifle and dressed in such a manner that onlookers thought Rambo had suddenly arrived out of nowhere — and we wonder what role, indeed, various films might have had in such a tragedy. But psychotic mass murderers have been with us long before today's omnipresent tellys and moving picture shows and youthful rock culture. Nor are the many efforts of social scientists to understand these matters all that helpful when it comes to the ultimate question of daily conduct. No question, often enough children exposed to repeated violence absorb that violence in various ways — register their experiences in the thoughts they have, the daydreams and, yes, the nightmares. But what psychologists create in classrooms or laboratories is not to be equated with what obtains in the lives of people. I know children who are exposed to plenty of media violence — and yet are thoughtful, decent, and well behaved. I do, however, know other children whose overall lives are in psychological jeopardy and who, in consequence, are all too vulnerable to the violence and sexual promiscuity, the emotional lunacy, they see and hear through the courtesy of modern technology. Already hurt, frightened, with poor prospects because of their social or racial background or their family experience, they can be seen copying the attire worn by a particular actor in a movie, can be heard reciting some awful lyrics — such as these words I heard recently: "Out go the lights / In goes my knife / Pull out his life / Consider that bastard dead." I inquired and found that we owe such unforget-table lines to The Motley Crue. The youth I heard speaking them has hurt no one but himself, and I suspect he will always be the major target of his own despair — a psychological inclination not caused by The Motley Crue, though they have helped many, one suspects, to discharge plenty of bile.

We all ought to be wondering, however, whether at a certain point in time, perhaps approaching us, the amount and intensity of media violence (including the sexual kind) will make a decisive cultural and psychological difference in our children's lives — affecting more and more of them in harmful ways. Even my lawyer friend, mentioned above, wondered how many in our society can escape the general impact of what the media increasingly give us — the effect on our sense of propriety and decorum, at a minimum, of all the sleaze sent our way by certain movie makers, television producers, rock groups, and so on.

Recently I read Tipper Gore's book *Raising Up Kids in an X-Rated Society.* It is, I think, first-rate — an effort on the part of a concerned mother to point out in precise detail what it is our children are be-ing offered by our so-called entertainment industry. Her analysis of the repetitive themes that keep appearing is thoughtfully done — the violence, the celebration of drugs, the bitterness and the preoccupa-tion in some quarters with nihilism, suicide, wanton promiscuity, and the appalling meanness, especially toward women. She furnishes the specific words used. She tells us of the efforts some have made not to institute censorship, but to make sure, at a minimum, that parents know what it is their children are seeing and hearing. She knows, of course, that those children who are at the greatest risk psychologically may well not have parents who are going to search out the often small type of an advisory warning. Still, she wants us all, as a nation, to begin making certain distinctions — and for so doing has incurred the suspicions, if not the scorn, of some entertainers and their business as-sociates. Perhaps because her husband is a U.S. Senator and has been running for the presidency, these critics (they do not include promi-nent civil libertarians, who have been appreciative of her efforts) have been especially jittery and nasty in their remarks.

There most clearly are political implications to what Mrs. Gore in-tends — and to the response she has received from her adversaries. It seems easier for Republicans to make the kind of criticisms she has leveled at a prominent part of our media and the climate of expres-sion it spawns. Many liberal Democrats, like my lawyer friend, shy away from the kind of firm stand against violence and pornography

Mrs. Gore makes in her book. All too many Democrats confine their righteousness to economic or foreign policy issues — as if the everyday moral struggles of ordinary families are beneath their scrutiny. Richard Nixon and Ronald Reagan, among others, have had no such reservations — and haven't, as a consequence, suffered all that much at the polls.

Moreover, the question of class figures prominently in this ongoing debate. With some success, Republicans have persuaded many voters that the socially privileged Democratic cadre — people who are the ideological architects of their party — has scant interest in many of the social and moral concerns of poor and working-class people. That lawyer once told me that his education, his job, and his money give him and his wife the time and the personal and economic leeway that enable their children to be "protected," as he put it, from the consequences of media violence, if not lunacy. But many other parents have no such control over their own lives, never mind their children's — and yet yearn for certain moral changes in this country, while fearing that those changes will never take place. This is why Mrs. Gore's observations are important and will be welcomed by many American parents.

April 1988

– 2 –

A Testing from God?

F OR MANY YEARS my mother and father went to hear the Boston
Symphony Orchestra on Friday afternoons. They loved doing
so, and over time managed to establish some firm and satisfying habits
for themselves. My dad would leave their downtown apartment, located on the waterfront, and walk briskly along some nearby streets,
often stopping to look at ships, engage in conversations with parents
and children similarly drawn to an interesting harbor scene. He was a
great observer and walker. He was born in Yorkshire, England, where
walking can be a sport, and had been a champion walker as a youth.
I have fond memories of trying to keep up with him as a child —
the fast pace of movement and the shrewd social and cultural observations as he took in everything, it seemed, and tried to make sense
of what he saw in pointed language a touch exotic in sound because
of his slight English accent. Even in his middle eighties (he died two
years ago at eighty-six) he walked long and hard until a last, brief illness took him. On Fridays, "symphony day" for him and my mother
forever, it seemed, he'd be out walking early, about eight o'clock, and
eventually would make his way to one of several restaurants he and
my mother had frequented over the decades before their joint walk
to Symphony Hall. The entire city of Boston seemed safely his for
exploration, and he grew to know and love that city.

My mother was far less interested in walking. Even on a delight-
fully warm but dry and bracing spring day she was content to "put
in a mile," to use a phrase my father often summoned, rather than his
six or eight. She loved finding a park bench; she loved feeding pigeons
out of a bag of peanuts, and remembering her sons cracking peanuts
when they, with her, rode the well-known swan boats in Boston's Public Garden, or when they sat and watched the Red Sox — oh, the ups
and downs of that love in a family's life! — keep trying to prevail. She
had her own shrewd capacity to take stock of people, places, things —
but she was quiet about her mind's activity, and far less interested than
her husband in sharing her thoughts with others. A ready, warm smile
was her way of greeting the world. A constant willingness to extend
herself on behalf of others was her way of indicating that the point of
her soft-spoken, even reticent manner was not stoic aloofness or self-

contained hauteur, but a certain skepticism about mere words, their flashiness, the boasting they occasionally do.

She was a generous person; she trusted people; she was ever prepared to help strangers who needed help — pick up a toy a child of strangers had dropped, serve people in soup kitchens, teach (as a volunteer) boys and girls going to woefully inadequate schools. "Your mother is a truly modest lady," the doorman to the building where they lived once told me, and I always thought the compliment was not only earned (and spoken with heartfelt appreciation) but of a kind she truly deserved — from someone who had occasion to know well the virtues and vices of innumerable people, and from someone she liked: no fancy airs, for sure, and himself one who silently did things for others all day long. On Fridays, as my father worked his walking way toward a restaurant, my mother would, to use an expression of hers, "have a gab" with that doorman, or with a man who sold flowers on a street corner near the apartment, or with a waitress in a small cafeteria who served her coffee. Unlike my dad, she would usually take a cab to their place of chosen assignation, usually decided upon on the spur of the moment, as the one left for his ambulatory challenge and the other lingered over yet another short story or chapter in a novel.

In 1985, both in their eighties, they were still following such a routine, no matter the snow and ice, the blasts of Arctic air which hit Bostonians hard in January and February of that year. One Friday morning in February each of them set out, hoping to meet the other at noon. It was a terribly cold day, and a six-inch snowfall had covered the streets of the city. Lingering ice from previous storms made any journey even more arduous and treacherous. Nevertheless, my dad stepped from the apartment building and made his way through the financial district, then the streets which offered department stores or somewhat smaller specialty shops, on his way to a fine hotel's most pleasant dining room. As he walked he wondered about his wife — whether she'd hazard so much as one step into the winter mess he was negotiating; or whether, more likely, a cab would bring her from home right to the restaurant. He decided that they would both certainly ride a taxi to Symphony Hall rather than pursue their customary after-lunch walk. He wondered, though, whether a taxi would be available. The weather was "bad," and few people were braving the elements in his manner. He even began to wonder whether his wife would arrive for lunch. She, too, might have trouble catching a cab. She could go take the subway, but to do so would have to walk a mile or so, no mean feat that day for her. He decided to call home, learn if she had stayed there or had returned rather than fight the weather and its consequences. No one answered the phone. She was somewhere in the city on her way to meet him. Good luck had graced her with a cab, he concluded. Some cabbies, he mused, will go out of their way to favor an old woman battling a fierce wind, coats of ice everywhere, a substantial snow.

In fact, she had decided to walk. There was a charge to the wind that she found appealing. She had woken up tired, but as the doorman let her outside, she felt wide awake for the first time that day. Moreover, she didn't like his assumption that she wanted a cab: "It'll take a half hour or so for one," he told her. "No," she replied, she wanted to walk, and would, and did. She girded herself, stepped forth, heard her mind wonder whether her heart would give out (she had suffered a heart attack five years earlier), but also heard herself say that a mile was really no problem for her, if she took her time. One block, then another — and soon enough she would see the subway station looming, its invitation boldly announced with a new sign.

The streets seemed empty, and she got a boost from that fact: others were intimidated by what was not in the least scary or inhibiting to her. She plowed on — one step, then another, careful each time not to slip, eyes intent on what was immediately ahead of her.

Suddenly she was conscious of her ears rather than her eyes. She slowed down, stopped watching, listened: steps behind her, fast moving steps. She moved her attention back to her eyes, but wanted them to look backward rather than forward. A turn of her neck. A fast glance: a man moving along behind her, catching up with her. Now her mind became agitated. She wondered what to do: keep walking; step into the street and hope a car would appear, so that she could try to flag it down; stop in her tracks and wait in hopes that acquiescence — as she had once heard — is the best policy? She decided to keep moving, but her heart was not in the decision. Her head, meanwhile, was conscious now of her right hand, its contents: a pocketbook. "He's black," she kept saying to herself. "After he's gone, I'll go back home," she found herself thinking — and then, he was there, right next to her, just as they both stood at the corner of a street.

For a second she searched the roads — but no traffic. No pedestrians nearby, either. Her hand released the pocketbook, just as the young man asked her if he might help her cross the street. When he saw the black leather pocketbook on the snow, he picked it up, gave it to her. Her hand trembled as she took it; she managed to look in his eyes for a second; she tried even to smile, but her face's muscles wouldn't respond. She felt his hand on her left elbow, as he guided her across the street. For the first time during that walk, she pictured herself falling, landing on some ice, even losing consciousness. In a few seconds, though, she was on the sidewalk, and the young man had bid her goodbye with that expression she had noticed more and more people use: "Have a good day." She tried to say something similar. She tried to say thank you. But now it was her voice that had turned unresponsive. She shuddered as she fought off a thought which nevertheless crossed her eighty-one-year-old mind: "Ought I have tried to give him something?" A second later she had pushed that question away, and replaced it with nothing.

She walked until she got to the subway, rather enjoyed the steep steps down, the ride to the station nearest the hotel where, she knew, her husband awaited her. On the train her mind took her South, to warm weather and beaches she remembered from youthful trips. At lunch with her husband she was quiet, to the point that he wondered if she was "all right." The answer she gave him went like this: "I thought I was until today." He pursued the matter medically, and got nowhere. She always had been a bit elliptical and moody at times, he reminded himself. He successfully diverted her with serious talk of financial matters.

"All during the Brahms Requiem I thought of that young man," she later told me. Then she added, "I prayed that God didn't have time to notice me." When I asked her what she meant by that remark, she explained tersely: "I'm close to meeting Him, and I'm sure this morning I didn't improve my chances of staying near Him for very long." As I tried to reassure her a bit, she stepped further into mystical speculation: had He tested her — as surely He does with each of us all along? "Maybe," was my feeble reply.

May 1988

– 3 –

Sinner Swaggart and Our Smugness

WHEN MY WIFE AND I read of preacher Jimmy Swaggart's abrupt decline into the role of a public sinner, we remembered the hold he has had on so many people we have known, not only in our country's South, but the South that stretches from the Rio Grande Valley way down to the Strait of Magellan. So many families we have met over the years have found Swaggart's performing skill irresistible. He has a way of collaring his listeners and viewers, insinuating his hyped-up alarm and foreboding into their nervous systems. He has a way of hitting a home run with his hysteria, evoking it in others, proving what Freud learned in the Vienna of 1900 — that passions denied at home or in the workplace can suddenly burst forth, inexplicably or in response to something...or someone. It is all too easy for someone like me to pursue the above line of psychoanalytic thinking, to render a discourse on the contagious power of religious emotionality on certain kinds of psychologically vulnerable people. It's rather easy, as well, to join the ranks of those who prefer a more sociological or economic or cultural mode of analysis — the ignorance and impotence, the near desperation, the edge of despair in so many men and women who can take little, indeed, for granted, who live in constant debt or with no hope of any real security, any sense of achievement. To pursue such inquiry is to risk the cool, confident self-importance of the quite privileged intellectual — one more "them" to comprehend, maybe pity, maybe keep at a distance as a negative drag on the kind of enlightened politics my kind proudly tries to favor and practice.

As I tried to discuss the foregoing with a few friends "up here" (in New England) as opposed to "down there" (in Louisiana) — ah, the occasional symmetry of language and egotism — I was met with a barrage of skepticism, if not scorn. Swaggart is a phony, a manipulative fraud, an exploiter of sorts. He rakes in millions, lives high off the hog, exudes contrived bombast, offers hurt and ailing people — well, the list is familiar — an opiate; false consciousness; illusions; a crutch; or as a friend of mine, a decent, hardworking psychoanalyst whose liberal politics and sane rationality I admire, put it in his quiet, understated Jamesian way, "some dubious satisfactions, indeed." Yes,

yes, I want to say, and do say — but. I stop with that small qualifying word, have trouble spelling out what "but" is meant to announce.

I am tempted, maybe, by my own condescensions, but certainly by my own memories — all those fervent people I've met, hard praying and hard working and poor as can be, with few prospects. Especially I remember the rural folk I've met in Nicaragua, or the *favelados* in Brazil — for whom Swaggart is the messenger of the existential Christ, as opposed to the sacramental or ecclesiastical Christ, not to mention the Christ endlessly examined by smart theologians: "I hear him [Swaggart] and I see Him, our Jesus — sweating and crying and trying 'to do right by God, Who sent Him here to suffer, the way we do. In his voice [Swaggart's] you can hear Jesus getting upset, and getting ready to fight all His enemies. I will look up at Him [the "well-known statue of Jesus, arms outstretched, atop a Rio de Janeiro mountain] when I hear this man from the North [Swaggart] telling us to watch out, because God will soon come here and straighten everything out."

She dearly wishes for that day to come, when a leveling will take place, when a topsy-turvy change will happen, when "the last shall be first, the first last." So it goes — an excited populism in the mind of this impoverished mother of seven, who has lost other children to miscarriages and to the deaths that go with hunger and malnutrition. She lives in a hillside shack which lacks adequate sanitation or clean drinking water. For her Swaggart offers a direct, energetic encounter with biblical emotion — unmediated by institutional coolness or arrogance. She explained her response to me once — after I had taken pains to tell her, in a soft-spoken but pointed aside, that this big-shot television evangelist, who pressed Jesus on half a billion people, lives like a king on the proceeds of all the humble families who pour out what little they have into his coffers: "Maybe he does live big. I don't mind. Look at all the people who live big, and they don't care about Jesus, or about us, either. They only care about themselves. I'm sure he [Swaggart] is a sinner, like you and me. But he speaks to us. We're sinners, too. The others [she pointed toward Ipanema and Copacabana, the affluent, educated secular world] don't give us a glance. They only call us their names — think bad of us. I'll take Swaggart the sinner to them."

I had my rejoinder, perhaps the same one many readers of these words would immediately summon. I reminded this woman of no schooling and no work and no money that Swaggart was not only rich, he was a hypocrite — pretending righteousness, yet shrewdly a self-promoter who drives fancy cars, lives in a mansion, wields plenty of power on his own behalf. I was not harsh, simply factual and a bit melancholy in the tone I used, as was the translator who gave her the thoughts and observations in Portuguese. She was not to be educated (or patronized), however. She told me that she assumed Swaggart did not live like her. A silence, as I digested that brief moment of wry understatement. Then, her outburst again — at the Catholic Church, and all its wealth, splendor, power; at some university sociologists and government officials, who keep coming to the *favela* and keep making various suggestions, but who deliver nothing tangible to her and others she knows; most of all once again, at the well-to-do people who live in the fancy neighborhoods of Rio de Janeiro, and who (she knows) would love to have the *favela* where she lives "cleared" — out of sight, out of mind.

My mind went back several years to those talks with her and others like her as I thought of Jimmy Swaggart prowling the seedy motels of the old Airline Highway, outside of New Orleans, the "city that care forgot," the city of so many sinners — and like those who sin in other cities, they are not just strippers or errant, hypocritical preachers. I remembered how "respectable" people, even those who ran newspapers and universities, didn't stand up to the mobs that heckled black children going into the once all-white schools of New Orleans, even as in my native Boston all sorts of respectable folks keep an arm's distance between themselves and the hard-pressed life of the city's white and black people alike. In our comfortable parlors, with our educated tongues, we deplore so many people, not only the Swaggarts of this world, but all who attend them, and all who aren't quite "up" to us — a pride, a sinful pride. Was my mother wrong when she admonished us children that of all sins, pride is the worst? Exactly how does one weigh the various sins: sinner Swaggart's sexual transgressions as against the smugness of self-satisfaction of some of us liberals who think we know what is best for everyone, who judge without worrying about being judged, and who call everyone to account, with no forgiveness in our vocabulary — except, of course, for ourselves?

June 1988

– 4 –

Preachers and Politics

WHEN I WAS A BOY I remember my mother reading the *Catholic Worker*, paying much attention to the message Dorothy Day and Peter Maurin offered — an everyday kind of Christianity meant to be lived in the secular world, and a Christianity with decidedly political concerns: to lobby, picket, protest, to stir up others in support of this, against that. I also remember my father listening on Sunday afternoon to the speeches of a Catholic priest from some place called Royal Oak, Michigan: Father Charles Coughlin. My mother disliked him, called him a "rabble-rouser." My father disliked him, called him "dangerous" — yet listened to him every week, and, I could tell, was somewhat fascinated by his passionate oratory.

I was six or seven, but I sure recall my father telling my mother that Father Coughlin was "saying things" a lot of people think but don't dare express. I recall, too, asking my father himself to "say things" — to spell out what he had just somewhat cryptically mentioned. But he wouldn't, nor did my mother want him to. Children, of course, often suspect there is more to say, so to speak, than gets said — and are often disappointed after their push for candor.

Years later, in college, I encountered Father Coughlin again — now in a history course taught by a young assistant professor who was much interested in "populism": the yearnings and fears and resentments of ordinary so-called working-class people. We read C. Vann Woodward's *Tom Watson: Agrarian Rebel*. We read *Millhands and Preachers* and *All the King's Men*. We read William Carlos Williams's *Paterson* — his fiery blasts at the university world, with all its proud gentility and, not rarely, pietistic egoism. We also read about Father Coughlin and others who criticized the New Deal or corporate America from one or another angle of vision, whether of the "right" or the "left."

The professor made a point of emphasizing the religious aspect of some of that criticism — the populism, so he argued, in the Old Testament (the prophets Jeremiah and Isaiah and Amos) and the New Testament (Christ's angry confrontation with the money lenders, and His defiance of various "principalities and powers"). As I listened to that professor explain Father Coughlin's critique of American power — especially the early broadcasts of the priest's, before he

28

embraced anti-Semitism and thereby discredited himself with many who had heretofore attended him closely — I began to realize why my parents had been made so nervous by him but (in my father's case, at least) found him hard to ignore. They were living a fairly comfortable life and, with respect to my mother, a life grounded in conventional Christian pieties. Here was a man of the cloth who on nationwide radio invoked Christ against capitalists. Not that Dorothy Day didn't do the same thing — but few paid her much heed, so she was less a part of the nation's political life. Father Coughlin was heard by hundreds of thousands and had become, really, a preacher much involved in the politics of his day, the 1930s. I still remember (and nowadays I especially remember) what our professor said about priests and preachers in American politics: "There is a strong religious side to our political life, but it's always struggling to gain our attention, because there's also a strong suspicion of religion in our political life."

Such a remark, in retrospect, is not all that original or revealing — and yet, as I've watched television of late, contemplating the Reverend Jackson and the Reverend Robertson, and listening, as well, to the other candidates as they gingerly deal with (or try to avoid dealing with) the so-called social issues, I've been remembering that teacher and his effort to help us students understand the complex matter of religion and politics in American life.

In years of work done in the homes of ordinary people, black and white, Northern and Southern, living in the East or way out West, urban and rural, I have constantly heard strong moral and religious views expressed, and connected to our country's politics — to the point that I've often wondered why some populist with a religious sensibility hasn't emerged at some point as a powerful American leader. (Though Jimmy Carter called himself a "born-again Christian" and once or twice, early in his 1976 campaign, a "populist," he never really espoused a heartfelt struggle on behalf of some of the "family issues" to which some political ministers like to pay close heed, and his economic positions were "conservative" rather than "populist," meaning he was clearly anxious to join the American secular "power elite" rather than take sharp aim at it.) Here is a Massachusetts Methodist, not a Southern evangelical, talking to me in 1980: "I don't like politicians. I don't like these two [Reagan and Carter] running. They're each trying to get to you, but I don't trust them. They try to talk as if they're praying hard to God to follow His example, but they're not convincing me. They're not the kind of religious person I'd like to see in the White House. I don't mean a minister, no [I had asked]. I mean someone who really believed what Jesus did, and was ready to live the way He did, and stand up for what he believes the way He did."

No big chance of such a person appearing, that man hastened to tell me then; and I rather suspect he is not any more optimistic, in that regard, in 1988. Still, there is among us a continuing hunger for a politics that connects with certain moral and religious values, hence the appeal of Robertson to one constituency and Jackson to another. The black people with whom I have worked love their ministers, and love to envision them holding political power. Many so-called working-class white families I have come to know are less comfortable with the idea of a minister being an office-holder, but are hungry for the expression and advocacy of certain moral and religious values in our secular culture, and have kept listening to various candidates for some clue that such advocacy will be forthcoming. True, there's a big secular vote, too — people scared out of their minds by anyone who even mentions the Bible (Old or New Testaments, both), let alone calls upon it, calls upon God, in a serious manner (as opposed to lip-service at the end of a speech). Yet, even among such people one can hear a yearning for a spiritual side to politics. Driving home one afternoon I heard a caller on a talk show mock both Robertson and Jackson, not to mention Falwell, Bakker, Roberts, and Swaggart — then say he was fed up with all the rest of the candidates, too. Whom did he want then, the host asked — demanded, actually, with that cynical petulance one occasionally hears on such programs. Well, said the caller, he knew no one to suggest. A moment's silence. I thought we would soon enough hear another caller's eager, performing voice. But no, there was a sudden exclamation: "Someone who's truly a man of God, but he doesn't have to keep saying so, because then he ain't." I turned off the radio, to let that one sink in deep.

July–August 1988

- 5 -

The Legalization of Drugs?

I N THE LATE 1960s I worked with elementary school children and high school youths in a Boston ghetto. I talked with those young people in their homes, and also at school. I talked with their parents and teachers, too. I was doing a documentary kind of child psychiatry — trying to learn how ordinary lives unfolded in a particular neighborhood setting. I especially wanted to know what those boys and girls found to be important in life — their hopes, their beliefs, their values, their purposes, if any. As I did my work I couldn't help noticing the widespread presence and use of drugs in that neighborhood. As is the case now in our cities, so it was back then — all too many younger children "running" drugs for dealers, and all too many young men and women using one or another drug casually, if not compulsively.

Later, in the 1970s, I worked in well-do-do, mostly all-white neighborhoods — now talking with boys and girls whose parents had lots of money, and all sorts of diplomas to their credit. In those privileged towns I also encountered drugs — used by high schoolers, even junior high schoolers, with alarming nonchalance, and sometimes, I thought, a near suicidal intensity, frequency. In the ghetto, I noticed, many youths already hooked on drugs were ignored by the police or school authorities — as if the problem of drug abuse was already unsolvable in such neighborhoods. In the rather wealthy towns I noticed that most of the youngsters who used drugs also went about their ways secure from arraignment, let alone prosecution. The few who were fingered by the law — or by a teacher, a headmaster — were quickly sent to doctors like me for "treatment." By then I had concluded that the use of drugs had already become widespread enough to give pause to our police, our sheriffs and prosecutors, our school officials — make them try only for a circumspect and occasional enforcement of the law.

Now, a decade later, I read that we are in even worse shape with respect to the drug problem among our young people — so much so that a growing number of political and cultural figures in this country, conservatives as well as liberals, seriously advocate one or another version of legalization, on the supposition that at least enormous criminal excesses of various kinds will thereby be eliminated — drug distribu-

31

tion as a major law-breaking industry, and the hundreds of thousands of thefts and assaults, if not murders, which individual drug-users commit in the course of their addictive lives. "We must be realistic," I recently heard one law school professor say — and then his punch line: "Overnight we'll be rid of drug wars, and the crime rate will drop significantly, because people won't have to steal to maintain their habit." I have heard, in this regard, serious scholars, medical and legal both, suggest that publicly supported clinics simply dispense drugs to those who claim a need for them and *presto* no more mafia drug lords and no more drug-hungry (and crazed) street robbers.

Meanwhile, in the ghetto where I worked, not to mention in every other kind of neighborhood across the nation, parents struggle on behalf of their children, sometimes with success, and not rarely with a sense of failure. Matters debated publicly by big-shot experts or politicians are also considered by ordinary parents, by their children, too. In a Boston ghetto these words were recently uttered by a thirty-five-year-old mother of four children, two boys, two girls: "I try to do the best I can for my kids. I try to teach them to be good, and to do good. But they leave the home and the street is out there, waiting on them. All the troubles. All the people with all the schemes they've got — to fool you and trick you and bring you down. I warn the kids, but how can you protect them against the whole world out there, lying in wait for you? On the television they'll warn you against everything, and they'll tell you they're trying to help you. They say watch yourself, or you'll catch AIDS. They say use condoms. They say you should say no to drugs. They say don't have a baby if you don't want it, and you own your body. I'm with them all the way — that we should go to school and stay away from drugs and wait until we're older and married for the children to come. I try to convince my kids, and I hope they listen.

"The other day on the news a man who's a professor said they should make drugs legal. He was talking a blue streak. He was smart, and he wanted to make everyone else believe he's smart. He kept talking about 'the drug epidemic' and the 'teenage pregnancy epidemic,' and he had the answers — make the drugs legal, and give the kids contraception, and if the girl gets pregnant, she can have an abortion. I sat and wished he was right here in my living room, so I could talk with him. I'd ask him if he had any kids. I'd ask him if he'd want us to make the drugs legal for *his* kids; and if he wanted *his* girl to use birth control, and go have an abortion. He's writing all of us off — we're below him. He doesn't give a damn about us — so long as we stay out of his way. Give them drugs and condoms and abortions and some welfare money! Just stay out of my way! And if my own kid gets in trouble — well, that's different, I suppose."

She had much more to say, but the essence of her remarks amounted to a pointed analysis of the way class and race affect our judgment as we contemplate certain important social problems, not to mention moral ones. For our own sons and daughters we want a decent, sturdy, solid life — no drug abuse, and a developing sexuality that is kept under civilizing constraints, be they secular or religious in orientation. For others "below" us, quite another point of view obtains: stop their pregnancies, and stop their stealing or violence by making drugs legally available. Were our own child sexually active at twelve, pregnant at thirteen or fourteen, we'd be on the phone to doctors: my child is troubled and desperately needs medical care, and maybe I do, too, as the parent. Were our own child using drugs, or involved in a drug gang, we'd also be in a doctor's office, pronto — determined with all our heart and mind to put an end to such an addictive process. But for "them": let us change our laws, modify our moral principles — anything to be rid of the consequences of their behavior.

What children of *all* classes and races need is a social order that responds to and clearly evokes a firm moral tradition. Children need to know what is right, what is decent and responsible — and also, what is wrong, what is harmful to themselves and others, what is not to be encouraged or allowed. Serious problems, both personal and social in nature, are not solved by repeated acts of moral surrender. The mother quoted above is crying for a world that helps her and others struggle harder and more successfully against a range of troubles at once cultural and familial, not to mention economic and political. She needs help in that fight, not a signal that all is lost and that an entire moral tradition is to be sacrificed in the name of expediency.

September 1988

6

Raymond Carver's Dying Chekhov

A T THE END of his collection of stories titled *Where I'm Call-ing From*, Raymond Carver breaks pace, leaves his own mid-twentieth-century American world of ordinary men and women — whose persistent hard luck, interrupted by brief moments of sat-isfaction, he has chronicled these past two decades — in order to enter another century, another country, another human landscape. "Errand" is Carver's farewell for this publishing occasion — an evoca-tion of Chekhov's last days, last moments. A master of short fiction, Carver attends a kind of literary and historical factuality — the great Chekhov's all too early, untimely encounter with death.

Carver obviously studied Chekhov's life carefully, but he does not write as a biographer. He has a dramatic presentation in mind — yet another of his unsettling penetrations of our moral and social compla-cency. He initially gives us the Chekhov of thirty-seven, who suddenly hemorrhages in a restaurant, the first sign of a tuberculosis which would seven years later claim his life. For a long time the ailing play-wright and storyteller tried to make light of his illness, even though, being a physician too, he well knew the serious threat it posed to his life. He did so not because he was psychologically in trouble, nor out of some fatuous inclination to hope against hope, no matter the obvi-ous progression of an invasive disease ever hungry for more and more lung *Lebensraum*. Nor did he do so out of religious conviction.

In that last regard, Carver gives us Tolstoy as Chekhov's loving ad-mirer and hospital visitor. "Tolstoy assumes that all of us (humans and animals alike) will live on in a principle (such as reason or love) the essence and goals of which are a mystery to us. . . . I have no use for that kind of immortality. I don't understand it, and he Nikolayevich was astonished I didn't." Chekhov's apparent indifference to the mor-tal jeopardy fate had presented him as an untimely offering was the response of a shrewd physician and observer of the human scene: we come, we go, and alarmed, wordy discussions or exclamations are to no avail.

Carver wonders whether Chekhov might have been inclined to "minimize the seriousness of his condition," but one wonders whether Chekhov wasn't as taciturn as some of Carver's contemporary Amer-icans in an effort to endure with a minimum of dignity a bad hand dealt. Yes, the dying Chekhov wrote to his mother that he was getting better, and Carver is right to wonder how an astute doctor could be so inappropriately hopeful. But what Chekhov knew for himself and what he said to others were not necessarily the same. He wrote lines for others to perform in plays and might well have had his own notion of how one behaves in public — whereas at night, in a world inhabited only by oneself, other kinds of assertions or acknowledgments can be made.

At the very end of his life, Chekhov was anything but fatuously optimistic. Carver is the wonderfully ironic and suggestive storyteller as he relates those last minutes of a particular life. A wife, Olga, calls for a doctor named Schwohrer; her famous husband has suddenly become delirious. The doctor arrives, starts doing his emergency work. He calls for oxygen. But now Chekhov is anything but the willing patient who dares hope for a miracle from medicine: "Suddenly, Chekhov roused himself, became lucid, and said quietly, 'What's the use? Before it arrives I'll be a corpse.'"

Now it was the doctor's turn — to speak, to act, to respond to a challenge both medical and moral, and certainly existential in nature. Dr. Schwohrer — in a scene worthy of a Chekhov play — makes a call to the hotel's kitchen. He orders the best available champagne. He asks for three glasses, too. He urges all possible speed — and soon the Moet arrives in room 211. Before Chekhov died, he and his wife and his doctor would drink that champagne. Indeed, his last words were: "It's been so long since I've had champagne."

There is more to Carver's "Errand." He is interested not only in Chekhov's death, but in the young hotel employee who brought the champagne to the room of a Black Forest resort near Basel. He is interested in a post-mortem drama of sorts — the way a youth's "errand" is part of a widow's response to death. When Chekhov died, his widow wanted to be alone with him. She and the youth were the writer's last companions on this earth. The doctor left, whereas the youth came back in the course of his hotel duties — unaware, at first, that someone had died since his earlier "errand" had been completed. For Olga, "there was only beauty, peace, and the grandeur of death," she would one day write in remembrance. For the young waiter there were life's small movements to execute — in the room and outside (another "errand," this time to the mortician's). All the while, though, Chekhov's spirit is there, prompting Olga's contemplative awe, and through her, a youth's effort to do his best in the middle of circumstances he cannot really comprehend. All the while, too, Chekhov's last farewell, enabled by his physician, lingers in the room: the empty bottle; the fallen cork, which the youthful waiter wants so earnestly to pick up — *his* goodbye, as it were, to a moment in life; and the wry meditative spell which a patient had set in motion through his final remark to a doctor.

The dying Chekhov Raymond Carver gives us is someone whose sense of proportion and humor prevail over the fear death instills in all of us. Moreover, and just as important, Chekhov's physician is utterly worthy of his patient. I don't suppose we are in any danger, these days, of witnessing a rash of champagne goodbyes in the wards of our hospitals where the terminally ill reside, though Lord knows, there are worse ways for doctors and patients and relatives to behave — all those tubes and procedures requested and mobilized in a futile effort to shake one's fists at Time, if not Nature's inscrutable mysteries. But as I read Carver's story — and remembered reading that he himself, of late, had been struggling with a lung disease, cancer* — I thought of my father's last moments. He asked for ice cream and let me feed it to him, as he talked with my son, his grandson, then a college history major, about the various kings and queens of England, where he'd been born and grew up. My son and I were amazed at how clearly an old and dying man remembered centuries of a nation's royal lineage. My father, recognizing our surprised admiration, smiled and graciously changed the subject: "Let's toast not only the past, but the future." He lifted his hospital glass, half-filled with water, and we scurried to do likewise — find a couple of cups, fill them with water. After the toast Dad slumped back on his pillows, and soon he was gone.

October 1988

---

*Raymond Carver died on August 2 of cancer at age fifty.

7

Raymond Carver's Death

ON MONDAY, August 1, 1988, I found myself writing some notes about Raymond Carver's stories. I had been immersed in them for weeks, and had written the column which preceded this one about "Errand," the final story in Carver's most recent, and alas, last collection, *Where I'm Calling From*. I had even begun to dream of meeting him someday—talking with him and learning from him.

I have spent a lot of time talking with so-called working-class people—men and women who show up regularly on assembly lines, on construction crews, in stores and offices, in gas stations, in trucks that crisscross America. I think I know some children who hail from that "middle America" fairly well. As I have read Carver's stories I've kept wandering back in my mind to certain homes I used to visit in Lynn, Massachusetts, near a General Electric plant; in Framingham, Massachusetts, near a General Motors plant; and too, in the South and the Southwest, where as one truck driver put it, "there are lots of folks who keep trying to get by, and sometimes they do and sometimes they don't." That mood—that mixture of stoic persistence and melancholy tentativeness — used to hit me in the face, sometimes, as I'd enter, yet again, a bungalow, a mobile home, a not very fancy apartment house. In Carver's stories I felt the same mood—a writer summoning his readers to a world he knew like the fingers of his hands. His people are holding on for dear life; some, in fact, are sinking fast, while others tough it out, day by day. They are not exactly the ones who figure in most American fiction today. They are not well-to-do suburban men and women, or fast-thinking academics or urban sophisticates. They don't even have race or geography going for them— the liberal fascination with one "them" after another.

On Wednesday, August 3, my fan letter to Raymond Carver finished in the rough, I sat down to the newspapers, and in one of them as I turned the page, I caught sight of this statement in the upper left hand corner of an even-numbered page: "Raymond Carver, Writer and Poet of the Working Poor, Dies at 50." I've been reading *New York Times* obituaries for years, and usually find them to be a brag sheet: all too predictably concerned with the pomp and circumstance of big-shot lives. Carver has, indeed, become a major literary presence, and so I suppose the significant attention paid him in our nation's leading

paper of record marked a final success of sorts. His smiling, hand-
some face is allowed a farewell to all those busy, intelligent readers.
Yet, the write-up of this prominent American short-story writer and
poet is surely one of the more unusual death notices to appear in
an important American paper. He is quoted this way: "I'm a paid-
in-full member of the working poor. I have a great deal of sympathy
with them. They're my people." We learn, further, that he was born in
Clatskanie, Oregon, the son of a sawmill worker and a waitress. His
father loved Zane Grey's many books, and read from them aloud; he
also hunted and fished a lot (Carver was an avid fisherman) and told
stories, such as the time an ancestor (the author's great-grandfather)
"stole a hog for the hungry men in his regiment."

As a young man Carver struggled hard to break even. He had married fresh out of high school and had two children to support. "Like
a displaced person," the *Times* obituary tells us, "he knocked around
California with his family, moving from one dead-end job to another
in search of a better life." He was a janitor; he worked as a farm
hand; he became a delivery "boy" for a while. He also drank hard
and smoked heavily. Alcoholics Anonymous gave him sobriety about
five or six years ago, and it is only in the last decade that his stories,
especially, and his poetry have earned him the growing and grateful
respect and admiration of many of us readers who look to people like
him, like Walker Percy, like John Cheever, for not only entertainment
but a clue or two about what matters in this life, and why.

As I sat at the breakfast table, saddened and even a bit numb,
and angry that his precious and singular life had been taken from
us prematurely, I kept thinking of some of the fine stories he has
given us, and a few of the memorable poems, too. I thought, as
well, of William Carlos Williams, whom I got to know in my early
twenties, and whom I admired beyond the power of words to convey, and whom I very much loved. Williams and Carver both tried
to connect some of us who live in relatively comfortable, privileged
circumstances with the lives of ordinary American men and women
who scrape by during good times, and are down on their luck when
things go sour in our nation. Both men knew whereof they spoke
and wrote — Carver out of personal experience, Williams out of his
decades of work as an old-fashioned general practitioner in northern,
industrial New Jersey, a doctor who put in countless unpaid hours
among the vulnerable, needy people of, say, Paterson or Hackensack
or Passaic. Both men wrote verse and prose; both had an instructive
and powerful anti-intellectualism at work in them, a kind of class animus: as if they willingly linked arms with plain and sometimes sorry

people as against the all-too-fortunate intelligentsia, with its not un-common susceptibility to smugness, pretentiousness, self-importance. Both men combined a romanticism that celebrated aspects of nature with a tough, unflinching realism that looked sharply at people and wasted no time getting at their central preoccupations. Both men were marvelously responsive to water, to rivers — and attended lost souls others were anxious to ignore completely or dismiss as beneath their concern; or put differently, these were two down-to-earth writers who had no use for the smug, snobbish world writers (among others) can occasionally be found inhabiting.

The West — Oregon and Washington — is far from New Jersey, yet in between are all the lonely or hurt people, the vulnerable souls who are as American as those who run things, own things — and it is such folks, trying to get through hard-luck days and weeks, whom Carver and Williams both addressed: the particulars of their lives, the frustrations and disappointments, the small moments of affirmation, if not triumph.

In another essay I will discuss a story or two, a poem or two, of Carver's, but first I want to mention the gratitude some of us have felt these past years for Raymond Carver's many gifts to us, and the sadness we feel that he has left us here on this earth; and too, I'd like to register a private hope, a daydream, I had as I read the *Times* obitu-ary and remembered reading the William Carlos Williams one — that somewhere, somehow, in some moment of God's time, some place in His kingdom, those two brave and strong and fiercely independent souls might meet, talk, laugh, exchange a yarn or two, and also get a chance to greet Anton Chekhov, the spiritual kinsman whom each so much admired.

November 1988

8

Raymond Carver's Heart and Soul

"A SMALL, GOOD THING" AND "CATHEDRAL" are two of Raymond Carver's later stories. I ask my college students and medical students to read them, an introduction to his particular late twentieth-century American world. Carver's people are, mostly, quite ordinary, and often enough down on their luck. Perhaps they drink too much. Perhaps they have never known how to get ahead in life — find a good job, make the kind of marriage that is satisfying and gives them a big boost as they take on bosses or fellow workers, not to mention all the annoyances, frustrations, and irritations that go with trying to make a living so you can pay your bills. Perhaps they are men and women who are getting by, maybe, but at a big cost — hence, lots of fighting at home, or an unrelenting boredom, or silence (the grim, tenacious silence of a nothing-time this side of death). Sometimes Carver is content to render such dead-end lives; but occasionally he moves toward some important shift that is spiritual in nature, as he does in these two stories, and of course, in "Errand," which I discussed in an earlier column.

In "Cathedral" a blind man enters the family life of a plain, working-class couple — no big-deal home, no pretensions to social success, to intellectual achievement, to cultural sophistication. The wife has known him for years, kept in touch with him — turned to him, really, as someone whom she could trust to hear her personal news, to respond with attentive concern. The husband (her second) is now to meet the blind man, who has recently lost his wife. The story takes place in a living room, a dining room. The husband is perplexed at his wife's obvious interest in, affection for the blind man. The blind man seems to be laconic, enigmatic. His eyes, obviously, tell nothing; a beard covers his face. To the husband he is at first "creepy." Carver more than hints at the familiar triangle — mostly rendered through the husband's rising dissatisfaction. But soon enough the story changes direction. The three eat a plain, hearty meal; the wife tires and goes to sleep; the husband and the blind man are left with that other great companion of our days and nights, television.

On the screen a program "about the church and the Middle Ages" comes on. The two men have been matching drink for drink, and it is late, and they too ought to be dozing off. But instead they resist sleep, pay closer attention to each other, respond to the television program — and soon enough the husband is drawing a cathedral, with the blind man attentively at his side, and eventually an awakened wife is there too. A man utterly indifferent to religion ("I guess I don't believe in it") has been prompted by a stranger to think carefully about cathedrals — how they look, their structural nature — and then convey that appearance on paper. The story ends with a threesome newly alert, with some mystery and excitement in the air. As in the Bible, the blind lead the blind — but now toward a new vision. Carver is too good a storyteller to load down this noumenal moment with preachy dogmatics. But the reader is prompted to think of things seen and unseen, of what he or she has or has not noticed; the reader, too, has been asked to consider what it is that might break the spell of indifference and isolation and loneliness that shadows us so much of the time. "Cathedral" at the very least offers a visual epiphany — and of course the story's title, the subject matter of the drawing, is of some implicit significance. One thinks of those distant ancestors of ours in southern France, untold centuries ago, marking the walls of the great cave of Lascaux, and perhaps asserting thereby their speculations and dreams, their questions about the world, about life's purpose and meaning.

"A Small, Good Thing" is that, indeed — a brief story of great suggestive power. A boy's eighth birthday approaches, and his mother goes to a baker to order a cake. But the morning of his birthday the boy is hit by a car, knocked unconscious, and rushed to the hospital, where he lies in an intensive care bed, closely watched, given all the maintenance support modern medicine can offer. The doctor is hopeful the boy will soon regain consciousness. He virtually promises the parents that such will be the case. They take the cue, feel optimistic, spend their time waiting, expecting a favorable turn. But time accumulates ominously, and the parents begin to hope against hope — join the ranks of all those who have paced hospital corridors, sat in them through long nights, sleepless and full of foreboding. One or the other parent dashes home briefly, to shower, change clothes, catch the merest glimpse of an earlier, once routine life. On those visits the phone rings. On one occasion the husband answers — hears about a cake, but knows nothing of it; it was his wife who had ordered it. Then the wife gets a couple of calls, which seem to her at the time to be inscrutable, then sadistic. She is on edge when the phone rings because she is awaiting (fearing) a hospital call; she asks if the call is about her boy, and is told yes. The caller, a man, asks if she has "forgotten about Scotty," her son.

The boy dies, "a one-in-a-million circumstance." The parents go through the last hell of such a hospital event; and then return home —

and again the phone call: "'Your Scotty, I got him ready for you,' the man's voice said. 'Did you forget him?'" The parents are enraged, regard themselves as the victims of a moral monster. Another call, and then silence: torment—but in a flash, the wife realizes who the caller is. She and her husband, in the middle of the night, go to the shopping mall, where the baker is alone preparing for the next day. What follows is a scene of unforgettable poignancy and power. The couple's anger at the baker turns to acknowledgment of suffering and tragedy. The baker gets them to be with him, to accept his rolls and coffee, to receive from him the "small, good thing" of bread. The light of his shop penetrates the darkness. The mother and father stay, talk, eat—a time of communion, of companionship. The author has taken us in his own fashion back to the literal meaning of that word: *cum panis,* with bread, as in Jesus ("the light of the world") eating with his followers. Yet again, no religious lecture takes place—only a story's healing glow: another threesome, another reminder of the redemptive possibilities in those humble moments of humble people, or of people humbled by fate.

Raymond Carver knew in his bones how intimately death lives with us, even when we think of ourselves as (temporarily) beyond its reach. At any moment any of us can be taken away—and he made no secret of his own alcoholism, a dangerously provocative gamble of sorts with one's mortality. Yet, in his poems especially ("My Death" and "Gravy") he is at pains to warn us away from indulging in pity for him ("try not to mourn for me too much. I want you to know / I was happy when I was here"). He was a proud man, who fought his demons fiercely, and in his last years emerged a clear winner — only to lose, as we all do. His poems ("My Crow," for example) offer his own measured, defiant assertion of a soul's singular sensibility; or they offer his unpretentious sensual joy ("The Party"). In the end he had found meaning in life's earthy particulars, in his beloved Tess Gallagher; the poet and his second wife, in the simple pleasures of food, in the sight of flowers, of the sea, in the tests of fishing. His heart and soul came to us in those poems, in those stories — a man with no claims to big-shot ideas, with no interest in big-deal people, with every wish, no matter his talent and success, to keep his attention toward those he knew so well from his early years: the hurt, the old, the sick, the vulnerable. His life was a special gift to us from on high; his life was that of the baker he gave us, or the blind man — he shed light on our darkness, helped us see a little more than we usually manage to do.

December 1988

9

On Simone Weil's
"Formative Writing"

Formative Writings, 1929–1941. By Simone Weil. Edited by Dorothy Tuck McFarland and Wilhelmina Van Ness. University of Massachusetts Press. 289 pages. $30.

WHEN SIMONE WEIL DIED in 1943, she was only thirty-four years old. She was living in London, and the Second World War was raging all over the world. She had come to England to join the ranks of General de Gaulle's "Free French"; to do so she had crossed the dangerous waters of the Atlantic — her parents left behind in New York City, to which all three had come as Jewish exiles from Pétain's France. Weil's father was a successful Parisian doctor, her mother a person of culture and refinement with a strong interest in music. An older brother, André, is still alive — one of the great mathematicians of our time and an emeritus professor at Princeton's Institute for Advanced Study.

Were Simone Weil never to have written a word more after 1943, but lived to the present time, then died, say, in 1989, at the age of eighty, she would be memorialized in country after country — the subject of long, admiring obituaries, followed, no doubt, by essays of reconsideration. There are, even now, societies devoted to her, and journals devoted to a continuing and mostly appreciative criticism of her work. Books with her name as author are in print the world over: she is declared again and again an important, a seminal twentieth-century figure — to some a cultural hero of sorts. Flannery O'Connor discussed her with great admiration in letters to friends. Camus, it is said, paid his respects to her mother upon notification that he had been awarded the Nobel Prize in literature — and before then had written of her with enthusiasm. T. S. Eliot offered a strong, erudite, affecting introduction to *The Need for Roots,* published under her name well after her death. She has become for many a moral beacon — her aspirations, reservations, doubts, worries, and enthusiasms examined ever so closely, her conclusions embraced with no small amount of fervor.

Yet, when Simone Weil died she was by no means the person whose

life and thought now inform the moral and spiritual assumptions of
so many of us. She died in a tuberculosis sanatorium, where the doctors had declared her a suicide because of her refusal to eat the amount
of food they wanted her to eat, so that her body would at least have
a chance of fighting successfully a major bacterial infection. She had
been living in obscurity in England. She published no books, and only
a few articles, in her lifetime. She had been a schoolteacher in France;
she loved working with children. She had also been a political activist
on the left — anxious to help the poor and working-class people of
France get a better deal out of a capitalist system that fought even
their minimal needs tooth and nail. She went to Spain on behalf of
the Loyalists, but got hurt in an accident and had to come home.
She worked for a time in one factory, then another, in the hope
that by sharing the life of ordinary workers she would get to know
their struggles and figure out what might be done on their behalf,
were any owners inclined to stop and think about those whose labor
enriched them.

By 1938 she was also preoccupied with religious matters. She was
especially drawn to the Catholic Church of the poor — to the faith
of hard-struggling men and women, a faith she both respected and
marveled at (as has been the case with certain intellectuals), and en-
vied as well. She held on to her political and economic egalitarianism,
and her social views fitted in with her religious sensibility. She also became increasingly frail. She was plagued by severe migraine headaches.
Her appetite was hardly hearty. When the Nazis approached Paris, her
family fled. During the initial Vichy years, she lived with her parents
in Marseilles. For a while she worked as a farm hand, evidence of her
persistent desire to share the fate of those who worked hardest and
got the least pay. Soon enough, with her parents, she was on the way
to America, three exiles lucky enough to find safety in New York City.

In Manhattan she was the same restless, intensely reflective Simone
Weil, now more fervently drawn to Christian meditation and prayer
than ever before. She also searched eagerly for a way to give of herself to others. She went to Harlem; she thought of going to Alabama,
to work in some way on behalf of sharecroppers. She went to church,
prayed long and earnestly, and, as she had been doing all during her
twenties, wrote in her journal. But such a life was not then for her.
She wanted to fight Hitler and all he stood for. She dreamed of getting back to France, of joining the resistance. Eventually, she secured
her way back to Europe and found a job as a functionary in London
for the exiled French government. But she was not satisfied with such
a position; she yearned for a fighting role. Might she be parachuted

behind the Nazi lines? Those asked such a question were incredulous:
she was obviously in failing health. When tuberculosis claimed her,
she had little strength to resist. She had been keeping herself on a ra-
tion no more substantial than that of the French who lived under the
Nazis. Her doctors tried force-feeding her, and regarded her as anorec-
tic, as thoroughly disturbed and deeply depressed. Her death did not
surprise them.

Now, she lives with us through her writings, all the posthumous
books that have given us so much to consider. There is, too, a substantial critical literature, and her friend Simone Pétrement's long and
helpful biography. Moreover, a number of editors have assembled
some of her shorter writings in such a way as to reveal a direction
of her thought — the scientific or religious or political or philosophical side of her, or the writing she did in New York or, before that, in
Paris. This book belongs to that last tradition — a collection of Weil's
writings penned between 1929, when she was only twenty years old,
and 1941, when she was thirty-two. The editors are two first-rate Weil
scholars, one of whom, Dorothy Tuck McFarland, published a study
of Weil in 1983. The editors provide a helpful introduction which offers a brief biographical sketch of the writer whose essays follow, each
with instructive prefatory remarks. The editors make clear that they
are more interested, for this volume, in the political and philosophical Weil than in the religiously inspired Weil; indeed, they venture to
claim — on what evidence, they do not say — that "the political activist and the philosopher/teacher," one side of Weil, "never caught up
in the public mind with the religious Weil, or were satisfactorily inte-
grated into the public perception of either her person or her thought."
Some of us, who first met Weil as a brilliant political theorist and an
extraordinarily brave and penetrating social and cultural observer, will
no doubt take issue with such a comment. In any event, this is a collection of essays that will prompt, yet again, a recognition of Weil's
distinctive genius.

At the age many of us were callow college students, scarcely certain of what to major in, Weil was writing "Science and Perception in
Descartes," an effort to affirm — with a boost from her reading of that
philosopher — the importance of the observations ordinary men and
women make as they go through life. She disliked the idea (maybe, the
reality) of a "science" understood only by an elite few, and tried hard
to connect the abstract, erudite comprehensions of philosophers and
physicists to the capacities she believed the rest of us have to fathom
the world. Often, of course, *she* is the layman — not exactly a stand-in
for many of us; but her intention tells us a lot about her values and

hopes: a belief in the capacities of her fellow human beings that contrasts with the opinion all too many intellectuals have of "them," the ordinary working people of the world.

We are offered other important, poignant essays — the journalist Weil's views of Hitler's rise, the working-woman Weil's "Factory Journal," a testimony of sorts to one soul's willingness to lay itself bare under great duress. How many others in any of the world's various intelligentsias have done as she did — sweated out assembly line work in order to learn from such a life, in order to test ideas and theories with a concrete, everyday laboring experience? In that journal she is, as always, the self-critic as well as the observer of others. She was always trying to evaluate the world's rights and wrongs and to change through actions the latter into the former. Her struggle with the notion of pacifism throughout the 1930s — given Hitler's increasing challenge to everything she held dear — is also part of this book's record: an honest soul, at once practical and idealistic, trying to figure out what *ought* to be done and what might have to be done under the extraordinary conditions that her beloved France (and the entire civilized world) had to face in 1939 and 1940.

So it is that we once again, through this book, meet Simone Weil, try to understand her complex, at times hard-to-fathom way of seeing things. She could be austere, even forbidding; at other moments she becomes decent and kind and compassionate — ready, it seems, to touch us mightily with her goodness of heart and soul. Above all, she took the biggest possible risks; she was thoroughly ready to stake everything she had in search for what matters truly. By the end of her relatively short time here it had become apparent to her that Jesus and His life had been the incarnation of what she had been seeking. The writings called by this book's editors "formative" were a prelude to a soul's discovery of its Maker — and so, inevitably, this book will be put aside by many for others, such as *The Need for Roots,* or *Waiting for God:* a soul now not in formation, but formed, a person now become, as Dorothy Day put it, a "fool for Christ."

January–February 1989

10

What Do Our Children Need?

I KEPT READING in 1988 that "children's issues" are newly important politically, that in certain respects America has no reason to
be proud when the lives of our children are compared to the lives of
children who live elsewhere — the infant mortality rate, for instance.
We regard ourselves as the world's richest and strongest nation, yet by
the millions our children don't fare well. Some, born into poverty and
ignorance, don't eat well; they live in an unsafe world of rat-infested
buildings, neither well heated in the winter nor well ventilated in the
summer. Many such children don't get adequate (or any) medical care,
and the schools they attend aren't comparable to those in well-to-do
suburbs. Such boys and girls have a lot going against them, and it is
right that some of us who know of their fate speak up loud and clear
on their behalf.

Other American children are also in trouble, some of them born to
parents who proudly call themselves middle class, even upper-middle
class. Many young American children, even infants, see very little of
their parents, week after week. They are taken to neighbors or relatives, or they go to day-care centers, a large percentage of which (by
the criteria established by local, state, or federal agencies) are inadequate. That is to say, quite young children spend their days in woefully
crowded, understaffed programs. I have visited a number of them in
various parts of the country, and I can only agree with the words of
one mother who described her daughter's situation (and her own) this
way: "I can't not work. I've got to work. My husband lost his job. He
can't get another one [they live in a Midwestern, so-called rustbelt
community] and if we're not to live on welfare, I've got to bring in
dough, because it's easier for me than him to find a job. He's got a
temporary job, but he's working for peanuts. It kills me to take those
[two] kids to day-care. [They are one and four years old.] I take one
look at the numbers [of children and staff] and I know the score; I
take a look at the room, and the stuff in it, and I know the score dou-
ble — a loser. I pay them big bucks, and what I get is someone to be
there with my kids. I can't leave them alone, can I! It's lousy — for
the kids and for me and their father. We hate it, and the kids do. And
we're supposed to be lucky — because we *have* day-care. My mother
had a stroke — or she'd be with my kids. She sits there in bed and

curses her illness. She says there's something wrong in America — that little kids, infants even, aren't with their families all day, most of the week. She and my dad — their families were dirt-poor during the Depression, but the kids in those families, the babies they had someone at home to take care of them. It's different now; it's no good."

I bring this woman's thoughts to this column because I believe she senses in her heart and mind what her own young children, never mind so many others, are distinctly lacking: a daily family life that lasts more than a few minutes here and there. She once told me this: "I'm with my kids a half hour in the morning, and an hour or two at night." Essentially she gets them up, delivers them to others and at night picks them up, brings them home, scurries to prepare supper, her husband helping her cook and clean up, and then puts the children (who are, she says, "utterly exhausted when they come home") to bed. Yet, our current national discourse has us emphasizing the matter of day-care in such a way that the family concerns of mothers and fathers like this woman and her husband are not part of the discussion. *He,* by the way, would gladly not work at all, would stay home with his young children; but again, they are proud, so-called working-class people who want to "do the best we can," they tell me — meaning, stay off welfare, at all costs, make as much money as possible, so that life can be as "comfortable" as possible (not especially unusual aims for millions and millions of us Americans). For trying to do so, these parents feel their children are in some jeopardy, and then I am asked for my opinion.

Often, I hesitate and mumble and try to change the subject, I have to admit. I am getting old, I tell myself, and what I took for granted others simply don't have to offer their children: a mother who was with my brother and me until we were solidly in school, and who was also at home when we came back from school, and a wife who similarly has been with our children in such a way. Moreover, my dad was constantly moving things around in his life so that he could be with us a lot. I've tried to follow suit. My parents divided up all sorts of chores and responsibilities, and they loved not only each other, but their joint obligations as parents. They were lucky, yes; they were not poor and had some control over their lives, and I guess the same goes for my wife and me. Yet, I have to say that my father did turn down several very important job possibilities because he didn't want to move and have us leave a world we knew well as growing children, and my mother encouraged those decisions. I think their example has very much informed my life and that of my wife.

When I hear talk of the needs children have — for day-care, for more medical help, for better schools — I quickly and enthusiastically assent. But I think, also, of families such as the one I've mentioned above, and of the one next door to them — where three so-called latch-key children live, two boys and a girl, all under twelve, who come home from school to an empty house. I think, too, of the many "adolescents" I know — youths who do, indeed, need lots and lots of time with their parents. Where did we get the idea, by the way, that "teenagers" require a kind of independence that translates into virtually no contact with their mothers and fathers? High schoolers need their parents very much — not in the way preschoolers do, or elementary school children do, but as important companions, ones with whom ideas and thoughts and yearnings and worries can be shared. A family can be rich and still, in a child's eye, a youth's eye, be judged extremely hard-pressed: the parents are so caught up in themselves and their own imperatives that the sons and daughters feel left out, cut off — no matter the "quality" of the day-care, or even the presence in the home of a cook, a cleaning lady, a gardener, and on and on.

I am making an old-fashioned appeal, I guess, for children: that they spend as much time as possible with their parents, and that we as a nation pose as a major problem the fact that such a family life — children brought up, in the main, by their parents — is less and less a possibility for more and more American mothers and fathers, more and more American sons and daughters. Two former students of mine, both just out of law school, now take their year-old girl to a rather fancy day-care center five days a week — and recently came to me in tears: they wondered "what this life is all about." I think of them, think of the much poorer couple I mentioned earlier, and sometimes ask myself the same question, and for the same reason. These young lawyers told me, right off, what their daughter needs: "more of us, day in, day out."

That is what our children need, all of them, all over the land, and I see little willingness in some quarters, both "liberal" and "conservative," for such a consideration to be put on the table for urgent acknowledgment.

January–February 1989

11

Memories of 1964

A S I WRITE THIS, America's magazines and newspapers are offering a fairly extended discussion of the movie *Mississippi Burning*. Critics argue pro and con — the movie as an important stimulus to social reflection (with respect to our national history of racial exploitation) or as an exercise in self-indulgent melodrama, with no serious effort to convey what happened in 1964, the year the civil rights movement in the deep South crested. The film is meant to tell today's viewers about a terrible tragedy, the murder (in June) of three civil rights activists (James Chaney, Andrew Goodman, and Michael Schwerner) in Neshoba County, Mississippi. Those young men, one black and two white, were the vanguard of the Mississippi Summer Project, a bold attempt on the part of SNCC (Student Nonviolent Coordinating Committee) to take on directly the then bastion of Southern segregationist power — the rural communities of a state long associated with fierce resistance to federal integrationist pressures.

I met those three men in Oxford, Ohio, where a number of us who had worked in the South — involved one way or another in the desegregation struggles of the early 1960s — were trying to prepare some five hundred student volunteers from all over America for what they soon might be experiencing. They were a diverse lot — Ivy leaguers, youths from small Midwestern Christian colleges, students from Berkeley, men and women connected with the Catholic Worker Movement. Most of them had never stepped foot in Mississippi; many had not once visited the South. They were a decent, earnest lot — but I remember well the words of Robert Moses, the SNCC veteran who had helped conceive and organize the project: "We originally thought we'd ask some idealistic young people to come to the Delta and live with the [black] people, and stand by them as they tried to register to vote. But now I realize we've got a major problem on our hands — how to educate these folks about where they're going and what they'll be up against."

Our hope was that clusters of young people from, say, New England or Chicago or the Western states, mostly white, would offer the hard-pressed and justifiably fearful blacks of towns such as Canton or Greenwood or McComb a sense of solidarity — would hearten those men and women as they contemplated the consequences of that long march up the stairs of one or another county courthouse in hopes of securing the right to vote. Moreover we not only had voter registration in mind that summer. We were going to do some teaching — Head Start had not yet come into being — and some medical work among families which, in the main, had virtually no access to any doctor, clinic, or hospital. But first came the "orientation" — talks by some of us, discussions among the young people, and some movies and newsreel footage to watch. Just before Chaney, Goodman, and Schwerner left, I had lunch with them. They kidded me: come along, and then we'd be a "real shrink team" — Micky Schwerner was a social worker, Andy Goodman's mother a psychologist, I was a psychiatrist, and Jim Chaney would be the "mobile clinic administrator." We had a lot of fun with that fantasy — Chaney, at one point, saying we ought to go "all over the South, to treat the craziness of racism." But in no time the four of us were remarking on the social and economic and political aspects of that phenomenon — lest an assertively unqualified psychology be allowed to strip a particular human scene of its thickly textured complexity.

I walked those three to their car, a Volkswagen, as I recall. We laughed about the sudden spell of hot weather in that Ohio college town just north of Cincinnati: wait until the unrelentingly sultry summer weather of Yazoo City or Itta Bena or Hattiesburg had worked its effect on all those Yankee nerves. "Your last chance," Jim Chaney said to me as they got into the car. "Come on," Andy echoed. Then, Schwerner's goodbye, which I can hear now, as I write it out: "Finish up here, and we'll see you there." Seconds later they were headed south and I toward a building, to continue with our orientation program. Days later hundreds of us had heard that Jim, Andy, and Micky had disappeared — and we had little doubt as to why. I sit here now writing — but have stopped to close my eyes, to go back to that moment in late June of 1964 when hundreds of us came together as a giant circle in the middle of a field, holding hands and singing the anthem of the civil rights movement, "We Shall Overcome" — over and over, as if to ask the Lord to take notice, as if, too, we ourselves, given what had happened, might be convinced.

As the saying goes, the rest is history — a history (with respect to Chaney, Goodman, and Schwerner) the movie *Mississippi Burning* makes no pretense at documenting in any scrupulous detail. The director of the film has made clear his intention — to reach in a dramatic, compelling manner the minds and hearts of the millions of whites who now, twenty-five years later, will be seeing this film: to stir in them currents of the moral imagination. In one sense, such a hope was also that of SNCC's leaders — as one of them made clear to me in the course of a long interview done in Canton, Mississippi, in early August of 1964, well after the Neshoba County tragedy: "I hope and pray these folks [the volunteers] get something out of this summer that lasts, that sticks with them when they go back to their Yales and their Berkeleys. We don't expect them to win this war here. The people here will have to win their own war, and it'll take years and years. But we — I mean, *they* [the local people] — need allies, and lots of these college kids come from families with plenty of money and plenty of clout. The other day I heard a few of them talking, and they were going to do *this* when they went back home, and *that,* and I thought to myself: if they do 10 percent of what they're now vowing to do, then that'll be good, real good, for our cause down here."

Later that year President Johnson would sign an important Civil Rights bill, and thereafter the voting rights of blacks throughout the South became increasingly protected — a big breakthrough. Still, as the leaders of SNCC well knew, the cost had been high in lives lost, in people injured, threatened, insulted, in churches and homes burnt to the ground. Nor would that summer be the end of it: "I think we'll be fighting this fight for a generation, for longer even than that," Bob Moses said toward the end of August, as one white youth after another departed for Jackson's airport, or by car for the interstates that headed west or north — and here we are, a generation later, discussing a movie titled *Mississippi Burning,* aware that things have changed enormously, true, but aware, also, of how persistent the racial discord the film portrays is yet among us as a people.

March 1989

12

Teaching Fourth Grade

FOR TWO YEARS I taught a fourth-grade class in a school just a few blocks away from the college classrooms where I give my twice-a-week lectures. I hope to continue that elementary school teaching, because, not only does it help me understand how children think — my job in life, I guess — but in addition I am helped by the spirit of those nine-year-old boys and girls, to the point that their words and reactions give me a much needed boost sometimes, when I find myself cringing with irritation, annoyance, or worse as I talk with someone called a professor or university student.

In our fourth-grade class I taught reading and I also brought over from Harvard's Fogg Art Museum some slides, which I showed the boys and girls each day I taught. I suppose during that time we were engaged in an "art history" class. I would project on the wall a picture of a drawing or painting, and then ask the children to respond as they wished to what they saw — to describe the scene, to speculate about the artist's intentions, to say what looking at the picture brings to mind. I was able to offer the children a range of pictures — those of El Greco and Rembrandt, those of Turner, Degas, Renoir, Cezanne, Pissarro, those of Picasso, Kollowitz, Rouault. At first I was timid; I showed only the most realistic of art. But in time I showed some contemporary art which gets called "expressionist" or even "surreal." I delighted in showing Edward Hopper pictures, because I love his work, and, accordingly, the children took to him, put *themselves* in those barber shops, drugstores, beauty parlors, tenement apartments, and those houses of his — large, somewhat imposing, sometimes spooky or haunted, or so the children thought.

One day, as we discussed Hopper's work, a girl who ordinarily kept quiet during most classes spoke up rather insistently. She wanted to know whether Hopper liked people. She answered her question as soon as she asked it — told us she thought the artist was "probably shy." A girl sitting beside her immediately had a question to ask her: "How do you know?"

The initial commentator was not at a loss for words: "Because, Silly, I looked, that's how I know."

"Well," said the second speaker, "I looked too, and I don't see any shy painter in that picture."

We all sat there, quiet — but now we looked at the picture on the wall with a new intentness and curiosity.

A boy across the room added his two cents: "Just because you don't know, doesn't mean you can't guess — [or] you shouldn't try [to guess]."

"Hey," said a boy sitting in a nearby desk, "you can guess, sure, but that doesn't mean you should speak like it's for certain, what you're saying."

A pause — then I expected more remarks, and so said nothing. But I didn't hear anything, and soon I heard those noises that told me I'd better get ready to open my mouth: the squirming of bodies, fifteen in all, on wooden seats, a cough or two; a giggle from a boy who's been known to get hiccups when he feels "nervous."

I spoke: "Well, are there any other thoughts?" Another pause, one that lengthened into a silence. I got prepared to make a comment of my own. I wasn't really sure what I'd say, but I'd been looking at books with Hopper paintings in them for years, and had lots of affection for the artist and an interest in what he did with such compelling originality and suggestiveness, so I was sure my head would come up with something halfway sensible for the children to consider. But before I could hear my words — learn what I had to say — I heard someone else's, those of the girl who had started us down this road:

"All I said was 'probably.' I wasn't saying 'definitely.' This is no college."

We sat there, the boys and girls quiet and not inclined to pursue the matter any further, and suddenly I awakened — surprised and amused. I wondered what to say. She had made her important point with respect to the adverb she had used earlier, and thereby successfully defended herself against all comers, so I thought, and against her classmates with me, I soon realized. But that final sentence had me all astir, and I wasn't sure what to do — pass over it without saying anything of the rush of surprise and delight and admiration I felt, or respond perhaps with a question meant to elicit an elaboration. In a second or two, I yielded to that latter inclination, if not temptation — to indulge my own interests, rather than assume that many of the children were ready to ignore or pass over that sentence, or, indeed, assume that they did not know what to make of it and weren't especially interested in being edified.

"What did you mean," I asked, "when you said, 'This isn't a college'?" A reply was quickly offered by Anita (by then I was paying close attention to her, and had summoned her name to mind, no matter the increasing difficulty I have with proper names in my middle-aged life):

"I meant what I said. That we're not a college here."

We were at an impasse, I realized, and again I wondered whether to let the matter drop, or pursue our so far awkward exchange.

"Yes," I observed, tersely, a safe rejoinder for sure. Now Anita decided to be the teacher of all of us with this:

"In college they know a lot, and here you can just have your guess."

"Well," said her neighbor, the same one who had doubted her in the first place, "just because they're supposed to know a lot, doesn't mean they do."

"You're right," said Anita, gratefully. "They *think* they know a lot."

The silence that fell on our room was not one many of us wanted to interrupt. No squirming. Lots of renewed attention to Hopper's magical revelation, still there on the wall. I found my mind wandering for a second or two to the big lecture halls of that big university a few blocks away, but soon enough I was also staring at Hopper's urban street scene, those store fronts — amid an utter stillness in both the picture and the room. No people in one, no words in the other — and for a few moments no need for any of us to do anything but look, take in the sight before us. We certainly *weren't* at nearby Harvard.

April 1989

– 13 –

The Day after Inauguration

O N SATURDAY, January 21, 1989, the first day of the Bush era, I rode my bicycle to downtown Concord, Massachusetts, where I live, to buy two newspapers, the *Boston Globe* and the *New York Times*. It was the day after the President's inauguration, a sunny day, and I looked forward to reading what those two papers had to say about an important day in our nation's history. When I got to the drugstore where I buy those papers every morning, I noticed that the *Times* was not there — quite unusual. It was not a foggy or snowy day, nor was any strike in progress — so, puzzled, I asked the store's clerk whether the *Times* was expected. He did not know — but it had been "a long time" since "this" had happened: the absence at 8:15 of that paper. I went home with the *Globe,* read it, set out again downtown, now in my car, to do various errands, and to check on the *Times* again. When I got to the drugstore I was told that the *Times* wouldn't be coming: some unusual foul-up in the Concord delivery for that day. All right, I thought to myself, I can surely do without that paper.

I went about my chores, then remembered that the town's library gets the newspapers through its own delivery network: even when the stores don't have certain papers or magazines, the library will have them. I went there to stop and read. I do so once or twice a week anyway — far less expensive than subscribing to this and that publication. I entered the "periodical room," sought out the *Times,* found the bamboo stick with the *Times* attached to it, but noticed it was Thursday's edition, that of the day before the inauguration. There was something wrong. The daily papers are always there, ready to be read, by 11:00 a.m. I looked around, then went to the circulation desk. I asked a young man working there if "today's *Times*" had come in. "Yes," he said. I explained what I had just discovered. He went with me to the reading room, saw the same thing, and then told me what he surmised had occurred: "Someone took it — and substituted an old copy from the stack." (A week's issues of the paper are kept in a separate pile, available for those who care to go back in time that way. There are, too, microfilms of months, years of the paper.)

I was confused and irritated, but the young librarian had a clear notion of what had transpired and was, I began to realize, a bit sad and bemused rather than angry or upset. He told me that he was "sure" that "someone" had decided to take the *Times* home — since no copies had been available in the local stores. That person had taken the trouble to connect a two-day-old newspaper to the bamboo poles, after removing from them the Saturday edition. I wondered why. The librarian gave me a look of slight surprise — as if I belonged, perhaps, in the children's room across the hall. Then I was offered a lecture on stealing in the Concord Public Library; the home of Emerson's books, Thoreau's, Hawthorne's, an institution that serves a quite comfortably middle-class population. Hadn't I noticed all the "security" in the building — all the machinery meant to catch thieves? Newspapers and magazines, however, can escape the detection of that gadgetry — and so, they are "often" taken, not returned. The librarian did permit himself this moral disquisition, which I can offer word for word: "Someone went to the drugstore, as you did, and saw no *Times*. He came here, read the paper, and decided he wanted it. For some stupid reason he didn't just take the paper. He went to the trouble of switching papers. I suppose he was afraid someone would notice the empty [bamboo] sticks. His mind doing tricks on him! A Raskolnikov! So, he made the switch and left with the *Times*. He didn't care about you or anyone else. He didn't care that now our microfilms will lack that day, unless we write to the *Times* and get another copy. All he cared about was his desire. And everyone talks about how safe these suburbs are. And in that police record you read in the weekly Concord paper, the only crimes are a few drunken episodes. If someone's house is robbed — oh, that's an outsider coming into the town! Concord's people are all well educated, respectable, and law-abiding."

We talked for ten or fifteen minutes. He told me what he'd been told by some of the town's storekeepers, including the owner of the drugstore where I buy newspapers as well as shaving cream, toothpaste, and such staples of contemporary living — the thefts that take place week after week: people who hide magazines or other objects under their coats, or slip them into their pockets; people who pretend to leave the right amount of coins on top of a stack of papers, but don't do so; people who go to a sandwich shop's counter and pocket tips left for the waiter.

That last sad bit of information brought to my mind, suddenly, John Cheever's compelling story "The Housebreaker of Shady Hill." Now a lot became clear to me; I knew where I was — in a territory occupied by sinful human beings, men and women no less selfish and self-centered and greedy and lawless, in their own ways, than those who live in "high crime" areas of our cities. To be sure, as the saying goes, there are crimes and there are crimes. I am certain some of my fellow Concordians use drugs, but we don't have the drug wars that plague our ghettos, nor the murders. Our kind of crime is, as Cheever reminds his readers, genteel, discreet, slyly self-protective (and self-aggrandizing) in nature — a paper stolen here, a grocery store article there. At work, of course, we take larger risks — the illegal stock deals, the lying and plagiarism and faking of data that has taken place in recent years at Harvard Medical School, among other places in the nation: "white-collar crime," one hears it all called, not the kind that lends itself to dramatic and unnerving television coverage.

I went home and sat in my study and looked out of the window. I read the Cheever story again — a melancholy glimpse at upper-class hypocrisy and duplicity. I tried to imagine that person going through all that humiliating, pitiable hanky-panky for a lousy news-paper. I remembered what I'd heard at psychiatric conferences — all the "kleptomaniacs," the "compulsive stealers" among the university students who inhabit Cambridge. I remembered one or two I'd inter-viewed years ago, youths from rather well-to-do homes who loved taking records or books from stores without paying: a thrill, a chal-lenge. "Pray for them all," my mother would have said, and I suppose she was right. But that day the best I could summon was a kind of disgusted pity, and an anger, too — that discussions about our "grow-ing crime rate" in America don't, somehow, take into account that slimy Concordian who kept some of us in the town from reading the highfalutin' *Times* on the day after George Bush's ascension to the White House.

May 1989

14

The So-Called Underclass, Part I

WITH THIS COLUMN I'd like to begin a discussion of the "underclass," a term used in recent years to describe the millions of men, women, and children in late twentieth-century America who seem headed nowhere. They are not only poor, or cursed by bad luck, or victims of a spell of unemployment; they are thought to be significantly outside our nation's social, economic, cultural, and, yes, moral mainstream. In recent decades other words or phrases have been used to describe such people; they have been called "illiterate," "culturally deprived," "culturally disadvantaged," or less pompously, "the poorest of the poor."

But the latest term, "underclass," has acquired considerable authority, and its widespread usage is itself of some interest — because "class" is now specifically acknowledged in a country that has not always been willing to give it much due. We are all "equal," so many of us insist; or we are, mostly, "middle class" — a term that seems to include everyone who has a halfway decent job as well as those who do, as it is put in the South, "right well," yet are not willing to consider themselves rich, a word shunned by many quite well-to-do families as applicable to themselves. I remember, in this regard, two comments made by Robert Kennedy in the last year of his life — words spoken as he toured the poorer regions of this country and tried to figure out how an effective political constituency might be mobilized on behalf of such neighborhoods: "When I was younger you didn't get far in politics talking about race and class; now we're mentioning race, but class still isn't up for discussion." Later that day he declared what so many Americans feel: "Everyone is in the middle class or wants to be there." He pulled back, of course, noted the many who know they are poor and the few who delight in being considered rich; but he was, as the narrator in one of Walker Percy's novels might put it, "onto something."

I have no wish to enter the various arguments about the origin and nature of the "underclass." I find the book of the black social scientist William Julius Wilson, *The Truly Disadvantaged,* persuasive; I also find persuasive this definition, offered to me by a thirty-eight-year-old black grandmother who was born in a part of Boston, Roxbury, commonly called a ghetto, and who expects to die there: "Hereabouts there's a lot of people who just aren't doing well, and they can't seem to find a way to better themselves, and I guess I'm one of them, myself. Some will try, I'll tell you, and they fall down. Some won't try; they seem to be beyond trying. I don't know what can be done [I had asked]. I've looked at the babies when they're born, mine and [those belonging to] others, and I've wondered if it's something they're born with; but the kids will be full of the devil, and I'll decide they could be fine, just fine, if it wasn't this world that doesn't treat them fine. It won't take a baby long to get the facts straight, about all our troubles here; and when they do, then that's the end of their trying to be like those nice people, living those nice lives you see on television."

She had a lot more to say, and sometimes — thinking the thoughts of the 1980s — I've tried to be skeptical, tough-minded. To be sure, she is a black woman living a life of poverty in a northern ghetto — but surely, with enough "drive" or "determination," I say to myself, she might have done better. Then I ask those rhetorical questions we have recently been urged to ask. Why did she have five children by two men, both of whom left her? Why didn't she try to get off welfare — perhaps by working part-time or even full-time, with her mother helping out at home? Why is it that her three daughters are on welfare, and haven't married, yet already have eight children, with two more on the way? Why has her older son become a tough, a member of a local gang, a drug user and dealer? Why has her younger son become so morose and sullen? Why has he fathered two children by two women, and taken no responsibility for the lives of either of the women, either of the children? What, finally, can be done for such people, who do not strike me as genetically flawed — in the sense that they are in reasonably good physical and mental health?

When I talk with each of them — three generations of American citizens — I get a sense of an adequate intelligence, though one not at work in the manner I observe in other (suburban) neighborhoods. Indeed, the drug dealer son is alert, savvy, shrewd, articulate. One of his sisters, the mother of three by two men, and on welfare, is wise beyond her twenty-three years. She can be observant, witty, knowing. But the doctor in me also concludes, at times, that she is not only overwhelmed as a mother, but disheartened, sad. Should I call her "depressed," I often wonder, and not only her — maybe everyone in her extended family — and thereby nudge my thoughts about the "underclass" away from an analysis of cognition and toward a psychiatric analysis? For many years, of course, I have emphasized neither — preferring to emphasize "class" and "culture" and "race," such "variables": the whole history of various groups of people in this nation.

The results of such work amount to lots of words, plenty of articles and books — one person's effort (shall I get fancy and pompous and pretentious and say one *researcher*?) to understand how children from various backgrounds grow up. Yet, I now feel at a real loss as I try to understand the woman I have just quoted and her family.

Well, all right, how do children of the "underclass" grow up — and why don't they grow up in such a way that they want to leave that "underclass," better themselves, live differently than they do? Is there, perhaps, some failure not of genes; not of psychology even, nor school experience for that matter, but of the moral imagination? After all — some teachers keep reminding me — plenty of boys and girls go through hellish times while growing up (Asian youths now in America, but once in Vietnam, for instance) and yet seem headed "upward," for all the trouble they've known and still know. I once heard the grandmother I quoted above say this, as if in answer to some of my questions: "I can't speak of others. Maybe they have their hope left. Me, us — it seems we've lost something somewhere along. I'm not hiding behind [being] black. Some of our people have made it good, real good. I look at the TV and see them living good. I'd like to live like them and my kids would too. I try to teach them to be good. But there's just so many of us — is my hunch — that can rise on up. I thought my bigger [older] boy would be the one — oh, he's smart! — but he's gone and fallen down. But, you see, he's got that money now. [He deals in drugs, a major business in the neighborhood.] He makes us all feel poorer than we are! I can't explain anything, beyond what I've said, no sir."

At such moments, after hearing such words, I can feel my body slumping, my mind tiring, my spirits falling. I lose my initiative in our conversation; my eyes drift toward the television set, which has never once been off when I've come to talk. I'm soon enough ready to leave for my own world, where a heady discussion of the "underclass" can be held in seminar rooms, or read between the pages of magazines, books, while sipping liquids, taking in good food. Once, though, that woman was forthcoming in a way that kept my interest somewhat longer. She said that she, and others like her, had "these problems," and then she added: "If we could be rid of some of them, just some, maybe we could do better." We proceeded to discuss "them," the various problems she had in mind, and I will try to do so in the next few issues.

June 1989

15

The Underclass, Part II:
Widespread Teenage Pregnancy

I N THE 1960s when my wife and I were living in the South, and later when we worked in Appalachia, we noticed that many of the white and black youths we knew got married while teenagers, or took up living together at that time in their lives. Often migrant farm workers became parents before they were twenty, and up the hollows of West Virginia we noticed a similar inclination of young people there to start family life, including child-bearing, considerably earlier than many who live in middle-class suburban neighborhoods think to do. A black minister who worked with migrant farm workers in Florida during the middle 1960s explained things this way to us one May day, after we returned from helping a public health nurse give shots to a substantial number of babies born to mothers we still regarded as, unfortunately, "drop-outs" from high school: "Hereabouts life goes faster than in other places. You'll see kids picking the crops early — no school for them. Why try the books? They're on the move from June to October, and they don't see another future for themselves. Sex comes when they're thirteen or so, and that's part of living. A lot will come see me and want to be married. Some don't get married, but they'll be together. Some shift partners. Everything goes faster for them. They die younger, you know. They don't live healthy. There's no doctors to see them. They're as poor as you can get. You say they're marrying young. I say they're well along in life. They've been working in those fields since they were seven or eight maybe, and by sixteen or seventeen they've got plenty of callouses to show they're all grown up!"

When we came back North and I began working in a ghetto neighborhood of Boston in the late 1960s and early 1970s I soon enough realized that the sexuality of the teenagers I met there was not the same as that of the migrant youth I had met in, say, Belle Glade, Florida. Of course, the 1960s had come and just about gone — giving shape to a more open sexuality all over America. Moreover, I had been working in the rural South at a time when strong social controls as well as racially connected strictures prevailed. The minister I quoted had enormous influence on his flock — not the least because he was an important intermediary between them and the white growers who controlled so much of the life of the Lake Okeechobee region. But in the Boston neighborhood where I talked with children, something else, too, was at work, I began to realize — something that went beyond the influence of the cultural changes of a decade, or the exhilarating consequences of shaking off segregation through a trek northward.

I will turn to another minister, a black Baptist who lives in Roxbury, where a lot of my research took place, and who in 1971 gave me the lecture of my life about the people I was trying to understand: "You have to realize that these folks are in trouble, real bad trouble. They've come up here, a lot of them, from small towns down South — where, until recently, they were watched over like animals. They had their own part of town. The police didn't care what happened there, so long as they behaved themselves in the white side of town. (What would happen in a white community if the police just shrugged their shoulders when someone did something wrong?) They went to lousy schools, and they couldn't vote, and every once in a while one of them was strung up on a tree, lynched — and even that wasn't treated as a crime thirty or forty years ago! Now, they've come up here. They came here to get away from all that second- and third- and fourth-class living: North to Freedom! Well, some freedom! They ended up in poor, poor neighborhoods — [they] used to be called slums, and now [they] get called ghettos. Down South, for all the troubles, there was a world they knew, and they had to control themselves, or the white man, he'd get them fast. Rotten controls, racist controls, outrageous controls, murderous controls, but controls. Up here, [the] white man says: you can have your freedom, but stay away from us. Down South [the] white man said: work for us, be close to us, sometimes we'll chew the fat together, laugh and cry together; we're not scared of your company, so long as you keep your place and mind your manners. Up here, [the] white man says go live where you can find a place to live, and stay away from us, because we've never had you around before, and we sure don't need you now or want you. You can vote, you can do as you please — just don't be bothering us.

"Well, we're up here, and there's lots of confusion, you see. People aren't the members of communities they used to be. Newcomers, immigrants, they're all dazed for a while. We're newcomers from our foreign country, the rural South. We've got to figure out a whole new life — and pretty soon, no, right away, we discover that it may be worse up here, in certain ways, than it was down there, yes, because it's getting better down there every year now that the civil rights struggle is being won, and it's getting worse and worse up here, more hate per square mile than anywhere down South.

"Back there [the South] back then [earlier decades of the twentieth century] we had our communities — in Talladega [Alabama] where I was born. We had the ministers, and people looked up to us. We had the insurance man, and the funeral director, and people looked up to them, and they talked about life and death, and people listened. We had our schoolteachers; we had our nurses; we had our grocery store folks — and if you had ambition, we had our colleges, every [Southern] state had them. Sure, terrible segregation, terrible poverty, terrible brutality. But we had our communities; even so, we had them. Now, we're up here, and it's a strange place, and it's every one for himself, and it's cold, man, cold, and I'm not just talking about the weather. Now we're not Uncle Toms anymore; and now Mister Charlies are gone (and some were nice folks, some); and now it's the alleys and broken-down tenements, with huge rats, and no heat, and the landlord you never see and he never comes within a hundred miles of you — he's in some fancy athletic club in a rich suburb, 'working out' — and it's kill or be killed, 'so harsh, so mean,' that's what a *girl* said to me, the other day, and she's got a baby inside her, and she's not yet fifteen, and she's hoping that finally she'll find herself someone she can trust, that baby, and finally she'll find meaning in life, but I'll tell you, she's sad now, and I predict, she'll be sad a year or two from now; and if she gets her welfare payment, that won't solve her problem, not really, not in the long run."

A long cry, an exhortation, an analysis, a series of observations, a lamentation — stopped by his melancholy awareness that the "girl" in question was his own step-niece. Nothing that he told me that day has changed all that much in the more than fifteen years that have elapsed. If anything, things have gotten much worse in his neighborhood — and especially the rate of teenage pregnancies. So many of the young women I've met in that neighborhood are, indeed, "sad." They may have been neglected, even abused themselves. They haven't become engaged with school work. They are hungry for love and desperately afraid of not going along with the social and cultural and sexual pressures that come to bear upon them on the street, where they spend so much of their time, gabbing, laughing, listening, watching, wondering — who is doing what where and with whom. They see little hope for themselves in the bourgeois world so many of us know so well and take for granted as our home. There are few successful businesses or factories to represent in a visible, ongoing way that bourgeois world. Those youths know in their own way that world —

its longstanding, essential disinterest (to put it mildly) in them. Indeed, such knowledge or awareness is a mainstay of black experience and culture — how to size up "the man" and come to terms with him. Against such a background (a cold, anonymous, hostile, death-like world of unemployment, of racist rejection), sexual activity offers at least the possibility of warmth, affection, and ultimately the "life" that is a baby, not to mention those welfare checks, as they go out today a pitiable, patronizing, degrading "industry" in itself.

My minister friend is right, though — as one of my sons, a medical student, has found out all too well these recent years as he has talked with the "girls" mentioned in the above quote. So often they tell him how frightened they are — and in low, low spirits. The new baby doesn't offer the New Jerusalem for which the mother had prayed. Such mothers all too commonly have little to offer their babies — little in material things, and little of themselves, because they, in turn, had been given so little, or had lost what little they once felt to be theirs. Still, the babies keep coming, so many of them. The young men want to prove they are young men. The young women want to prove they are young women. The young men, sometimes, smile brightly at their baby child — but turn elsewhere in response to the fast pace of adolescent life. The young women beam at their children, but also feel the downward tug of a particular life. My minister friend, again — now speaking in 1987: "The glow of sex, of a child born, dies out. They're back to 'reality' — these streets and themselves, poor, poor ghetto kids, more and more of them, with no place to go, no sense that anyone cares where they go, a dead-end street ahead of them." I hear such words and lower my head; I remember all the statistics I've read — of infant mortality and unemployment, of the number of single-parent families, of school drop-outs. I am glad, with such thoughts crossing my mind, to have a nice car nearby, which will take me swiftly, comfortably to another part of America, where I can sit quietly and write words such as these, and wonder what will happen to "them" — though, because I realize "we" have a lot at stake in this, too, I wonder what will happen to all of us, to our country, if somehow so many of those very young mothers and fathers I know, and their babies, don't find different, better lives to live.

July–August 1989

16

The Underclass, Part III:
Drugs

S OMETIMES AS I WALK in a so-called ghetto, or drive through its streets, I have to stop and scratch my head or shake myself out of an incredulity that has seized me, no matter years of work in such communities — the sight of ordinary men, women, and children going about their perfectly ordinary and quite normal lives. We have had good cause, of course, to think of ghettoes as a dense, melancholy tangle of accumulated psychological and social pathology. But often, I fear, we let such awareness distort our sense of what actually obtains in neighborhoods which become, even for the best intentioned of us, a foreign territory of sorts, a far distant "them" among whom all is decidedly not well.

The other day, standing on a street easily describable as one more corner of the American underclass, a street known for its "drug-related violence," a phrase I keep seeing in the newspapers when reporters refer to that street, I found myself noticing the humdrum, quite delightful particulars of weekend familial life. Mothers *and* fathers were walking with children. Boys and girls were playing the same street games my friends and I did in our white suburban heaven over forty years ago. Some elderly women stood outside a store boasting of the virtues of their various grandchildren. Bike-riders added their vitality to the human parade. Shoppers were carrying home their weekly supplies of food. A group of five girls, all dressed up, were obviously on their way to some special ceremonial occasion. A pizza parlor, its smells inviting to my empty stomach, was accommodating its patrons, and several of them, full of anticipation, had just left for home as I walked by.

A ghetto? The underclass? Such abstractions are pushed our way by journalists and social scientists, who command so much of our attention and have become the chief interpreters of our social reality. But as I stood at a particular intersection in the afternoon of yet another day in my lengthening American life, I thought to myself: There is a life here best observed and conveyed by those who don't make it their business to be "experts" on "ghetto life" or "the drug problem," and who don't herd people into "the underclass." I thought naturally of Ralph Ellison, what *he'd* tell us of that scene, or yes, as improbable as it seems, of John Cheever and Walker Percy and Eudora Welty, not known for including such neighborhoods in their fiction, and yet such marvelous witnesses to human variety, complexity, ambiguity. We are not, alas, about to turn toward such novelists for the help we need in understanding our social problems — a pity for sure. I'd bet on their vision, though, if it were focused on the urban poor as well as on the bourgeoisie, who are so used to being attended by storytellers.

The foregoing may strike the reader as a long and irrelevant wind-up to a column with this one's title, and yet I worry that we seem to have a language that in itself precludes the kind of life I have just described. For example, when I was working with black families who lived in a certain Boston section, I was constantly reminded that "drugs" ruled this or that street, to the point that all the life I saw there got banished by my singular ongoing preoccupation with those "drugs," not to mention other "variables," such as "race" and "violence" — even though, every day, I met utterly sane and sensible and law-abiding and decent and hardworking people, going about their ways in the manner the rest of us do: working, eating, sleeping, dreaming, hoping, worrying, trying to get through this life from day to day. Still, there *were* drugs in that part of town (and there are plenty of drugs in well-off, white, suburban towns, though we don't stress such a presence when we think of those residential areas). By no means did those drugs control everyone's life, but they most definitely have taken possession of a growing number of lives, and we in this nation now wonder what ought to (or, indeed, can) be done.

How else to think of drug use — by anyone, living anywhere — as but the most obvious evidence of nihilism, of despair? When one takes drugs one engages in an assault on one's brain; one does tricks with one's consciousness, with one's conscience, with one's ability to do everyday tasks. Societies, in many ways, try to protect people from all sorts of dangers, and the ingestion of, say, cocaine or heroin certainly qualifies as one of them — in fact, of a life-threatening kind. *Why* do people take to drugs, we ask our secular authorities, our doctors, our surveyors of social pathology? The usual, and in part correct, answers make mention of psychological words such as anxiety and depression — or, more sociologically, of a sense of futility about one's prospects with respect to work and a halfway useful, respectable life. Still, I am haunted by a question put to me years ago by an elderly black woman, a grandmother who had known the toughest and meanest of life: "Why do drugs have that pull on our kids — when it's better up here for them than it ever was for us in [rural] Georgia [where she was born and raised]?" I knew not what to say. I knew to toss the question back to her — a tic of my kind. Her response: "Up here they give you just enough to kill you." What did she mean by that? She wasn't sure herself, but she allowed for an amplification: "The young folks here, they can get jellies and kits and things [contraceptive devices]. They can get welfare checks. They can get drugs, or go take drugs [methadone] to get them off drugs. But they don't have something that's more important than a check or drugs or 'safe sex' around the clock; they don't have the belief that they're good, worthwhile folks, and the world is smiling at them, and the Lord is watching over them, and this is their country, as much as anyone else's. Back when I was a kid [in Georgia] we didn't have much, and the country wasn't nice to us, and it all looked terrible lots of times, but we had our Lord, and we had the faith of our momma, telling us to get on with it, every day, until we would one day meet Him, our Lord, and find His peace, the peace of the Lord."

In her own not especially didactic way she was telling me that a certain moral and religious life was absent in the Boston neighborhood where we were talking — not to mention other neighborhoods in America. She was telling me, too, that drugs are for some "all the sun they can see, all the peace of the Lord" they seem able to discover. Are we to let the matter drop there — offer drugs, as some would advocate, to such people, who are so often the first to tell a trusted person how forlorn they feel? The longer I struggle to understand the use of drugs in ghetto communities, the more I fall back on the woman I have quoted above, who on another occasion pointed this out to me: "We have plenty of good people right here, and they could be helping out, if they had a little encouragement. If we had more of us here looking out for others, it would be better, but you can't look out for others if you're not on solid ground yourself. I look at the people on drugs, and I know they need salvation, that's what they need, not in the next world — that salvation is God's to give — but in this world, and in this world we got to save each other, and to do that you need your strength, that's for sure."

She has had the idea of an "army" of sorts, all the "solid folks" linking arms in order to find a collective strength for those who drink too much and snort and shoot up. Indeed, as she talked I thought of Alcoholics Anonymous, with its strongly spiritual and confessional emphasis, and of *The Autobiography of Malcolm X*, with its story of re-demptive religious conversion. All rather visionary — yet one wonders what short of such a moral and mobilized community response will even begin to work with people daily driven to knock themselves out, destroy their will, their self-regard, their hold on the everyday routines that constitute the life most of us gladly take for granted.

September 1989

17

The Underclass, Part IV:
Schools and Mentors

ANY DAYS I wonder what real hope, educationally, there is
for the poor children I get to see in the course of my work.
Earlier this year I spent time every week in an industrial city north
of Boston that has a substantial Spanish-speaking and black ghetto. I
talked with high school youths and elementary school children. I was
trying to learn from them what prospects they felt they had, what
hopes and aspirations, what worries or wishes. Often as I sat in the
high school cafeteria or library listening to a particular young man or
woman talk, I noticed my head dropping or, more to the point, my
spirits sagging. The person before me seemed so grim or doubtful
about life, so silent — or, indeed, all too powerfully, cynically articulate, and not rarely, rather skeptical of or hostile toward me and my
kind. One late morning, over a pizza, I heard this: "Don't be worrying about us. [I'd obviously given him just cause to conclude that such
was my overall attitude, one of apprehension, alarm, perplexity, fear.]
We'll run in our marathon, and down where you live folks will be running in theirs. [I was grateful that in the second half of his declaration
he stopped just short of arraigning me, personally] It's two different
races, and the teachers, they're always trying to tell us it's all the same.
'In life,' our history teacher keeps saying, and I want to stand up and
say, 'In whose life, buddy?' But I won't win him [over], and he sure
as hell won't get me put in his pocket.

"You want to know why I still come to school? I'll tell you: the
company, some friends, and there's a girl I'm after, and she's here. She
says she wants to be an actress. Can you beat that! She's already one!
She strings us all along! She's the one who's keeping attendance up!
If she left, a hundred of us guys would be on her trail all day. I'm
not kidding."

In fact, he was kidding. Underneath his callous, wry, ironic, teasing
manner I thought I detected a sad and frustrated teenager whose very
sardonic repartee indicated that somehow, in some manner, he might
be "saved." What do I mean, though, when I use such a word — saved
from what, or for what? I tried to get the answer to such a line of
questioning from the student himself, and one February morning —

the snow covering a drab neighborhood with its temporary blanket of white, a wind stirring things up, and some dogs fighting noisily outside his home — I heard this: "You hear those animals barking? It's like people. We bark, too. We fight for what's ours, what we want; or we figure there's nothing to fight for, so you just try to stay alive the best you can. In school they tell you the sky is the limit if you'd only use your head. I've tried; when I was a little kid, there was a teacher, and I liked her, I guess because she liked me. She'd get friendly with me; she'd ask me about my family. She told me she thought I was 'smart,' and I could be 'a good student.' I tried. I was 'a good student.' She wrote a note to my mother, and I brought it home. But my mother was sick. She was throwing up, and there was blood coming out of her [uterine bleeding]. Besides, my mother is a 'case' [has psychological difficulties: depression]. Maybe I could have said to hell with everyone in my family and become a teacher's pet for life. But the next year [in school] the teacher hated every single one of us, me included, and we all knew it; she was an old hag, waiting on retirement. She didn't have to say a bad word; her face told us everything. That's when I said so long to school. If I hadn't [done so], I don't know; I'd be a good student, and maybe go to a college and get a good job. If I'd stayed with that teacher, the one who was nice to me, maybe — who knows? — I'd be different. You need someone to help you, if you're going to try living different. You can push on your own so far. Sure, some can push all the way, and they don't need anyone's help. But they have confidence in themselves; they must, or they're just going for broke, and if they win, great, and if they lose well, they've got nothing to lose. For me, it's not been worth the fight. I look at those teachers and their books, and I say: man, you're out in space, and I'm where I am, and there's nothing between us — nothing, no one. I don't even hear them a lot of days. I'm just sitting there, looking at the girls. My mind is on them, or it's on after-school: we hang around, and I deliver pizzas. I could do better — boy, could I! — delivering other stuff [drugs]; but I'm not into that yet. That's another step; I don't know if I'll take it."

He appears to be a youth of above average intelligence who has a conscience, who, in fact, has resisted the various blandishments of the drug culture. Perhaps his intelligence and conscience, plus memories of one teacher who paid him considerate and substantial heed, still keep him in school, for all his sadness and growing skepticism, if not despair. The long and short of my own conversations with him persuaded me to try to connect him with a "mentor" program — college students who become "big brothers" to youths such as he. I cannot report a glowing miracle, but I can say that a young man who is a junior in a nearby college has, so far, in his talks with this high schooler, gotten well beyond the kinds of discussions I have just set down — has heard less truculence and sarcasm, less talk of what might have been, more inquiry about what might be. Not that it has been easy.

I fear that many of us who want to lend our eager helping hands to ghetto youngsters are all too naive or cocksure, or we are optimistic beyond all warrant — a measure of our own experiences in life, soon enough headed for disappointment, if not outright despair, that more than matches the kind we notice in those we aim to "help." Still, with modesty and patience and persistence, and with carefully measured efforts to make specific, concrete achievements, a "mentor" and a "mentee," or better, a pair of human beings, can first learn how to work together rather than in tandem, and then begin to connect intellectually as well as emotionally. "I don't think I'm doing as well in school as he'd like," the young man quoted above told me recently, but, significantly, he added this: "He's trying hard, and he makes me want to give him a break!"

I was fascinated by that comment — a cool, sardonic intelligence at work, testing, always testing the world, but moving ever so tentatively and warily toward the recognition that there might, there just might be a chance for a "break" to be made with things as they have been. How else do we take a chance on "life," so to speak — except through the help of others? One-on-one, as the expression goes: that I-Thou the existentialists have kept mentioning is a distinctly redemptive possibility for any of us, anywhere, including in our ghettoes, as any number of "volunteers" have, thank God, kept discovering.

October 1989

18

The Underclass, Part V:
Children and Violence

I N THIS LAST PIECE on the so-called underclass, I would like to look back at my work in Boston over the years, and address the matter of violence — its presence in ghettos, among other places. For nearly a quarter of a century I have been working in parts of a Boston ghetto, trying to understand how black and Spanish-speaking children grow up. I came to Roxbury in 1966, upon my return from the South, where I watched the civil rights struggle unfold — school desegregation, the sit-in movement, the various marches, the Mississippi "Freedom Summer" — days of pain, but a time also of important political success and moral victory. Again and again I was told by segregationists in obscure Alabama, Georgia, Louisiana, and Mississippi towns not only to get the hell out, to go "back home," but more significantly (in retrospect, at least) to go take a close look at what I'd left to come "messing in other folks' backyards." Soon enough, I had indeed returned to my native Boston — just in time to discover what the sheriff of McComb County, Mississippi, told me (one July day in 1964) I'd find out, if I would only be willing to do so: "It's great the way y'all go around down here pointing out our troubles and our mistakes. Be sure to look hard around you when you're back there in Yankee heaven."

The violence that accompanied attempted school and residential desegregation in the North, in cities such as Boston or Chicago, took many of us by surprise. For one thing, the South had been regarded as the last bastion of segregationist resistance; now, it was cities whose sons and daughters had gone to Selma, to the Delta, that were caught in a cross-fire of fear and hate. I well remember sitting with Dr. Martin Luther King Jr., listening to him talk of that fateful trip to Chicago he took toward the end of his life — "enough to make you want to go hurrying back South," he said with a wan, wry smile on his face. Moreover, that sheriff had made a point to me that may well have accounted for the reluctance of many of us Northern folk to take a careful look at our own, nearby world: "Down here, rich or poor, we know each other, the colored and us, we live with each other every day. Up there, you have your well-off people, they buy their way out of what they don't like, and they never have a thing to do with anyone colored."

For years in Boston I watched a politics of both race and class play out — the bitterness and jeopardy felt by whites who worked in factories or service jobs, the earnest, high hopes of black integrationist leaders, the dreams of black parents that those Southern triumphs would soon come North. But as Boston struggled with school desegregation, I watched whites who could afford to do so move to so-called blue-collar suburbs; some blacks also moved, often to liberal, white, well-to-do suburbs, but most blacks, of course, have had nowhere to go. Let a black man in his late fifties describe what he has seen happen since he came North to Boston after the Second World War: "I came from just outside Greensboro [North Carolina] and we had a quiet life there. I drove for the undertaker. I always wore a suit that way! But I wanted more than the suit, and him telling me he'd bury me real good, 'a dandy job,' he'd say. I wanted to live good, not just die good. So, I went up North. I had a cousin who'd been stationed near Boston during the [Second World] War and he stayed, and I figured I'd go follow him. He was living near Columbus Avenue in the South End. He'd gotten a job in a gas station; I believe it was called Merit gas that they sold. I got me a place near him, and I got me a job in a restaurant. White folks would come there — steppin' out, and you could see them being curious and excited: 'the best fried chicken in Boston,' someone said in a newspaper. Where I lived, there were some white folks — boarding houses, mostly elderly, but some young ones, I remember. The South was in me: I'd tip my hat to the white women. I didn't do that with our women. But then the civil rights movement back home got me thinking, and so one day I stopped tipping my hat.

"All of a sudden [the early 1960s] the whites were getting out of where we lived — too many of us. We moved to Roxbury, and there were still some white folks there. It was peaceful. Some of the old apartment houses, and the triple deckers, you could feel the ghosts there, of the Jews — and all their stores on Blue Hill Avenue, some were still there. There were some Irish around, too. We lived together for a while. My kids knew some white kids, and I'd tell my sons and daughters, the Jews are a high-class people, they believe in the mind, and I want you to be like them. I had a job for a while as janitor: the folks called me 'superintendent.' The landlord, he was Jewish, and he treated me nice, real nice. He'd been living in [nearby] Dorchester, and then he moved over to Newton, 'the big jump,' he called it. He said we [blacks] could do the same some day — but I'm not sure it's true, no sir. We have some professional people here in Roxbury, and in Dorchester, and they move to Mattapan, and that's as far as they can go. You try the suburbs, and they'll fight you.

"It's been downhill here [in Roxbury and Dorchester] the past twenty years. I thought it would get better for my kids, and even better for *their* kids, but that's not so. I'm not educated, so I don't know the reasons, but everything's gotten worse here, to my way of seeing it. The buildings are in worse shape. The shopping is worse — lots of the stores are gone. You don't see white folks at all, and your own people, the good ones, if they can, they try to leave. The big business is drugs. The kids, they're in gangs. They've got guns. I walk down near the park [Seaver Street, along Franklin Park] and I say to myself: What's this all about, and why, for crying out loud, did I come up here? I go back to see my brother and sister [in North Carolina], and I'll tell you something, their kids and grandkids, they're living in a better world than mine are up here in freedom land.

"One of my grandsons, he's ten, and he'll tell me about shoot-outs and drug deals. He's seen both. Half the time he's scared; half the time he's excited. The other day the boy said to me: 'Grandpa, they shoot the guns, just like on TV, and they have $100 bills, the kids do, like the rich have them, and if you fight them, you're dead, and they [drug dealers] "own" some cops.' That's what I heard from my grandson. I told his daddy, and his daddy is strong, I'll tell you, and he said, 'I know, I know,' and then he said, 'I'll take care of the boy, I will.' I hope he can. He's a hard worker. [He works as a bus driver for the city, and in the evening protects a supermarket and helps resupply its stock.] But he don't see the kids all he should, and their mother comes home tired. [She has a job at a day-care center with mostly white children whose parents work at Harvard Medical School and its teaching hospitals.] There'll come a time when Jamie [his grandson] will be out there on the streets, like kids are when they're growing up. And then what?

"The streets aren't what they were just ten years ago, never mind twenty. You have violence everywhere. It's guns. It's drugs. It's gangs. It's lots of cash, and lots of shooting, and lots of shooting up. I can't sleep, thinking of it all, thinking of my kids and my grandkids. I try to figure out what the answers are, and I don't come up with them. If we had the money, and could move somewhere else, that'd be our answer. But we don't have the money, and there's no place up here for us to go. My brother says, come on back, and I've gone back. Last year my mother passed, and we all went — and Jamie, he said, 'Grandpa, I like it here; let's stay.' I know there's trouble everywhere, but more

here than there, and that's the truth. The biggest trouble up here —
it's that there's nothing a lot of people believe in, nothing and no one,
except to have the dough to buy things, and to dress themselves up,
pretty themselves up, and feel 'good.' That's what I hear them all say:
'As long as I can feel good sometimes. . . .' There isn't the respect for
the other person; there isn't the respect for God; there isn't the fear —
that you're afraid to do wrong. 'We're not afraid of anything,' I'll hear
young kids say. My Jamie sees kids his age on the street with guns
and stacks of $100 bills. There's no rule of law. There's no belief in
anyone's laws, not man's, and not God's."

I listen to him, remember his self-effacing modesty as he defers to
"educated folks," keep in mind his reluctance to offer "answers," yet
wonder whether all the social science books I pick up and read have
any more to tell us. He has a shrewd eye, can see what the sociologists and psychologists and psychiatrists would notice if they were
around — the poor neighborhoods, the widespread unemployment,
the inadequate schools, the welfare dependency, the single-parent families, the drug culture, the gang culture, and the threat that such a
world presents to children who see not only violence on television and
in movie houses, but on the streets where they live.

Most of all, though, he takes notice of a moral chaos which he connects not to "drugs" or to "television" or to "welfare" — the standard
explanatory abstractions — but to a loss of moral values, of religious
belief. Once he even played, *seriously* played, with that old phrase "law
and order" that the civil rights movement faced head on — the sheriffs
demanding "law and order" all right, the segregationist kind: "Back
then there were our ministers and undertakers and schoolteachers, and
there was *their* 'law and order,' not only the police watching over us.
We said no to our kids, and they listened. Now, we're up here and I
look at the kids on the street, a lot of them, and there's no one who
gives them the slightest pause, not the slightest. Not the ministers any
more. Not the schoolteachers. Not the undertakers. You know [I'd
asked], we looked up to those undertakers; they guided your body
to the grave, and they guided your soul toward God, that's what my
granddaddy told me, and my momma. A man who sees death every
day, he'd stop and think, and he'd make you stop and think. Now,
our kids see death every day, and there's no hush, there's no — well,
there's none of 'God's majesty,' our minister used to say, for us to call
on when someone's life was passed. There's just the police wagon, and
they'll send the men to sweep up the streets afterward."

As I talk with the children whose future he regards as so bleak,
I hear sad confirmation, week after week, of his social and cultural

analysis, and too, his moral diagnosis. Last year in a fourth-grade class I was teaching as a volunteer, a child took me aside — after I'd shown the class some Edward Hopper pictures which seemed rather melancholy to me (the urban loneliness he knew how to evoke so masterfully) — and said she only wished she lived "in one of those places" depicted in the book I'd brought to class. I asked her why. She answered immediately: "Everything seems quiet there — no hassles." For her, in contrast, any day can bring sudden, inexplicable violence, even death. "It's no fun," she once told me, her quiet understatement all the more memorable in view of the subject at hand.

I got to know her well enough to learn more — the grim consequences of a neighborhood's street life: scary dreams, nervous rituals (checking locks over and over again), constant worries about relatives and friends, and, not least, daydreaming, some of it understandably escapist, some of it evidence aplenty of an agitated sadness that, as she told me, "comes and goes." She was talking about her "moods," and elaborated this way: "I wake up and wonder what it'll be like, the day. I hope everything will be okay — you know, no one getting hurt. I hate seeing someone get hurt. I don't want to get hurt. I try to remember some [television] program or movie where people are nice to each other, and I put myself in it [the television program or movie]." Again and again, ever so poignantly, she has told me that in her head's daydreams those stores and hotels and tenement houses which figure in Hopper's paintings are not as desolate as they sometimes seem to me, but are havens for her, places whose very anonymity and stillness seem comforting indeed — certainly a contrast with what she sees and hears every day.

I often wonder what will come of her, and of my friend's grandson, Jamie — witnesses to constant terror and violence — even as I wonder how to make sense of the widely reported violence (the rape of a woman jogger by a gang of boys under sixteen) that took place in New York's Central Park, or in a pleasant white middle-class New Jersey suburb (the rape of a somewhat retarded girl by three high-schoolers) — all of the foregoing a national puzzle of late, and the occasion, yet again, for a parade of experts to come forth, each with his or her explanations and solutions. Who and what to blame, and why?

Well, for starters, with respect to all such incidents, those who perpetrated the deeds ought to be locked up for a long time, even as that girl in my class has told me several times of her all too conditional wish: "If only they could get all those people with guns and knives and drugs and lock them up for life, for every day until God decides He'll take them and judge them." An almost quaint way of talking — a great-grandmother's biblical oratory that lingers across the generations. Who, these days, among secular liberals, suggests some fire-and-brimstone, backed by strong police clout as necessary — the moral resurgence my black grandfather friend born in North Carolina looks in vain to find for his children's children?

Yes, of course, and unsurprisingly from my mouth or pen, there are the debilitated schools to be mentioned, the rundown housing, the "employment opportunities" or lack thereof. But something else is amiss in those ghettos, the elderly man keeps telling me, and I rather suspect not only in those ghettos. Nor do I mean the reflexive invocation of white violence, as in the Queens mob that set upon blacks, virtually driving one to death before an oncoming automobile. Many of the problems we associate with ghettos are by no means absent from well-to-do suburbs, in New Jersey or elsewhere — drug use, alcoholism, a callous or exploitative sexuality, and certainly, various kinds of violence. Youths kill themselves or others while driving cars crazily, drunkenly. Parties in fancy homes deteriorate into episodes of wild, destructive behavior. A policeman in one of those Boston suburbs: "These kids here [in the town where he works] are left with their parents' homes, and they go nuts. They're determined to leave everything in ruin. They can be as mean as prisoners on a riot in a jail. The parents — they're 'away.' But it never makes the press, what these kids do."

For a long time, when I worked in such towns, talking with children from quite affluent families, some sent away to boarding schools by mothers and fathers with their own "priorities," I heard such stories from teachers and maids and gardeners, from "the help," but also from children themselves, who were trying to make sense of a particular and often puzzling world. When I go to psychiatric and psychoanalytic meetings, I listen to discussions of youthful violence, the kind committed in well-to-do neighborhoods. I hear mention of "peer pressure," "acting out," "hostility and aggression" — and of course I hear of "therapy" as the solution: "When these [suburban] kids destroy property, they are displacing the anger they feel toward...."

As I recently heard those words my mind drifted a few miles east to a ghetto — where for most people there isn't so much property to destroy, and no money for psychiatrists. The street becomes a living room, and the court probation officer the therapist. I'd better, at this point, let an elderly suburban resident speak, a pediatrician and a grandmother and the moral equivalent of the black grandfather I quoted earlier: "I'm not a gloom-and-doom person, but I'll tell you something, this is sad — the rule of the *self* in our town. Once this was a community; we all knew each other, and we were interested in each other. Now, we're each 'into our own thing.' I *hate* that expression! In America today the politicians don't stand for anything but to get elected. Give them a poll, and they'll vote its numbers! We've had scandals in the church, in business, in the universities, in government. Cheating, lying, stealing — no good! Then, we ask why some of our kids are so selfish and mean and inconsiderate!"

There was much more — interrupted, at last, by her decision to switch tracks, emphasize the "upbeat," as she put it. She was right, by then, to do so, and so ought we all at certain moments, after much despair is expressed: remember the children in our ghettos who may observe violence, yet try to shun it, try to grow up decent and thoughtful; remember the children in our fancy suburban towns or urban townhouses who are also trying to be decent and sensitive individuals — no matter the greed and self-importance they observe, the violence of callousness, of selfishness, of smugness.

What to suggest, to do? Some recommendations are all too familiar, though they don't quite address the worries of the two watchful grandparents I have called as witnesses. Ghetto children need better educational and economic prospects. Many suburban children need from their busy, successful parents "quality time," and some could be helped by "counseling." But I wonder whether such liberal pieties, declared by me and my kind with conviction if not passion over the decades, really address one very important part of this matter of violence, be it in the ghetto or in our various better-off neighborhoods: the inner emptiness, the waywardness if not outright anarchy one hears children themselves directly and indirectly describing, never mind some of their worried elders.

Do secular liberals even have the vocabulary to begin addressing such matters? Will psychotherapy truly provide what is needed by our affluent young people, who for years have learned to become first self-indulged, then self-obsessed — and the devil on anyone who gets in the way? Will more condoms, more abortions, and the incredible latest suggestion, the publicly sanctioned availability of drugs, truly provide what our ghetto youth need? Will the language of the social sciences, so familiar, so readily (and dreamily) trotted out in public emergencies, help us all that much? Or new "public policy initiatives"? Is it more psychological and sociological explanations we need — and their antecedents, the always expensive "research data"?

Might we do a lot better with a rereading of *The Catcher in the Rye* and *Invisible Man?* Are we not only adrift morally and spiritually, but so lost we don't even know to ask how we can find our bearings, can reach out to one another, including our sons and daughters, in such a way that — to use an expression — we live kinder, more gentle lives?

December 1989

19

The Underclass, Part VI:
What Is to Be Done?

I AM STILL STRUGGLING with the phenomenon of the so-called underclass — struggling with the question of what ought to be done, what can be done, once the nature of such human suffering and jeopardy has been described, analyzed. When someone like me poses such a question (to himself, to readers) or when others, such as public officials, pose such a question to me, a so-called expert, the temptation to self-important pronouncements becomes substantial — and often they include no small number of banalities and pieties. Who in his or her right mind, for instance, wouldn't recommend the availability of more jobs for our ghetto youth, or better education, or improved housing, or programs that offer drug counseling? Not that our country has shown any great interest in such efforts in recent years — hence the final political exhortation: the need for a shift in "priorities."

Yet, when I pose the question of what is to be done to parents and grandparents of ghetto children, and to the boys and girls themselves, I hear a different kind of expert comment. They are witnesses with their own shrewd wisdom; they speak not to earn the praise of others, not as an act of self-enhancement, but out of a desperate knowledge earned every day in a particular world. One listens; then one listens with a certain quiet awe, one's own ambitions, one's proposals, and, yes, one's conceits as a researcher and writer for a while subdued by a cry from the heart, a statement that becomes, finally, a life's testimony.

"I don't know enough about things to give you the answer [to the question as to what ought to be done], but I'll tell you this" — and a pause by a twenty-eight-year-old mother of four, a black woman on welfare living in Roxbury, a Boston ghetto. In ten or so seconds she resumes: "I hear talk of more jobs and better schools, and I sure agree. But let me tell you something: There's people here, there's some of us, that's beyond that — I mean, there's kids who are so bad and mean, and there's kids that are so confused and scared and 'out of it,' that they don't really go to school, not regularly some of them, and not at all, some of them, and they're just lost, that's what I think, and the same with their families. Look here, we have people who are *so* lost

81

here, you've got to figure out a way to go find them, and get them listening to you, not to the drug dealers and the pimps, and not to the gangs, fighting each other like crazy.

"How? [I'd asked her how "we" might get to "them."] I don't know! They've dropped out; they'll be nine, ten, and they're running [for drug dealers], and they're already in gangs. They'd put a knife to their own blood [family members]. You know how some of them get 'saved'? They'll get to jail — finally, they will — and the Muslims will come along and talk sense into them. I know — a kid across the street, I watched him from a baby grow, and turn into what he is, and now he's got religion, and he's behind bars. Some of them, I see them come out [from jail] and the religion sticks with them, if they've got it, and it makes a difference. But you just try that [preaching religion] to these young kids. They'd laugh you all the way to nowhere!

"You should be worrying about all us folks who are scared! The ones who scare us — they're past anyone worrying! Our kids, they get caught — there's not much pulling them that's good, that they can see ahead nodding, and saying yes, you bet, hold on, it'll get better. There's a lot pulling on them, pulling them down and down — telling them they'd better play along, or there'll be a bullet in their head, and that's what happens here!

"If they could round up the gang people; if they could have the teachers come here, and the folks to help us out with the kids [a nurse and doctor whom she sees in Boston's Children's Hospital, because one of her daughters has a congenital digestive disorder], then maybe we'd feel stronger — there'd be some hope, right before our eyes. There's a lot for us to do better, I know; trouble is, we can barely keep up with today, so we don't try to get an edge on tomorrow. If there was folks here to help us get on our feet a little; if they got rid of the drugs and the gangs — those are mighty big 'ifs,' though!"

Allowing for her wise cautionary reminders, I don't think her suggestions are beyond realization. In the course of my work these past years, I've talked with many an urban policeman who knows the ghetto score, and all tell me of their constant fantasy: that "a couple hundred 'worst of the worst' somehow be removed from the streets," the words of the most experienced policemen I have met. When I was a resident in child psychiatry I worked with *very* tough delinquents who had been sent to a so-called industrial school in lieu of jail, and there we had some success with some of them — a mix of a work-camp, an educational program, and a psychiatric clinic, all enabled by the power of the law: Either be there or behind bars. Such places, by and large, are a thing of the past but might be reinstituted in ways meant to respond to youths under sixteen, and so not yet adults, but already well along as actual lawbreakers.

As for those "scared" — or laid low by life, hence apathetic, locked into despair, not headed anywhere — there are ways, surely, in which that woman's suggestions might be heeded. I know, after thirty years of work with children like hers, how hungry those boys and girls are for people to give them a hand, even inspire them, *even as* those same children may not only be "scared" but suspicious, withdrawn, sullen, hugely indifferent to a society which the rest of our young people have learned to regard with high hopes of future membership. When I see children already dropping out of school, for all practical purposes, at ten or twelve, when I see young people in need of the advice and care nurses and doctors can offer with respect to their personal hygiene, their various ailments and difficulties and worries and fears, I wonder whether somehow a cadre of teachers, doctors, nurses, and job counselors might not leave our schools and hospitals and city hall offices for particular neighborhoods, for apartment buildings in those neighborhoods: an on-the-site, visiting presence for some children who otherwise simply won't "connect" with the established institutional life of our cities.

Many of my students would be eager, indeed, to work with those "scared" children, with boys and girls battered by life, but not beyond the response of a society really determined to reach them, offer a few concrete alternatives. That mother has directly and indirectly suggested to me a strong initial effort to clear the streets of gangs — to work with gang youth in a contemporary version of the old detention camp or industrial school — and then an attempt to teach, to advise, to heal in a vigorous door-to-door way: "barefoot" and on-site teachers, doctors, nurses, and job counselors working in the least bureaucratic manner possible, even working as home visitors first, then as companions to families in a program that offers them, at once, a new kind of neighborhood school, clinic, job-training center.

Is America prepared to make such an effort? So many young people I know (undergraduates, medical and law and business and nursing school students, youths wanting to teach) tell me they would want to take part in such an effort, not for decades, many of them say, but for a few years, yes. Perhaps our businesses and universities can initiate such programs, become partners with various "layers" of government many of which have their own sad ways of making everything seem so hard, so entangled in mandated routines, in regulations galore.

March 1990

– 20 –

On Ideological Conformity

[The following is the author's contribution to a symposium organized by the *New Oxford Review* — preceded by the review editors' introduction to the symposium.]

T*he respondents to this symposium don't fit the conventional ideological categories of "Left" or "Right." Nor are they merely "moderates." They are usually regarded as being generally to the "Left" in terms of politics, economics, and/or foreign affairs, while to the "Right" in terms of sexual morality, cultural issues, and/or theology.*

Five queries were offered to guide their responses: (1) How did you come to adopt your unusual stance? (2) Are you often misunderstood or mistrusted? How difficult is it for you to maintain your stance? (3) How do you connect your "leftist" views with your "rightist" views in a way that you find consistent? (4) Why is it that so many people fall into rigid left-wing or right-wing ideologies, such that if you know their position on one issue you can usually predict their position on virtually every other issue? Why are so many people prone to be "politically correct," whether Left or Right? (5) What are the prospects for getting more people to transcend ideological conformity?

Respondents were given the option of answering the queries in a more or less point-by-point fashion, or addressing themselves generally to the issue at hand.

For my wife, Jane, and me, American politics continues to be a constant seesaw. We side with so-called liberals and the Democratic party in their strong concern for this country's vulnerable or excluded people. But we believe in the centrality of family life, and worry hard and long about the intrusive (and often, plainly arrogant) power of bureaucrats, however laudable in name their purposes. We worry, too, about what remains these days for all of us to hold dear, never mind holy and sacred. Prayers are no longer spoken in our public schools. The flag, for many urbane and influential people, means very little. Stories and novels are constantly "deconstructed" — their larger and shared moral significance ground analytically into the dust of academic abstraction. What remains is a pervasive skepticism, even cynicism, and no small amount of smug secularism, insistent consumerism — the divine "self" and the body as something to obsess us to the very end. All of this was described in the nineteenth century by Kierkegaard — his wonderful diatribes against the Copenhagen burghers whom he observed closely — so the issue may not be American life in the last days of the twentieth century, but the apparent eternity of Kierkegaard's "present age": that is the gripping tug of self-absorption on all of us who live in the comfort of the modern industrial world. Kierkegaard's psychology precedes and matches Freud's, and Kierkegaard's social and economic analysis surpasses that of Marx or Weber.

So often Jane and I wish American conservatives worried harder about those who are in need, who are hurting badly, who have grim prospects for whatever reasons; we wish that conservatives remembered and tried to pursue the righteousness of Isaiah and Jeremiah, of Jesus of Nazareth — indeed, tried not so much to talk up their biblical words, but tried to live as those prophets did. So often, too, Jane and I wish American liberals stopped chasing every social or cultural or sexual trend or fad or pressure group, all in the name, so often, of being "open-minded" and "tolerant." Where now, in America, is the indignation of those prophets of Israel who speak in the Bible — the indignation with respect to self-satisfied power and wealth, the indignation with respect to personal self-indulgence and prideful self-assertion, self-preoccupation?

So many of us who call ourselves "conservative" seem so hardhearted; so many of us who call ourselves "liberal" exult in a kind of openness to anything and everything, not to mention what George Eliot, in *Middlemarch,* taking canny aim a hundred years ago, called "unreflecting egoism." When Jane and I read newspapers and periodicals today, we sift and sort, and, often enough, turn away only half satisfied or sadly disappointed — and yearn, we sometimes say, though with no confident expectations, for an American populism that espouses a cultural conservatism and a political liberalism and an economic egalitarianism connected to the Jewish and Christian moral values espoused in centuries of study and contemplation.

October 1991

21

Vulnerability

IN RECENT MONTHS, as I believe readers of this magazine were told, I suffered a good deal of back pain. I am a physician but have always been loath to visit any of my colleagues, and I have never been one to take medicine with any relish. My parents, mildly puritanical, were also stoics: pain is part of life. My dad regarded even that all-purpose staple of American life, aspirin, as something to be resisted. My mother, too, had no interest in frequenting drugstores, and when a doctor came or wrote her a prescription, I remember, she used to keep it on her desk a good long while before making the decision to throw out the piece of paper or take it to the pharmacist. If she chose to do the latter, we always knew she was quite ill. When doctors offered either of my parents painkillers, toward the end of their lives (both of them died five years ago in their eighties), they were inclined to want something "not so strong," a phrase I recall my mom using when a doctor, sensing her acute pain, wanted to help with codeine. The very word sent her reeling back to the virtues of aspirin, virtues I'd never before heard her celebrate.

This past year I began to realize, yet again, how much I was their son as I, too, was offered a variety of painkillers, only to shun them. What I received, as a reward for such a posture of long-suffering self-control, unassisted by modern medicine, was not only plenty of pain, but a sense of vulnerability that had its own instructive impact on my sense of things, on my way of being. Now, the world seemed less inviting: now, I had to be more tentative both in how I moved, and, more broadly, in what I regarded as possible, even desirable — and the latter (what we regard as within our capacities) often follow the former (what we, in and out, can manage to do), testimony to our ability to accommodate ourselves psychologically to the physical reality of our lives. In no time, I was watching my step, as the saying goes, both figuratively and literally — and in so doing, so being, I was becoming all too concerned with myself, a kind of self-consciousness, if not self-centeredness, I had also learned from my parents to struggle against with all my might.

Under such circumstances, I turned to certain stories for relief — for some instructive reminders about human frailty and vulnerability: what we might try to do or have to do redemptively, we who are fated to find ourselves in that kind of condition. I read both Tolstoy's "Death of Ivan Ilyich" and his "Master and Man" several times — indeed, began to think of the central figures in those stories as my comrades. I was not mortally ill, as was the case with the lawyer Ilyich, nor was I about to die in a fierce snowstorm, a central occurrence in "Master and Man," but an ailing back had curbed me, confined me — taken away many of the rhythms and motions of life that keep us properly busy, and, no doubt, amount to an important and fulfilling part of our overall achievements as the particular persons we are. Yet, much that keeps us occupied, if not preoccupied, is mere busywork — distractions meant to help dissuade us from thinking about what really matters, what we believe to be truly significant. Entire lives (as many of us know, as Tolstoy reminded us, and in the essay "Confession" reminded himself) can be given over to such earnest evasions of moral and psychological introspection.

No wonder, then, that an illness can generate enormous apprehension — as one youth I came to know years ago (1970) in rural West Virginia let me know while he lay in bed, partially paralyzed in consequence of an injury sustained while working (even though he was only fourteen) in a strip mine: "I'll be here, lying on the bed, staring up at the ceiling, or looking out the window yonder, to the hill. I get to thinking. I wonder why I was ever born — if there was a reason. To end up like I am now? I wonder if it makes any difference if anyone is ever born! I mean, a hundred years from now, we'll all be gone, and if anyone has any idea who we are, it'll be because he stumbled on a grave, or he saw a picture in someone's scrapbook, like I do sometimes when Grandpappy comes visiting, and he shows me *his* Grandpappy.

"When I look out there, I see the trees and I figure they must know something we [human beings] won't be told. They just stand there, and they wear their leaves, then they let go of them, and they build up their sap, then they yield it, and nothing seems to bother them, while we're running all over the place. You cut into them and mark them up [he was referring to his own habit of using his knife to put his initials on certain trees] and they don't say 'ouch'; maybe they feel sorry for you, that you have to do that!

"It's the start of the day that I notice most of all. I never did [take such notice] before. Now I'm up, because there's only so much sleep you can get, and I'll be lying there in the darkness, and my mind is having these thoughts, like why was I put here in the first place, and when will I be going, and does it make any difference, that I'm here, and is there a God, and has He got the time to pay any attention to me, what with all the other folks, so many of them, all over the world.

All of a sudden — it sure happens every time! — there's a shift: It's not so dark as it was, you begin to realize. It's 'the first light,' my mom calls it. You know what she told me: It's the Lord coming on his visit, his morning call to us, checking on us! I think she's being the joker she is, but she's serious, too. Our dog doesn't miss that time. No sooner does the light come [into the room] than he'll stand up and come and pay me a visit. He sniffs me, and licks my hand — he's telling me good morning partner, there's another one [day] coming around the corner, for both of us to have for ourselves! That's what I imagine him thinking! Sometimes I even will think of him as having even more on his mind, like: Partner, it's all right, you can get used to being like you are, the way I have — we're all part of the place here, and if you're giving orders, it shows how much you need people to take hold upon you, and if you're taking orders, it shows how much you're needing help for direction, and so there's no one who isn't in some kind of need, and that's the biggest need a person has, to understand that."

There was much more, the ramblings, I suppose some would call them (at times hard to comprehend; at times utterly lucid, compelling, suggestive comments), of an utterly uneducated, "backwater" Appalachian youngster who knew well how much of a just beginning to life he had lost, who knew with a shudder at times how tenuous his hold on life was, and who, nevertheless, found himself not so much disheartened or sulky as awake to all sorts of nature's nuances, not to mention his own mind's expressive, evocative possibilities.

For some reason, of late, I found myself remembering him, asking my wife to dig up the transcripts of our talks with him, discussing with her his words, his outlook on life; his character, his virtues. At times, in a fit of imaginative flight (and indulgence, perhaps), I connected him to Tolstoy, even constructed a lively exchange between the two — soul mates, happy together, I presumptuously thought of them as being. The youth's vulnerability had become, I realized long ago, had long forgotten, and now was remembering, a new path for him: toward the trees, toward that precious first appearance of the day that visits us so regularly during our stay here, toward his beloved companion dog, toward all sorts of memories and meditations. In a second, he would have given up these newly acquired psychological or spiritual possessions for the vigorous ambulatory life he'd had abruptly snatched from him — but, as he told us one afternoon, "you don't get a chance to look over God's shoulder, you just take what life gives you on the chin, and you try to hold it [the chin] up high, no matter your luck."

That quiet, accepting resignation, coupled with an energetic inwardness, was a new experience and accomplishment for him — one his mother acknowledged in her own terse, impassive way with these words: "His nature's changed." So it had — and so it does, so it can, for others, too — as one by one we find ourselves given this or that pause on life's way and, such being the case, discover parts of ourselves previously unknown to us, or long lost to us, conveniently set aside by us for the sake of the daily tasks that come to us with each sunrise. It is, perhaps, when the sun begins to set on our lives (whether for a spell, only, or for good) that we have a chance for the kind of visionary glimpse of things that youth found: those Tolstoyan moments of escape, of release, of birth — almost as if the visit of death brings with its arrival a new life, one to be tasted even here, never mind thought of as a possibility in some beyond whose nature and contours, of course, will never be ours to know, short of arrival there.

November 1991

22

Life and Death

I N JULY OF 1984, a Brazilian winter month, I was working in a *favela* of Rio de Janeiro which, ironically, commanded a magnificent view of the Atlantic Ocean. I was talking with a number of children about their lives, their hopes and worries, their beliefs and fears. I also met their parents and grandparents, and soon enough would hear them, too, speak about their daily struggles — terrible poverty, marginality, and vulnerability as a way of life. Death haunted every shack in that one hillside slum — miscarriages; babies dying of one or another untreated disease; children chronically ill, and often telling me of the "departure" of this or that age-mate, a friend or neighbor; and, of course, parents who were sick, and near the end of their lives, not to mention grandparents.

"To die," a ten-year-old girl told me, "is what can happen to you any day — that we know." When I heard her say that I thought to myself, initially: yes, of course — pure common sense. But then I remembered her face, the resigned shrug of her shoulders, and I realized that most of the children I'd worked with as an American doctor did not speak such words, ever; nor did they spend their time having such thoughts, as that girl most assuredly did. Nor do many of us who live comfortable lives in this country know whereof we speak on the subject that child addressed, as she most certainly did: "My father died before I was old enough to call him by his name. I was a year old, I think. My mother will soon join him, she says. She wanted to stay with us [seven children, fathered by two men, of which she was the second eldest], but she tells us she's also counting the days until she leaves our home for the last time — because there is so much pain she has to carry, from the moment she gets up to the second before she nods off. At night, we hear her; we should be asleep, but we worry about her, and we listen to her crying. But she doesn't want us to worry about her. She says she wants to let out her tears in the dark. All day she smiles, and talks with us, and tries to teach us all she can. I'm a better cook since she got sick! I'm better with my little sisters and my brother. I'm better — well, I'm better all the way around! I don't mean to brag, though; that is just what has happened. My mother tells us: she has one more thing to do before she says goodbye — leave us with her words and a picture of her in our heads!"

There was much more, long descriptions by her about what was happening to her, to her mother, to her sisters and brothers and her stepfather, who would show up, hang around a day or two, then, inexplicably, pick himself up and take off. She once summarized her own remarks (her colloquial, earthy Portuguese was wonderfully translated for me by a half-American, half-Brazilian physician friend, who accompanied me and my sons on many of our expeditions up to that *favela*). I had asked her if there was some "central message" she had for us Yankee visitors — some way of describing the gist of her life. She wasn't sure how to answer. She asked me a question meant to clarify: "You want me to send my heart's signal?" I couldn't understand what she meant. I tried asking my question again — edging nearer to my own "heart's signal," as she had poignantly put it: "I was wondering whether there's some message that you've learned, going through all this — in your life; one message, maybe, your mother has taught you that means a lot to you." Now she understood; now she could smile as an indication that she was aware of what the visitor had in mind, and could reply with ease: "Oh, yes — I can give you what you want to hear; I can tell you what our mamma tells us — she says there is life, our visit here, and then we leave. She says you should be glad to be here — but don't forget: We're only here to visit, and so be prepared, every day, to say goodbye. She says she's doing that now, and each second more she has — that's good, because the longer we remember her, the stronger she'll be, her memory, in us. She says the pain is terrible, but when she sees us she's proud, because she sees us loving her, and then she knows why she was born — so that we'd be born, and then there will be our kids [little ones] one day."

I recently took out the transcripts of our many conversations, to read them again — pages and pages of her reflections, observations, aspirations, apprehensions, given forceful, blunt, earthy expression — an impoverished, illiterate *favelada* (inhabitant of a slum) who, nevertheless, has her own capacity to wonder about things, think them through with clarity, intelligence, openness. Her mother died only days after the words above were spoken. I was not there, but I heard about the death-bed scene — a family, a community assembled, a woman of thirty or so in great agony, yet trying until the end to whisper advice and instructions, or to admonish and warn about one matter, then another. No doctor was there; no priest, either. My young friend — informant, teacher — quoted above was reported to have addressed the Jesus who towers over Rio de Janeiro, His arms outstretched, with these words: "She's on her way to You now — so be ready for her!" To this day, I think, occasionally, of that response,

those words and especially when I think of a book titled *Final Exit,*
now a bestseller, whose subtitle is *The Practicalities of Self-Deliverance
and Assisted Suicide for the Dying.*

Those who seek such a "final exit," and those who assist them, emphasize the "rights" of the individual — a person's freedom to choose
when he or she has had enough, wants to end it all. The emphasis,
too, is on control — a person's wish to assert authority over suffering
and pain, do an end run, literally, lest further and worse deteriora-
tion, heartache, misery, tribulation take place. Rather obviously, what
is at stake here is the very definition of what life means — whose life,
and for what purpose. Also, at stake is the very definition of a profession, medicine, not to mention words such as "husband," "wife,"
"friend" — what ought we do for others, and what ought we not do,
and for what reasons? I cannot in this present column discuss (and
take issue with) the various rationales for suicide or euthanasia as they
have been assessed by certain doctors or those who write essays or
books such as *Final Exit,* but as I made my way recently through that
book, I thought of the poor and humble people I have met, young
and old, such as the *favelado* family just mentioned; I thought of
dying patients I myself worked with, when a medical student or a
young doctor in postgraduate training; and I thought of certain important pieces of literature — Tolstoy's well-known "The Death of
Ivan Ilyich," for instance, or Raymond Carver's "Errand."

I remembered the children I came to know as a pediatric resident —
dying, they were, of leukemia, then a disease whose fatal outcome
we could not prevent, as we so often can successfully manage to do
now; or the "terminal" patients I attended during a fourth-year medical school stint of two months in a ward whose inhabitants were all
near death, due to one or another form of cancer; or the elderly men
and women I came to know in the early 1970s when I lived in New
Mexico and talked with Spanish-speaking children (and their parents,
and their grandparents) in small, mostly impoverished villages well to
the north of Santa Fe. Many of those people, young or old, of whatever social or economic or cultural or racial background, were losing
their grip on life, were enduring great suffering (and without the kind
of medication for pain we now can take for granted) and yet struggled
hard and long not only for a little more life, but for a sense of meaning with respect to the life they already had lived. Put differently, they
remembered the past, what had happened before they fell sick, and
they discussed (with themselves as well as others) what had mattered,
what had not mattered: a sifting and sorting of a particular human
experience, as it was drawing to a close.

To be sure, there were "down" moments, plenty of them; but there were also times of self-recognition, of reminiscences shared with others, of hopes for those others given expression, not to mention much love conveyed through words, through stories, through a look, a wink, a nod, a smile, a turn of the head, an elevation of an arm, an embrace. "What would I do, where would I be, without these last days with you," a thirty-three-year-old woman, dying of ovarian cancer, an awful affliction, asked (told) her husband, who repeated the words to me — immensely grateful, no matter all *his* agony, grateful that his wife, in her own manner, was taking both of them through so very much that was important, even redemptive, for both of them, and yes, for their children, who had their own way of needing to look at, comprehend, an illness and its consequences.

That is what Tolstoy asked us to consider, too — the lawyer Ilyich's grave illness and its consequences. He had lived an aloof, ambitious, ostensibly successful life. In fact, he was smugly isolated from his colleagues, even his wife and children, long before he fell ill. The sicker he became, the more withdrawn he became — an instance of a disease calling forth a truth already worked into a life. At the end, though, a servant's goodness, his kind attention, awakens a heart long since closed to the world. A dying man, after a fashion, comes alive — reaches out with love to a world he had for so long (maybe all his life as a grown man) kept coldly at a distant remove. Tolstoy's title proves deeply, instructively ironic: on the occasion of the death of Ivan Ilyich, a man is born — his spirit, his soul, comes to life. The question that humble patient of mine had put to her husband might well have been Ilyich's — the transfiguration of suffering at the end of a life, the moral redemption of a life earned in its last earthly moments.

No wonder Raymond Carver, in his story "Errand," has Chekhov's widow, as she sits aside his dying body, then his dead body, think of "beauty, peace, and the grandeur of death." A beloved and wise man had left her, left us — and so doing, given us yet more to contemplate: all his wondrously gifted existence had offered. In story after story (those beautifully subtle, unnerving tales, those touching plays) Chekhov's approach to life is not that of the imperious lord, anxious to take charge, to assume utter sovereignty; rather, he looked respectfully at the characters he created, accepted with wry humor, with amusement, with immense satisfaction or with sad regret, the inevitable ups and downs that come their way. Chekhov's end, in Carver's portrayal, is of course Chekhovian — a man who knew how to yield to death without a great show of egotism (which can take many and sometimes devious forms, such as the melancholia of self-pity, the rage that culminates in self-destruction). A wonderfully knowing and wise man, Carver tells us in his evocation of Chekhov, knew how to render life with masterful precision as well as great compassion, and also knew how to leave it with dignity, thereby giving his wife, giving us all, his final example and lesson: an instructive, memorable nod, on his part, to life, as he took leave of it. Such a lesson, I fear, is all too desperately needed by some of us alive now at the very end of a century whose first years, only, Dr. Anton Chekhov glimpsed.

December 1991

23

Moral Anarchy, Moral Necessity

F OR MANY YEARS, with the help of two of my sons, now medical students, I talked with teenagers who were pregnant or already mothers, and with their boyfriends. We were interested in learning about the lives of these young women and men — their hopes and wishes, their worries and troubles. Not that the widespread occurrence of "teenage pregnancy" has been denied attention by newspapers, magazines, and radio or television networks. Long ago I stopped clipping journalistic reports, some of them first-rate, with their stories of twelve- or thirteen-year-old mothers — and fathers no older. Periodically I watch "special reports" on television devoted to the same general subject matter.

Rather often, such coverage emphasizes, correctly, the social and cultural and economic side of things, or of course the psychological forces at work among these children, really, who are themselves now parents of children. By now, for many of us, a picture of sorts comes to mind: an urban ghetto, with minority families living hard, even desperate lives, among them youngsters old enough to be sexually active, to create children, and yet still children in so many important ways. By now, too, all sorts of diagnostic and prescriptive formulations and theories come to mind. We have been told and told, for instance, that these youths need more and better education — that they need to stay in school, need to learn all sorts of lessons there, not the least of which are those that have to do with "personal hygiene" and "sex education" and "birth control." We have been told and told that these youths also need "more opportunity" — need to have better prospects available to them: jobs and more jobs, especially of a kind that hold out the hope and the reality of a decent, solid life. We have been told and told, as well, that many of these youths (even given such an improvement in what is possible for them) have substantial trouble taking advantage of what the world offers them — are fearful or all too apathetic or sullenly cynical, hence woefully unprepared for the world that might well be more beckoning than they realize. Such being the case, we are reminded of another need those youths have — for what gets called these days "mentoring": careful, sustained, edifying, sensitive, kindly (but of course firm) consideration and attention and devotion from teachers, social workers, and volunteers who will take them in hand educationally and emotionally.

Surely, such recommendations, the stuff of numerous research projects and commission reports, are utterly worth being realized — though, needless to say, many of us who have worked in shelters with the families who live in them are well aware of how hard it is to find the kind of people who will be able to "deliver" the kind of "services" required: a special sort of commitment from a special (and all too rare) sort of person. I have to say, though, that after a thirty-year effort to work with and try to understand what happens to poor and vulnerable children of various kinds in various parts of this country, I sometimes get a bit bleary-eyed and dazed as I read about yet another panel's recommendations, yet another tough, probing survey, be it the work of a resolute journalist or a determined social scientist.

The more I read (or the more I hear, as statements are made to reporters, to politicians, to me and my kind) the more I hearken back to the fiery, impassioned words of a black mother and grandmother I heard ten years ago in Roxbury, the heart of Boston's impoverished community. She was in an impatient, even truculent, mood as she rendered her analysis, made her judgments: "All the folks are wringing their hands and saying something is wrong, really bad wrong, and something has got to be done, and right away. Yes sir, I'm with those folks — you bet I am! Who would want to argue with them? We need all the help they want to offer — and then a little bit more, I'll tell you! We need schools that aren't falling apart, and our kids need the doctors to teach them what's right to do, how to take care of themselves, all that, and boy, we all need jobs, the more of them for people the better, and the better the jobs, the better for us."

She stopped, took in a big breath, looked around at us who were listening. Then she lifted her right hand high, held it up for a second or two, let it come thumping down hard on a nearby table, and thereupon turned on herself equally hard for a few moments. She told us she was tired of hearing herself talk as she just did, tired as well of seeing her eager, attentive listeners pay close attention, nod knowingly, if not gratefully, at her strong, even unsparing message. I remember, at that moment, thinking she was winding down, even as I debated whether I ought to feed my tape recorder yet another cassette, or assume that one more day in my working, listening life was near an end. Suddenly, though, she took in a deep breath, lifted that right arm up high again and then let it really come crashing down on that not very sturdy table, which trembled enough to call itself to my attention. I can still remember myself looking at it, then staring at the tall heavy-set woman standing beside it, then paying heightened attention to her remarks which poured out, even as I scurried to make sure my machine would capture them for later consideration: "I'm sick and tired of my own words. Later, I'll think to myself, I've said the truth, but there is more, a whole lot more, that I haven't said at all, and it's then that I feel that I'm scared, that I'm afraid to speak from my heart, that I'm afraid to tell the truth, that I'm a coward."

She paused only for a second — she was gathering her own force, I realized later, rather than awaiting the reassurance of others. Then she spoke her piece: "I don't know what has happened to us here, but it's terrible, terrible — worse than I can say with all the words I know! People tell you our kids need everything, and they're right — our kids need so much, I can't list it all, for then we'll be here for hours, and my voice will give out on me. But it's not just money and jobs, all the things people say we need — it's not just the schools and the clinics; it's something else, and no one can give it to us: We've got to find it for ourselves, and if we don't, then it's too bad — it's worse than too bad, it's the end of everything for us, it will be, that's where we're going, we're headed. If we can't learn to behave ourselves; if we can't learn to do what's right, no matter what; if we can't get hold of ourselves, and become the masters of our house; if we can't get some discipline in our lives, then I'll tell you something, all the money in the world, all the tea in China (like they say) won't be of real help to us, because it's not the help we've got to have. People want to give us something, to make up for all we've never really had. Fine! But I'll tell you: Where is the faith that we need in ourselves, and where is the voice telling us to behave, to do what's right, not just the easy thing? There's right and there's wrong, and if we don't know the difference, if we've forgotten how we should behave ourselves, and if the devil has taken over, taken us over, then it doesn't make any difference whether they boost the welfare, and bring us to the clinics, and give the condoms to the guys, and the sex teaching for the girls, and all the rest. God spare us, if we go on being the way we are! God give us the strength to obey His commandments, that's what we need more than anything, anything else: the strength to obey God, and be good people. If we don't learn that — then it's all over for us, I'm afraid. I look at our kids, our kids having kids, our kids sleeping around, loafing around, our kids on drugs, our kids beating up each other (and worse!), and I say to myself: Lord save us, and only He can; Lord save us, and give us the power to pull ourselves together, so we can be — ourselves, rulers of ourselves, the boss of our mind, not run all over by this and that coming into our head. That's the choice for us — to be rulers of ourselves, not slaves to ourselves."

With that passionate outcry she was through. She sat herself back in her chair, and looked across the room, out the window, her eyes resting on an apartment house that blocked what lay beyond, the sky. Meanwhile, I thought of the moral anarchy she mentioned, the moral necessity she described — and I realized how hard it is for people like me to say what she said, even, often enough, to think what she thought, then declared, no matter our protestations of compassion, concern, and personal or political camaraderie.

January–February 1992

24

Not Only a Disease

WE ARE IN THE MIDST, these days, of a rational (and natural) preoccupation with AIDS, and its prevention. A terrible disease, all of a sudden out of nowhere, came upon us a decade ago, killing thousands here, even more thousands elsewhere. The way this disease gets spread has given it a special place in our moral and psychological and cultural life—sex and drug use are now wedded in our thoughts and ruminations to the ravages a particular virus inflicts on its victims, most of whom, in this country, are gay or addicts. Many of us feel compassion as we contemplate a growing medical and human tragedy, while, of course, not a few people have shown themselves able to be cruel, condemnatory, or indifferent — as if a plague of sorts had found deserving targets.

I am ashamed to put before the reader some of the remarks I have heard, in recent years, from grown men and women, all too eager to denounce others (alas, not rarely, in biblical terms) for their sickness and, needless to say, for much more: the way they have lived their lives. I suspect that some politicians know that such animus is not uncommon, know that one's personal worries and doubts and fears, one's social and economic vulnerability, crave expression—hence the various cursed outcasts we summon for ourselves: one or another "them." When life itself (or rather death itself) seems to be making such a selection, then moral energy can fuel to a pitch the various private apprehensions we may otherwise suffer in relative silence. Talking in 1989 with a devoutly churchgoing computer programmer who had just lost his job (the collapse of the "Massachusetts miracle" which a governor had hoped would propel him to the presidency), I heard a torrent of abuse directed at "deviates and druggies," culminating in an appalling (but also candid and instructive) call to a so-called religious truth, a phrase explored this way: "You have to be honest, and say what you believe. This [AIDS] is a disease that hits people who are doing the wrong thing. They're homosexuals; they're shooting up drugs. If God watches over us, judges us, He's watching over and judging them [AIDS victims]. That's the truth — that's a religious truth. Yes, I agree, you can't say that every time someone gets sick, it's because they've done something wrong. But here, it's different:

The people who are getting sick are getting sick after they've done something wrong!"

He wasn't a "fundamentalist"—as some of my well-educated, outraged (and agnostic) Cambridge friends were quick to say when I told them what I had heard, showed them a full transcript of the remarks. That word "fundamentalist," in the hands of the liberal intelligentsia, can itself get turned into a means of ostracism and condemnation: a swear word, for some, as sweeping and divisive in its intent as any denunciation of those with AIDS, those susceptible to AIDS, in the name of a morality, a received body of scriptural truth. Rather, the man I was hearing speak his contempt for others was a proud burgher suddenly in trouble, in jeopardy, and searching, searching ever so hard, to locate others in even worse straits, whom he could rebuke and scorn. When he was reasonably successful, working at good pay and with good health and retirement benefits, he could be easygoing and tolerant—able to express "pity" (he once called it) for the poor and, too, those who had contracted AIDS. After he left his job and realized he wasn't going to be able to find another one like it for a long time, he contemplated moving to another part of the country. But his parents, who live nearby, are old, sick, quite dependent on him emotionally; and so it goes, too, for his wife's parents, who also live nearby. "I've come down in the world," he once told me—after announcing that he had, at last, found himself a job: "Now I drive a truck—and I'm lucky to have the job. [He got it through the efforts and influence of his brother-in-law, himself a truck driver.] But I get less pay, and I've got the lousiest health benefits they [the company] can offer, short of giving us nothing at all! I look at people passing me in their fancy cars, and I say: Good luck, Charlie—and I feel real 'down,' real low. But then I try to give myself a pep talk. I say: Listen, buddy, things could be worse, a hell of a lot worse! You could be some drunk, or some druggie; you could live in some ghetto; you could be sick, and not able to work. Your kids could be sick—or in some kind of trouble!"

When he had finished that enumeration, he sat back and pulled on his cigarette repeatedly, and let me know, once more, that he was a solid, determined person ("as hardworking as can be"), that he wanted no "handouts," that he would "somehow get by"—after which he repeated the word "somehow," a moment of doubt as well as stated determination. Soon enough, he was drifting from righteousness to self-righteousness — declaiming the virtues of his ethnic and class background, casting scorn on those who live across various kinds of railroad tracks (racial, cultural, sexual, socioeconomic). In no time, it seemed, he was reminding himself and me, once again, how lucky he was to be "healthy." That good fortune was then bolstered, I began to feel, by his angry outbursts against the victims of AIDS: their disease a judgment on their lives, "except for the ones with that blood disease," he added as an afterthought (hemophilia as the basis for merciful understanding, even forgiveness).

Sometimes, as I listen to others, much better off, bemoaning the recession that plagues our nation, I think of that man and his hard struggle, as he put it once, "to keep his head above water," and his struggle, too, he reminded me, for "respect" when "things aren't going well." "AIDS isn't just a disease," he told me — and then he added this description: "It's something that's hitting a lot of people who could have gotten themselves in a lot of trouble, even before they got sick." Such a way of putting the matter, for him, proved to be a relatively tolerant pronouncement — less inflamed with accusations, less of a moral diatribe. As I heard his words I realized that they could be used, more or less, to describe millions of jobless people, or millions of others living by the skin of their teeth: employed now, but all the time in danger of being fired. No wonder so many of us are tempted to turn our backs on various others, by virtue of how they look or talk, or where they pray, or, indeed, what ails them — a moment's sad kind of self-satisfaction for those of us who are closer to the edge of things than we dare acknowledge, or so close to the edge that only smugness and malice seem able to keep us half-way at ease with ourselves.

March 1992

25

A Last Conversation
with Anna Freud

S EVERAL TIMES in these columns I have mentioned Anna Freud, who did so very much to connect psychoanalytic knowledge *about* children (learned from the memories of adults) to psychoanalytic work *with* children. So much of the understanding today's child psychiatrists possess was enabled by the work she did for over half a century with boys and girls troubled by virtue of their experiences in particular families, or as a consequence of the Nazi air assaults on London during World War II, or, horror of horrors, as a result of living in concentration camps during that same war. To such children Miss Freud, as she was called by so many of us for so long, gave all she had: a brilliant, knowing mind; enormous, unflagging patience; and the consummate skill she had as a clinician — able, I often noted, to get to the heart of the matter with a child, with his or her parents, in what struck the rest of us as no time at all. Toward the end of her life (as happens with some of those men and women who have not only learned a discipline inside out, but come to realize how much they still don't know, how much is yet to be discovered), she had about her a real wisdom — not the feigned or pretentious wisdom of yet another late twentieth-century secular guru, but a quiet, humble, wry, though still passionate, interest in the world that got translated, at times, into remarkable observations, which she made unselfconsciously, with no eye to who might be ready to venerate and celebrate what had been spoken.

My last visit with her was in late 1980. She would be dead in less than two years, and was already in failing health. I had known her, by then, almost fifteen years, and had much treasured our times together, our correspondence. The latter could be edifying beyond expectation — long letters, sometimes, or brief ones with candid, occasionally brisk and sharp observations, not to mention constant reference to her work as a child psychoanalyst, all delivered in the clearest of narrative prose. During our last meeting (and I knew then it would be fatuous to expect there would be any more) she was quite willing to review some of the past discussions we'd had — about the ways children come to personal terms with those "variables" called "race" and "class," and about the lives of two individuals who meant a lot to me, and about whom I told her a lot: Simone Weil and Dorothy Day.

At one point, as I was talking about those two women, yet again, and more broadly about the way all of us (including children) formulate our religious or spiritual yearnings (or, for that matter, most emphatically formulate a lack of such yearnings), she had this to say: "It comes as no surprise to many parents that a child is for them an opportunity: to discover themselves, their own childhood, once again; to find the only 'immortality' most of us can ever hope to see, in the children we see before us, as I heard a mother once say, 'carrying on, where I'll leave off' — a very tactful way of talking. I am getting around to saying that we can find in children what we are looking for (within limits, yes); and the reason is, we have put there [in them] what we're later so surprised (sometimes) to notice! I'm afraid this [formulation of sorts] applies to us, too [child psychiatrists and psychoanalysts]. We have found in children what we suspected — an endlessly complex psychology. When you started your own work, you found what you suspected: sociology, race, the circumstances in which a family lives — all that has a life in a child's mind. Before any of us [psychoanalysts] appeared on the world scene, others knew what they were looking for: a capacity to *believe* — and they certainly found that capacity in children and learned themselves to work with that capacity! Now, more and more, I hear about biology and the brain, and surely children will help out those [biologically oriented investigators] who are looking at them from that angle!"

She paused long enough to see on my face a mix of consternation and anxiety — as if I were hearing an indictment of all of us who spend time with children: We impose on them, so I feared she was implying, our own agendas — the child as a mirror of us observers, if not an instrument of our ideological passions, maybe even our ambitions. But no, she had something quite else in mind — and she had a way, I'd noted for years, of quietly seeing through someone else's confusions, and without mentioning them, or in any manner putting the person in question on the spot, clarifying her own remarks in such a way that the one she was with, suddenly, was with her, so to speak: "It is natural, all this [that she had described]. What is sad is — when we don't quite realize what we're all doing. Maybe *that* is what my father did for us, after all — give us a way of being more aware of what we do, so we're not so surprised when we finally understand not only what others are doing, but what *we're* doing!"

She was not at all interested in reserving for herself the privileged position of the one who is beyond the limitations and blind spots to which everyone else is heir. Rather, she was reminding herself, never mind me, toward the end of her life, that psychoanalysts (and social scientists, and all sorts of other theory-bent individuals) can single out and explore what is there in the world, but also miss what's there or, alas, dismiss what others notice and regard with great interest as not being worthy of much notice, hence to be put aside with one or another pejorative description: religion as a neurosis, for instance.

During that same meeting, a short one (by our standards) of less than an hour, she came as close to a full and sympathetic interest in spiritual questions as I'd ever heard her manage to do: "The longer you live, the more you realize how little time there is — and how little we really know about this universe! It is impressive — the way some people can put distance between themselves as believers and themselves as human beings, with all the passions we have as human beings. I suppose that is the soul [in them] at work: their ability, at times, to be bigger morally than they usually are. It's a struggle — but they have moral passion, working in the interest of certain ideals. I am not interested in *explaining* those people — only saluting them, some of them, who are such good men and women, and have found for themselves a faith that inspires them. I am not sure there are too many [such people] — I think there are plenty of churchgoers, but maybe far fewer people who really take to heart what those churches were once meant to be!"

Silence, then her signal to me that she was tired: an offer of a refill of coffee. I said I had to go. She said she too "had to go." As I left, I heard myself saying (a free association!): Yes, so do we all, in time, "have to go." As I left, too, I saw, still, her face after she had spoken those last words, made that last observation — a certain wistfulness, an ironic detachment, but also, I thought, a kind of yearning: the great joys of honorable and decent spiritual transcendence (a commitment to the beyond) that some can find, but among them not her.

April 1992

26

Remembering Walker Percy

I WRITE THESE WORDS as the second anniversary of Walker Percy's death approaches, and as my mind still lives intensely with its memories of him, not to mention his six novels, random essays, and interviews — a late twentieth-century American novelist, essayist of a very special mind, heart, soul. For many of us came to regard him as a gift of sorts, a messenger, even, from on high: someone graced *with a wisdom that was extraordinary, someone, and so we sometimes* reminded ourselves, God-given in nature.

I first met Dr. Percy (he was a physician in an early life) through some of his essays, especially "The Man on the Train," which appeared in *Partisan Review* during the middle 1950s, when I was learning to be a psychiatrist. I read that essay many times; it connected with my life — the relatively affluent self-preoccupation and moral drift evoked: plenty of ostensible success, but no real purpose in life other than going through the usual rounds, so to speak, meaning a compliance with every norm and convention around. At that time, and later, when I was stationed in Biloxi, Mississippi, and working at an Air Force psychiatric hospital (all of us had to give two years to the military under the old doctors' draft law) I went to the movies a lot. While in the Air Force I went to New Orleans often, attended medical and psychoanalytic conferences, visited various fine restaurants, and always took in a movie, or two, or three — to the point that when I started being psychoanalyzed in New Orleans (I decided to stay there, after I left the Air Force, and study school desegregation: a whole new life, of course) my analyst called me jokingly, but, of course, with some interest in my motives, "an apparently compulsive moviegoer."

No wonder, then, I was stunned, one day, to see a novel on display in a New Orleans bookstore titled *The Moviegoer* — a book I quickly bought and eagerly, even hungrily read, and a book which would become a companion of sorts to me for the rest of my life. I have read it through several times; I go back to certain passages in it constantly. I teach it to my college students, my medical students, and others I teach elsewhere in a university. Indeed, I would go on to be a committed fan of Dr. Percy's writing — always on the look-out for his articles, always ready to celebrate the publication of one of his novels, or book of essays. (There were six of the former, two of the latter). Eventually, like in a story, the young admiring reader got to do some occasional writing of his own, and one day, when an editor for a major magazine for which he was doing such writing asked whether there were any "special interests" that might become, in time, "magazine pieces," the writer (his heart beating fast, and a gulp in his voice) mentioned a name: Walker Percy — and connected it to the word "profile." Several years later *The New Yorker* published a long (two-part) profile of Walker Percy under the title of "One Search" (as in the old existentialist search for meaning in life).

To do that writing meant to get to meet Walker Percy, and (the greatest luck possible) to become friends with him, and, indeed, I am writing these words now not to offer an exegesis of his extremely important novels and books of philosophical rumination and speculation, nor to give a chronicle of his achievements, a sort of late obituary to a wonderful life. Rather, I am sitting at my desk and remembering a very special person, and concentrating on the very special message he had for all of us late twentieth-century American secularists, whose measure he had taken ever so well. "I tell you," he once told me, "the crazy thing about a lot of us in this here and now is that we sure as hell know how crazy a lot of them are, but we're not on to how deaf, dumb, and blind we are to ourselves, about ourselves — how lost we are, no matter how clever we think we've become." Pure Percy — we'd been sitting and talking about schisms in religious institutions, schisms in psychoanalytic institutions, schisms in universities and various professional associations, and finally we turned away, in relief, to the great music of Benny Goodman, and then Glenn Miller, and then Ella Fitzgerald and Billie Holiday, all heard to the accompaniment of some good sipping bourbon — and then that comment, the speaker tilting his head a bit, scratching his head a bit, then lifting his head back, to accommodate another swig.

I remember other great times — walks by the bayou in Covington, Percy's home; walks in Baton Rouge, where we were at a meeting; walks in New Orleans; walks into a nice old "country" bar, where we could sit and talk, and always, laugh it up. He had a great sense of humor, Walker did — the greatest; a sense of humor that hit upon (knocked all the hot air out of) the underlying pretentiousness of so much of our present-day life — a cover-up, in turn, for the melancholy aimlessness, the moral confusion and drift that characterize a good part of our lives. He knew how to keep hold of his medical skills; he was ever the diagnostician — and too, the healer. He had figured out how starved we all are, spiritually — so starved, we've forgotten what it's like to break bread the way Jesus and His friends did; and he had tried not only to address our desolate and desperate situation (the ulti-mate stage of it: we don't know of it, only know how much we know, what big shots we've become) but give us a few clues as to a way out. Lord, he never preached, never gave us those dreary psychological and sociological "stages" and "phases," those catchword phrases, that come and go across our cultural screens these days. He did, though, evoke the ironies and complexities and paradoxes and inconsistencies and ambiguities of our contemporary existence, and so doing, with penetrating, sometimes mordant good fun, helped us to look more directly and fully at what has happened to us. His was an honesty, a clarity of vision, of special distinction; and when coupled with a brilliant, well-educated mind, an accomplished, deft storyteller's ways, his was a voice thoroughly special and rare, one much needed and, now, achingly absent. He had a vast impatience with the hifalutin, a wonderful down-to-earth eagerness to enjoy the ordinary, to cel-ebrate it. He had a mind just as capable of enjoying waffles in the local Toddle House, and enjoying, too, the people who go there, their talk, their manner of being, as it was able to take in the most com-plicated of Kierkegaard's ideas, the most demanding of moments in Dostoyevsky, Camus, Sartre. He searched his soul scrupulously, but with wry amusement, too, and he gave many of us a big assist in that direction, mostly by winning us over to the desirability of making the effort through his wonderfully suggestive narrative presentations: a lively, discerning intelligence doing its work ever so shrewdly and knowingly, and in the end, contagiously. I miss him all the time and a lot, and I sure realize, these days, how much the country needs him and, will continue to need him, and therefore, misses him, will miss him.

May 1992

27

Gang Members:
Their Street Education

I N RECENT YEARS I've become much connected to some black
ministers in Boston and, as well, to some youth workers who are
white and black — all of whom are trying, in turn, to connect with
youngsters who have dropped out of school, who are gang members,
and who more than flirt with law-breaking (violence, drug dealing)
as a way of life. My youngest son, now only recently out of college,
was the one who first helped me meet such young people — he had
done volunteer work with them: taught in a program aimed at school
dropouts, at children dismissed from the public schools as "unmanage-
able," as "violent," as "severely disturbed." I had become quite worried
about my son, not the boys and girls he was getting to know: what
could he, a mere college student, do to be of help to such stubbornly
uninterested students, almost all of them black — and not least, I have
to add, what might happen to him as he ventured into neighborhoods
regarded as beyond the pale, alas, by so many people in the Boston
metropolitan region?

My son came back to his dormitory, and to our home, with stories
of fear and danger, sometimes, but also, of sadness and frustration:
how to work with youths defiantly uninterested in education? He
would try exhortation, not often to any effect. He would try intense efforts at engagement, personal and intellectual, not often to
any effect. He would try a kind of crude pragmatism, or a more
elevated version of espoused practicality — not often to any effect.
These boys and girls shrugged their shoulders, turned their faces away,
as he recited moral truisms, educational pieties; as he tried to establish working involvements or alliances; as he spoke of the economic
and social possibilities that literacy, that diplomas can offer to young
people. Finally, in desperation, he tried to put aside for a while his urgently felt need to tutor, to educate children much in need of learning,
and instead sought some, any common ground: things to discuss, and
even more important, things to do that would keep him somehow in
touch with "them" (what he realized those boys and girls had become
to him, a collective "other," alien, frustratingly hard to figure, never
mind reach, influence).

I still remember my son Michael's accounts of what he called "progress" — some conversations with youths as he played basketball with them, as he taught them hockey in a rink. They had inquired about his life, his interests and hobbies. He had told them what he was doing — his activities, his course of study. He had managed to go further, mention what he hoped to be doing in the future — a career in medicine. One of the boys, at ten a "runner" for a big-time drug dealer, asked how one becomes a doctor. Mike responded with information in a matter-of-fact way — even as the two of them shot baskets. A week later, the boy was interested enough to bring the subject up, ask more questions — while all the time insisting that school, any kind of school, was simply not for him. Two months later, though, Michael had shown this boy a hospital, introduced him to some doctors and nurses, explained to him how various clinics work — their purposes, the kinds of people who come to them. Gradually, the boy began to turn toward schooling, as Michael presented it to him — a book they looked at together, some newspapers and magazines they jointly read. Finally, Michael volunteered to do some explicit tutoring in English and math, and the offer was accepted, though with hesitation. A later summary description by my son went like this: "It took three months of being challenged, tested, doubted, put in my place, before we could even begin to work together academically."

A year later I became involved with a group of black ministers in Boston, who in their own manner are taking on struggles similar to those my son Michael has been waging. These black men are determined to try to reclaim the streets of their parishes — and to do so, are willing to go many extra miles: middle-of-the-night outreach efforts with gang members; educational, medical, legal assistance programs that are church-based, but include home visits; a public posture that mirrors the private conviction that one has to find a credible means of initial engagement with young people who are significantly "outside" a society's institutional life (its schools, its organized athletic and social activities, its businesses) and, too, connect with such individuals morally as well as intellectually or legally or medically. Put differently, these youths may well be in trouble with the law (or headed that way); they may have medical problems, drug and alcohol problems; they may be school dropouts already, or well down that road — but until they not only learn to talk with some of us who want to work with them, *and* listen to us, hear what we are saying, trying to accomplish (and why), there is scant hope they will be persuaded to change their ways, the direction of their lives.

Slowly we have realized that our best hope with these gang members, these school dropouts, is to walk the streets, work with those youth workers who are doing just that — taking a chance (taking the risk) of informal neighborhood conversation, encounters, in stores, on playgrounds, in homes. Each of the ministers has described what amounts to a kind of conversion, a time when he realized that the pulpit, the church school, the conventional programs and activities simply were of no avail — these children, often, slept by day, lived (gabbed and fought and "dealed") by night. Particular youth workers, particular ministers or teachers, particular volunteers, such as my son, have reached some of those children by putting themselves "out there," "on the line": a departure from the established routines and customs of a city's institutional life.

This summer, thirty years after the Freedom Schools of the Mississippi Freedom Summer, we are hoping to establish street academies on that model — places where young people might assemble to talk, to listen, to learn, and, yes, to teach. My son has kept telling me, reminding himself, how much he has come to know, courtesy of his young athletic colleagues, his informants, his regular acquaintances, if not, eventually, friends. Their assumptions, their values and expectations are important to understand for those of us who hope to persuade them of the advantages and virtues of another life. An especially knowing youth worker, Jim McGillvary, made the same point as he prepared to introduce me to some gang members one early evening: "Try to get them talking to you, ask them questions that will send them the signal that you're interested in them." Yes, I thought, easier to say than to do — even as I was quaking in my (teacher's, doctor's, white man's, suburban) boots. But no matter the barriers, Jim was there to start us out, and soon enough I was hearing (the two of us white men were hearing) twelve- and thirteen- and fourteen-year-old black youths give accounts of their ongoing lives, and their sense of what lay ahead: not all that much! Underneath all that street jive, that sullen braggadocio, that "hey, man, what's your deal" mix of cool and insolence, was another story, waiting to be told, entrusted: I'm a decade old, and I may not last another decade, and so, I'm scared out of my mind, but I see no way out, and I'm not sure what to do, where to go, whom to believe.

These are children much in need of moral and civic education, yet adrift and scared, eager to find a family and protection in a gang. Will all the well-meaning efforts at gun control, at condom distribution, at "violence prevention" reach such youths, make a difference in their lives? They are already at a remove from all that, from our schools, even. In some schools, of course, habitual truancy is a fact of daily life — and not an occasion for concern, for an attempt at outreach. "I try to make the cash I can, and I hope I stick around, that's what I try to do" — those words a response to this question of mine: "What do you hope to do when you get older?" An eleven-year-old gang member, drug dealer, school dropout letting me in on things — but a month later he did say that "maybe" he'd be on the lookout for a better deal, if he saw one. He wasn't quite ready, I knew, to have that kind of vision (there are "better deals" around him, *I* know!), but we hope that by this summer, our "freedom schools," our "street academies" will be available for children like him — informal places where he and others can meet with some ministers and teachers and college students and medical students and law students willing to be there, to hang around, to offer their interested selves as a "line," a moral connection, to our world, which some of those kids (I've heard them do so commonly) will call "that other place," meaning where all of us, black and white, rich and poor, try to live lawfully and with some reasonable hope in our lives.

June 1994

28

On Divorce

WHEN I WAS A SMALL BOY I lived in a quiet, comfortable town, on a street lined by single-family homes — a Norman Rockwell America amid the widespread suffering and vulnerability of the 1930s. We all knew one another, the children and their parents. We knew about one another, too: the boy who had rheumatic heart disease, and might not make it to ten, then a distant age for some of us just starting school; the girl whose dad had a rare and puzzling illness which I now realize to have been multiple sclerosis. We knew, as well, that so-and-so drank too much, that a particular set of parents didn't get on — fights overheard during those summer evenings when open windows allowed the sound of radios and of live human beings to travel far and wide. Still, every single family on the street had two parents — until, one day, we all learned that a tragedy (the word our parents kept using) had taken place: Buzzy and Sally, a boy and girl of our approximate age (five to seven) were losing their father — he had moved out, was asking for a "divorce." To this day I can recall the shock, the confusion that word prompted in us children — a strange word, a charged word, a scary word. I remember my brother and I asking our parents about it — what a divorce meant, why it happened. I remember their surprise, their sadness, their dismay — not a response, I might add, based primarily on religious disapproval, but one grounded in the secular values of that time: divorce was a rare step, a drastic one, an occasion for a good deal of soul-searching and regret among neighbors, never mind the two adults involved, and never mind any children they might have.

Now, of course, as I write the above, I feel like a survivor from another world, one that disappeared a few centuries ago. Now, divorce is everywhere — one of two marriages ends in it. Now, the intensely felt sense that a marriage is a lifelong commitment no longer dominates most neighborhoods, as was the case in the one where I grew up and learned what to value and why. Now, in fact, my profession of psychoanalytic psychiatry is often summoned to defend particular divorces, even the more general phenomenon of divorce, as a readily available (and far from objectionable) alternative to what is often called a "bad" marriage, meaning, of course, one in which psychological pain is to be found.

No doubt, many marriages are, indeed, a terrible burden to both partners — occasions for constant fear, suspicion, bitterness, even hate and violence. Who would want such so-called unions to be held in travesty by not being challenged psychologically, socially, legally? Put differently, some marriages are so destructive to the humanity of all involved, each parent and any child of theirs, that they are simply going to end — and even the Catholic Church, which decidedly shuns what our culture has done with divorce (turned it into yet another of those "options" that go with "freedom," with "progress"), has had to respond with its own "release" of sorts for such men and women (and their children): the increasing prevalence of "annulments," which permit a couple not only to divorce (that is possible as a separate matter), but to remarry.

I have in mind, though, the many, many marriages (the great majority, I suspect, of those headed for divorce) that held together in my parents' generation and that wouldn't stand a chance these days, when half of all newlyweds are headed for lawyers and the breakups they help negotiate; I have in mind, really, the social and cultural climate in which we live: a world that tell us in countless ways that our individual psychology matters, our "autonomy" matters, our "rights" matter, but is far less interested in emphasizing the obligations and responsibilities that go with living in this world; a world that has knocked down a million constraints, scorned any inhibition in sight, doted on what used to be called the weird, the aberrant, the preposterous, to the point that such words, with their implied moral judgments, have given way to others — how *interesting* or how *cool*. Throughout the day, in a parade of talk shows, people eagerly make public their inclinations and experiences, no matter how bizarre, are congratulated for doing so, are offered interpretations by eager self-proclaimed experts as they do so: a circus of hyped-up, applauded subjectivity, attended by cannily seductive ringmasters — all of that interrupted by ads telling us that if we eat this, drive that, wear one or another thing, travel here or there, we will really be in there pitching. When the evening comes the news give us the usual fare of phony politicians, talking down to audiences, talking out of both sides of their mouths, and, always, talking themselves up — and then, the sit-coms, where anything goes, even as the movies want to make explicitly available to us every wish, fantasy, and act known to the human mind. Under such circumstances, why should two individuals who are married, and going through a spell of trouble, feel they ought to stay together? They live in a society that celebrates the validity and importance of impulse, of feeling, of desire, a society that promises (through pills, through palaver, through

purchases) an end to pain: swallow this, talk about that, buy everything in sight with every credit card thrown your way — and you will
be, thereby, a part of the nineties, a part of the economic recovery, a
"with it" person.

I sat in a courtroom a while back, listening to ordinary men and
women convey their reasons for wanting a divorce through lawyers,
who were all too glad for the paid chance to be of help as spokes-
persons. Occasionally the lawyers were pushed aside by the judge,
who wanted to hear a man, a woman address the controversy in question. All day I heard the holy self summoned — one problem, another
problem, one emotion, another emotion. The stories were, these days,
unremarkable — the usual conceits and deceits of this life, the usual
betrayals and deceptions and lies, the usual illusions embraced, then
set aside for new ones. There were tears. There were angry outbursts.
Again and again men and women told of their "feelings," told one
another off, told the court that he, that she needed "help," required
"therapy," ought to be in "treatment." Indeed, by the end of the day,
I realized what a bonanza those courts are for my ilk — we are the
ones who get the patients, who are appointed mediators, who decide
when the children should visit which parent: mediation in the name
of something called "mental health."

Watching, listening, I wondered who "we" are, all those counselors
and therapists, all those court-appointed mediators and supervisors —
what do we believe in, what do we stand for, uphold? We are the
"value-free" ones, who in the name of twentieth-century relativism
summon psychological and sociological words that have become
pervasive pieties: "do you own thing," "let it all hang out" — as
Christopher Lasch so tellingly called it, "a culture of narcissism,"
wherein standards and values are as various as the individuals who
may (or may not) choose them. God forbid that someone in that
courtroom (the judge, one of the doctors or psychologists, or social
workers who worked in a nearby clinic, one of the lawyers feeding off
the trough of assembled family disarray) stand up and cry in sorrow
and horror — remind all of us that we all have our ups and downs,
with ourselves, with one another, and that marriage is a solemn and
sacred step, taken (as the old vow says) for life, "in sickness and in
health, 'til death do us part." God forbid that someone point out
what divorce can do to people. Even social scientists have had second
thoughts about the matter — Judith Wallerstein's extensive, pioneer-
ing work (*Surviving the Breakup*) has reminded us of the long-term
consequences a divorce has for children. But are we only to measure
life through the prism of personal problems? When do the moral,

the spiritual enter this discussion — when do we think of marriage as a hugely important good, to be nourished and sustained with all possible conviction, energy, passion?

I am not interested in confronting those who seek or obtain a divorce with tales of a future hell, but I wonder whether we are well-served today by a prevalent notion that the institution of divorce, so highly developed, so readily summoned by us, is a measure of our progress. Many marriages would last and last were we all encouraged to regard divorce as a serious, a grave step, indeed — and a moral tragedy, rather than as evidence, merely, of the psychological hang-ups two individuals happen to have. I realize that such a hope, on my part, is quixotic, to say the least — pure fancy, it would seem, in an age of (talk of self-congratulation!) "psychological enlightenment." Still, I remember with increasing wistfulness the social and ethical constraints that surely gave many husbands and wives plenty of pause, and surely saved many a marriage, even as I fully understand why some marriages — in their sum, pure horror — ought to be ended. Nor does psychology, which carries the mantle of "human understanding," work in a social or moral vacuum. Once we healers felt impelled to try at all costs to help marriages work; now, all too many of us regard ourselves as there to heed the call of mood and instinct, of changed minds and casually errant hearts. Conscience and its necessary demands becomes a quaint, an obsolete construct, while we negotiate the practicality of the passions — how to permit them to have their day, their sway — and let our nation's moral life, its family life, its children pay the costs.

July–August 1994

29

Ralph Ellison's Angle of Vision

F OR MANY YEARS I have taught Ralph Ellison's *Invisible Man* to college students, and each time I discuss the book I find myself yet again the grateful reader who is both entertained and instructed. The novel was published in 1952, when I was just starting medical school and with little time for reading on the side. I did have a few minutes, now and then, to converse with my parents, both avid fans of fiction, and I well remember my mom recommending the Ellison novel to me in the course of a hurried phone conversation. I promptly forgot her suggestion, however. I had long biological lists to memorize, if I was to be a physician, and my interest in such study could never be taken for granted, to say the least — so, I had to give what time I had to those text books, given my low level of "efficiency," a matter of boredom doing its undermining work. My mother kept trying, though — her apparently casual asides, suggestions a legendary part of our family's life: we knew how reluctant she was to abandon an idea in which she believed. But as her son I had learned my own, responsive stubbornness, and the long and short of it was that I turned a deaf ear to her prodding with respect to *Invisible Man* — until, one day, it arrived in the mail, with a long letter from my mother, which both offered apologies for what got called "an intrusion," but submitted, as well, a passionate plea for what she kept calling "a close look at our country." That phrase was all mom — a modest, unpretentious way of saying more than is at first apparent. This was, after all, a novel whose title told of invisibility, hence the blindness of others — and there she was, using a visual image in her appropriately casual advocacy.

I read the novel during the summer of 1953 — an occasional stolen hour while rotating through a clerkship in pediatrics, which even then I knew would be my chosen branch of medicine. I carried the book with me, actually, in my black doctor's bag, full of those instruments which not only help a medical student examine patients but are a badge of honor: here I am, headed *there!* One day, as I was examining a ten-year-old boy who had cystic fibrosis, and therefore, poor prospects for an extended survival, I found myself emptying my bag, in search of my stethoscope, which had become entangled with other diagnostic devices in a limited space. As I did so, I pulled out the novel, and the boy wanted to know what it was. A story, I told him. About what? Borrowing from my mother: about America, a look at it. Oh — is the guy a shadow? There, I draw a blank — puzzle at the reference, take it literally, say no, a real man, even if a lot of people don't consider him so, and ignore him. I don't want to go any further, though — I have work to do, and I'm already behind schedule. But the boy won't let up — he tells me about his dad's favorite radio program when he was a boy, "The Shadow." I smile. I tell the lad that I also used to listen to that program. For a second or two I'm forgetting about the novel, remembering "Lamont Cranston, man-about-town" and his girlfriend, "the lovely Margo Lane," and remembering, as well, the creaky, creepy voice of "the Shadow," and the mystery of it all: Cranston become invisible, and in that form, morally knowing, and yes, invincible — he could spot the crooks, take them by complete surprise, undo them.

After a minute or two of talk about "the Shadow" I have forgotten about Ellison's novel, and I presume the boy has, too. I prepare to listen to his lungs, but he wants to use them in further conversation: *well*, is the "invisible man" in that book someone who "catches the bad guys"? Condescension drops upon my thoughts — I smile in order to mask my impatience. I am convinced that there is no way that I can explain this novel to this lad, so it's best to move on, proceed with a necessary evaluation of his medical condition. But I can tell that the boy wants his question answered, and so I nod — signal the novel as yet another radio crime story that has a happy ending. The boy thankfully loses interest in further questions of any kind — the silence of a sick child, worried about his fate, descends on him, on both of us actually. *Invisible Man* moves far from my consciousness as I go about my work.

Later, in the evening, I have some spare time, and I go back to the novel. For some reason, as I turn the pages, that young patient of mine keeps coming to mind. I can hear him asking about the outcome; I can hear him wondering whether the Invisible Man, like the shadowy figure of the radio program, "catches the bad guys." I am still the patronizing older person, all too ready to dismiss that line of inquiry — yet, it won't let go of me. Finally, I stop and think; I take the boy's question seriously — and realize that Ellison's anonymous protagonist does, indeed, "catch" those many "bad guys" who populate the novel — he sees *through* them, catches sight of them, is a witness to their phony, pretentious, greedy, manipulative, mean-spirited ways, even as they pay him no heed, are blind to his presence, his humanity, his right to be taken into consideration, given notice. Who are "they"? Without favor Ellison dares show us warts and worse among the rich and poor, the powerful and the weak, and yes, black people as well as white people — his is a vision of things that is by no means shaped by the confines of race. His is a moral vision — hence the appropriateness, I begin to realize, of my patient's question. His is the outsider's peculiarly privileged vision — as in Dostoyevsky's "Underground Man": the world passes him by, but he keeps his eyes open, keeps observing how people behave, what they do to one another, and the result is the narrator's progressive enlightenment, in the tradition of say, Dickens or George Eliot or Hardy, his melancholy awareness of how things work, of how people get on with one another.

By the time I finished the novel, I had connected it unforgettably to that youngster I had come to know in the hospital, who in his own way was trying to sort things out, distinguish between the good and the bad, the heroic and the malevolent. The novel, after all, is one of innocence gradually lost — every child's daily experience. Ellison has a youth at a school in the rural South go North, and as he moves across the American land, meets people high and low, he begins to understand what he (and many others) have to keep constantly in mind — the consuming egoism of so many, a nervous smugness that deprives them of their humanity, hence their inhumane behavior, demonstrated in ways large and small.

Even as that boy, with his heart-of-the-matter question, made me squirm, retreat into a medical egoism, Ellison's college youth hasn't quite learned to go along with all the lies and pretenses, the fakery called normality to which he is exposed, and so we readers are made to squirm, to laugh nervously and, maybe, to recall our own time of relative naiveté, even sincerity, when the world seemed trustworthy, reliable, decent. Soon enough, the fall — our growing realization of what is out there, meaning what is inside the minds and hearts of so many, a darkness that has nothing at all to do with the skin's pigment, that belies all appearances, that can take utter hold of us, and in Ellison's imagery, blind us, so that we see no one, really, but ourselves, and ironically, become thoroughly blind to ourselves, as well (because we don't recognize, really, what has happened to us).

Not that such a growing moral awareness on the part of a humble hero makes for a finger-pointing stiff narrative, or precludes irony, ambiguity, and humor. *Invisible Man* is not, ultimately, a novel about race (only), and it certainly does not give us a black-and-white view of human affairs. The novel's anonymous observer finds all of us flawed, but there are good moments that befall him — he meets individuals who work hard, who have acquired an earned wisdom about life. Moreover, his growing shrewdness brings with it a capacity to smile, if not laugh at the craziness of things — the blind leading the blind, as the saying goes, in endless circles. The one whom nobody cares to attend, pays the closest regard to everyone, everything; and consequently, a talented storyteller, of broad sensibility, gives the reader an anthropologist's as well as a moralist's view of mid-century America — the details, as only a novel can supply them, of everyday life. Page after page of revelation: music discussed, food described, variations of language rendered, gestures and mannerisms depicted, exact scenes of many kinds portrayed — all that goes on as people try to make do, some of them as bosses, most of them as vulnerable common folk, trying to take one step, then another, get through one hurdle, with the sure knowledge that another one is around the corner.

Invisible Man is meant to be a picaresque novel, though it is not the protagonist who is the rogue — rather, he traverses a roguish world, discovers and then marks out for us its contours. The result is, again, one man's enlightenment (literally, electric lights shine in his bunker, where he hunkers down, at the end of the story), and presumably, ours as well: to use the verb of that boy I long ago came to know on a pediatric ward, we catch hold of what Henry James called our "American scene," plenty of two-faced folks, plenty of double-dealing camouflaged by pietistic avowals and disavowals, but also the strange beauty that can come out of pain and suffering, as in jazz and the blues, both of which figure prominently in this novel, as they did in its creator's life. Speaking of that life, for years after *Invisible Man* was published the world awaited its successor. Again and again, Ralph Ellison had to hear critics, interviewers ask *when*. At his death, at eighty, in 1995, it became clear that there would be no "when"; that in regard to fiction, he had given us his all, with that one novel — and in this instance, "all" turned out to be more, much more than enough.

October 1994

30

Remembering Erik H. Erikson

Iₙ 1965, my wife Jane and I were living in the South, trying to learn how school desegregation was working and trying to be of help to SNCC, an acronym for the Student Nonviolent Coordinating Committee, a group of white and black youths determined to confront segregationist laws anywhere and everywhere — even in the Delta of Mississippi. Those men and women were the architects, then the builders of the Mississippi Summer Project of 1964, a critical moment, indeed, in the civil rights struggle. By then I'd wandered rather far from my chosen profession of child psychiatry and psychoanalysis, and not only out of a strong involvement in an ongoing social and racial struggle. I had gone South, initially, as a young physician who had to put in his two years in the military under the doctor's draft that then fingered all of us as we finished our internships or various stages of our residencies. I had started out becoming a pediatrician, and ended up a child psychiatrist — and so doing, witnessed the good and bad in a particular profession: the opportunity to work with children, learn from them, offer back to them such knowledge, and offer, too, a chance for shared contemplation, introspection; but also the temptation, not rarely embraced, toward smugness and self-importance, toward an overwrought intellectuality that took the troubles of families and made of them the stuff of clever, overblown, overriding theory. It was such a pleasure, during the couple of years in the Air Force, and those later, the years of working with Southern children and young activists, to be at a bit of remove from all the heavy conferences, the heady colloquia with concepts and generalizations and abstractions around everywhere and all the time.

Still, the civil rights struggle slowly began to achieve its initial political purposes, and many of us white folks began to realize by the middle 1960s that we'd best try to figure out how to resume our lives — say goodbye to the intense (at times, nonstop) life of political struggle that had engaged us for so long. One day in the spring of 1965 I received a letter from Erik H. Erikson — a short one, indeed. He had heard from a mutual friend of the work Jane and I were doing, and he wondered if I would ever be near Cambridge — if so, he'd like to meet. A great and wonderful surprise for me — I had admired his *Childhood and Society*, his *Young Man Luther*, and to hear from him (he was about thirty years older than me) was to hear from a great man, a god-like figure in my professional life. I was stunned, then nervously apprehensive. Who can ever live up to the expectations one develops with respect to one's heroes — meaning, ultimately, one's expectations of oneself?

In no time I was sitting in Erikson's Widener Library study at Harvard. I'd come there as he was approaching sixty — he who had never gone to college, let alone graduate school. (He lasted less than a decade as a professor — he could be quite impatient with academic pride and pomposity and pretense, as many of us who listened to him sound off got to know.) He asked me if I'd be interested in teaching in his undergraduate course, and I accepted the offer eagerly, hungrily — a chance to go back to school, read books that mattered, study again, now with a psychoanalyst who had dared take seriously not only the workings of family life, but the influence exerted by us on the world: one's class and race and sex, as they give shape to one's life; and yes, one's religious and spiritual life, for that, too, Erikson knew, matters a lot, has a lot to do with our values, our choices, our manner of living.

Erikson himself had stumbled into psychoanalysis at its virtual birth. He was a young artist of considerable talent, German born, who happened to hear of a good summer job in Vienna — to teach children at a private school organized by the American analysands, who, in the 1920s, had started coming to Austria to work with Freud and his colleagues. After a summer with those boys and girls, Erikson had intended to go back to drawing, doing woodcuts, but Anna Freud, who had observed him as a teacher and who was beginning to organize a training program for those who wanted to work psychoanalytically with children, had an alternative suggestion: a career as an analyst. By 1932 Erikson had graduated from the Vienna Psychoanalytic Institute — only to realize what was happening to the north (Hitler), to the south (Mussolini), and to the east (Stalin). Soon enough he and his wife, Joan, a Canadian dancer and sociologist, were on their way to the United States with their two sons, Kai and Jon (a daughter, Sue, would be born a few years later, in New Haven).

Shortly after his arrival here Erikson surprised his colleagues by his willingness to leave places like Harvard and Yale, urban centers of psychoanalysis like Boston and New Haven and San Francisco (he worked in all three of these cities at various times) for Indian reservations — the Sioux in South Dakota, the Yurok in the Far West. He had begun a lonely trek as an analyst much interested in anthropology, in history — he had begun to develop, really, a new way of viewing human behavior. Even young children, he knew, live at a particular moment of history, in a particular place, among particular relatives, neighbors, and with certain prospects likely theirs, or very much out of reach. Gradually, such knowledge — a kind of common sense, of course — began to appear in Erikson's writing as something else: a major effort to connect Freud's theories of childhood to the on-going reality of childhood as it so variously gets lived. Put differently, Erikson respected Freud's observations, speculations, but wanted to ground them in the ongoing actual experiences of boys and girls, of youths, of parents, too — the web of human (and social) relatedness that slowly locates us psychologically.

The above is now utterly uncontroversial — the received wisdom our time can accept as obvious. Yet, a half-century ago, as Erikson staked out his theoretical territory, many of his colleagues turned on him — some even in that peculiarly reductive *ad hominem* manner to which psychoanalysis lends itself in certain callous, or vulgar, or plain mean-spirited and envious hands. I well remember him talking of those early years, and a reading of *Childhood and Society* (especially the epilogue) more than conveys the combative direction he was compelled to take, on occasion, as a writer who wanted to uphold a point of view at all costs. Here he is, at the very end of the book, a brilliant, knowing essayist orchestrating a powerful farewell, and so doing, making a few thinly disguised polemical points: "The various identities which at first lent themselves to a fusion with the new identity of the analyst — identities based on talmudic argument, messianic zeal, on punitive orthodoxy, on faddish sensationalism, on professional and social ambition — all these identities and their cultural origins must now become part of the analyst's analysis, so that he may be able to discard archaic ritual of control and learn to identify with the lasting value of enlightenment. Only thus can he set free in himself and his patient that remnant of judicious indignation without which a cure is but a straw in the changeable wind of history."

The word "identity," so crucial to the argument, was distinctively Erikson's — he spent decades fleshing out the meaning of the word, even as he lived out what he would describe as an "identity crisis" (a phrase now practically a part of everyday speech). He had Jewish and Christian forebears, and in Central Europe, during the first half of this century, such a background brought with it plenty of vulnerability — out of which, in his case, came a great deal of sensitivity, a heightened awareness of what is, of what has been and might be, and, yes, a breadth of interests, as if all those different ancestors of his, uncommon (at that time) in their connectedness, had given him many voices and visions as a collective inheritance.

He put his idiosyncratic life's story to good use, indeed. He told us about Luther and Gandhi (*Gandhi's Truth*) — their effort to take issue with established power and authority. He told us about young people as they do the same, so often — say many no's as they struggle to say yes to life and its hypocrisies and duplicities, as well as its opportunities. He became, ultimately, a psychologically subtle and astute moral essayist who breathed life into a profession seriously in jeopardy of getting lost, a victim of its own parochialism. So it can go, the one-time vigorous, bold rebel gradually becomes revered — those he regarded skeptically, to say the least, now more than reconciled to him, even grateful for the necessary ethical direction and leadership he has provided.

The last thing such a historical figure wants or needs is an absorption in a culture's iconography — though, perhaps, that is the price of intellectual endurance. When Erik H. Erikson died, at ninety-one, he had been silent for many years — the impact of old age and its consequences on his body and mind. Yet, at once he was everywhere: America very much paying him notice at his departure — he who had done so much, as an immigrant, to try to understand this country and convey to others the knowledge that came from that effort. But he went far beyond psychological exploration and clarification; he dared link (in *Insight and Responsibility*) self-understanding to moral awareness; he dared insist upon the importance of a readiness to stand for something beyond one's own egoism, however well explored. No wonder he was so fully acknowledged at his death — this man of the mind who kept telling us Americans, increasingly the victims of a secular culture, all too proudly "value-free" in its self-descriptions, that there are ideals and ideas worth embracing, worth living for, worth, even, the giving of one's life in order to further, to protect.

November 1994

– 31 –

Talk Shows

I HAVE BEEN MAKING some snide remarks in recent columns about the talk shows that now take up so much time during the morning and afternoon on television, and I want to bury the subject, now, with some further comments, prompted actually by those of a friend of mine, who kept asking me in various ways why I objected to such characters as Oprah and Phil and Geraldo and Montel and Rolanda and Sally-Jessy and Vicki and Maury (I'm sure I'm omitting a dozen or so others) when they, after all, offer thousands of ordinary folks a chance to be seen, to be heard, surely a democratic aspect of our popular culture. Yes, indeed, all day long that is what happens: People of no great wealth, power, fame, achievement — plain people, even humble people — get to sit on a stage, seen and heard by others, also unknown and far from mighty in their background. Why not be glad therefore — the elitism of experts and big shots of various kinds, who have constant access to newspapers, radio, magazines, never mind television, replaced by the appearance of Mr. and Mrs. America, the average ones who live in small towns or working-class suburbs or urban neighborhoods inhabited by people who wear blue or white collars?

Of course, there *are*, rather often, "experts" on those talk shows — a seemingly endless parade of self-proclaimed "psychologists," or "therapists" who specialize in this or that aspect of human behavior, the kind being featured on the particular program they are called to grace with their important presence. Not that the hosts of the shows lack their own claim to psychological authority — all the time, in fact, they draw on the phrases of our contemporary support groups. These are hosts who nod knowingly, utter "uh-huh" eagerly, prod their guests to say more (and more, and more), raise their eyebrows and lower their heads or shake them, a beguiling spectacle of the earnest listener who in a flash becomes the earnest (and compassionate or remonstrative) speaker in a conversation that is utterly public: the studio audience, whose members (hope against hope) await *their* chance in front of those mobile, ever panning cameras; and you and I, we who watch and watch, who don't know, commonly, whether to laugh or cry or scream, who keep on tuning in, however, we of the mainstream who by the millions mainline the stuff, no matter its

124

slick banality, because it's hard not to wonder when the apparent limit of one barrier will yield to another — the "seething cauldron" of the unconscious that Freud described as utterly beyond our recognition now turned into a shared narrative of deed and event. Once upon a time we in psychoanalytic psychiatry spent months, years, exploring gradually and tactfully (we hoped) the buffed fantasies and impulses of our patients, who had every reason (social and cultural, as well as personal) to keep such matters under wraps, keep them out of sight and mind, both. Now, the most offbeat explorations and discussions that took place in those medical offices, or at professional meetings, and were described in various journal articles or books, all seem quite quaint, surely not worth the attention of today's emotionally hyped audience for whom every once unimaginable form of sexuality and violence — every kind of human behavior formerly regarded as wild, utterly and thoroughly loony — has become unsurprising, even old hat. The "polymorphous perversity" of Freud's unconscious, the lusts and envies and hates, the bizarre passions, the cruelties and betrayals that once belonged way in the back of our minds, are now openly related as if they are the very stuff of ordinary American life.

I ask myself as I view those shows (and as I write this, now) what has happened, what these talk shows have to tell us about ourselves — with their parade of the hurt and the scorned, the violent and the violated, the goofy and the nutty, all rendered in the slick language of a popularized psychology that has become a secular obsession, if not a religion of sorts. Over the years, both before and after the arrival of Oprah and her ilk, the newspapers have yielded their precious print and space to advice columns (and now, of course, advice books are a mainstay of publishing, and the bestseller lists). I well remember my dad's scorn for them — and my effort to counter it with explanations of human need and vulnerability. Here, from memory, is how we talked about a development which prefigured what now has become a casual norm of our culture. Him: "These articles, these columns are insulting to the intelligence of the reader; they offer small-minded platitudes, empty psychological rhetoric dressed up as scientific truth." Me: "A lot of people out there are in a lot of trouble, and they need whatever help they can get. What is obvious to you may not be so evident to them. They need someone to direct them toward a point of view, a way of seeing things, and, more concretely, toward specific agencies or clinics."

A polite pause, as my dad took note of a certain patronizing tone in my way of putting things, and then: "Yes, I'm sure *all* of us could use some 'help' now and then; but I read those 'advice' columns, and at their best they offer homespun, folksy words of reassurance or explanation — probably better given by friends, neighbors, relatives. I worry, though, about the false hopes raised, the false promises made: If you consult this authority, that kind of doctor or psychologist or clinic, or read someone's book — in five steps, or with ten points — then you will have your foot in the door of heaven itself! What happens to the notion of will, of self-reliance, of common sense — of humor, even? Where is the good laugh directed at the psychological simplifications, the glib and reductionist interpretations offered in the name of the latest knowledge? Life's complexities and inconsistencies and ironies and mysteries (in George Eliot's phrase, 'life's indefiniteness,' which she knew won't ever be banished by the latest outburst of persuasion, of 'guidance') will always be with us, and to know that, to be reminded of that, is the greater need."

A moment of silence from me — and then I try a personal tack: "Dad, you are a fortunate man. You've been reading George Eliot and Dickens and Hardy and Tolstoy all your life, and those novelists inform it. Lots of people aren't so lucky — and they aren't as lucky as you are in other respects: Their lives are hard and the consequences are severe. You've had a happy marriage, and a successful career — think of those who are overwhelmed by various personal and economic and social struggles, with no one, really, to call upon for assistance." Him: "I understand what you're saying, but I tell you — to switch to your mother's religious talk — it's a sin to condescend to people, underestimate them: Isn't that an especially wicked kind of pride! *That* is what troubles me the most about these 'mental health' people, these 'advice' people, with their daily offerings in the paper: They are the ones, actually, who are making worse the very problem you mention by emphasizing our psychological helplessness or blindness, by giving us less and less credit for what is possible for us, personally or emotionally, by insisting that even teachers or lawyers or doctors or judges need 'help,' need these 'experts,' these 'guidance' people. We all become diminished thereby, diminished with respect to what we expect of ourselves and one another; and we turn to — well, whom? Exactly who *are* these people we're now to count on, and what are they offering us, and what does their prominence in our culture tell us about it, about us? In that regard, your mother is aghast at the way the clergy, of all people, are the most gullible — they parrot the nearest psychologist they can lay their hands on, turn their ministries into endless 'counseling sessions.' God forbid that we should ask of people, speak to them as the biblical prophets did, or our own founding fathers — assume in them a substantial rationality and a moral capability, and these days a moral thirst, a hunger that goes unappeased, amidst all the 'value-free' or 'neutral' positionings of these self-declared 'therapists.'"

I now decide I have one last tactic to summon, an ironic one, indeed: "Dad, you are being 'hostile,' 'defensive'; *you* need 'help' — you are showing 'resistance.'" Him: "I hope so — I *am* troubled and worried by all this. The issue is not the legitimacy of psychology or psychiatry; rather, the issue is the moral and cultural vacuum in our society that those disciplines have been allowed to fill — it's no good for *them,* either: They've been sucked into something, a consequence of the decline of religion and literature and philosophy as our guiding spirits. Nowadays, even scholars of those disciplines or 'fields' turn to psychology and psychopathology — give us 'deconstruction' and 'situation ethics' and agnostic skepticism dressed up as theology, or as an impenetrably abstract philosophy that shudders at the thought of taking a firm stand, saying no or yes to anything. Is it any wonder that these newspaper columnists write all that psychological drivel and readers flocked to them — and now the disease has spread to television!" Me: "I surrender!"

Even now I think of Dad, no longer here on this earth, as I watch those talk shows; and I think of my friend Walker Percy, with whom I used to watch some of them — his sad laughter as he mourned for all of us: the melancholy nonsense of so much of it all! Once he said, cryptically, "a circus" — we'd watched dear Oprah and some exceedingly hyped up folks who shouted, cried, poured out the secrets of their lives for millions to slurp up: one more hour's consumption, the studio audience chortling, applauding, with God knows what echoes in home after home across the land. He was being quite literal, Dr. Percy was, I later realized — the people on those talk shows become performers, led through their respective acts by the trainer, the handler, with assembled onlookers to cheer, to enjoy the proclaimed, enacted distress, craziness, wildness. In the ancient Colosseum, animals were turned upon citizens, while the crowd roared its delight; today citizens are egged on to tell unashamedly of their animal-like emotions and actions, while (courtesy of technology) just about everyone in the world can take it all in, hour after hour of weird confessional melodrama put on public display — a circus, all right, a peculiarly American one that has seized the day in these last years of our second millennium.

December 1994

– 32 –

On Birth Control

IN THE EARLY 1980s I spent a lot of time in Brazil, trying to learn how children of a particular Rio de Janeiro *favela* lived — exploring not only the physical circumstances of their lives and, too, their psychological response to an especially hard, unpromising fate, but the moral and spiritual side of things: the manner in which certain boys and girls made sense of things, sorted out rights and wrongs, responded to the religious traditions of the Catholic Church, which had an outpost of sorts at the foot of the *favela* in the form of a soup kitchen run by two wonderfully kind and sensitive and generous nuns. I got to know many children, many families in the course of that work, and all were quite poor, with virtually no prospect of ever rising to a more privileged situation in a country where a small number of people are enormously rich and the vast majority utterly impoverished. I remember, even now, one mother of eight children, who had, besides, lost several others to miscarriages. Once as she and I talked about her daughter Maria, then ten, and her delight in drawing pictures for me, I was asked this: "Do you think God wants us to have children every year, every other year?"

I was surprised at that inquiry, and for a few moments, speechless. With me was a Brazilian doctor, half American, a friend who was acting as a translator. When, finally, I begged off, shrugged my shoulders to indicate an inability to say anything, my colleague, in English, intervened: "Come on, tell her what you think — she wants to know!" Instead of doing so, I pleaded for time and mercy: "I don't know how to answer her. Who can speak for God?" Then, I blurted out this: "She already has too many children. She is overwhelmed by them — by everything. She keeps telling me that her life is 'to stay ahead of the Devil,' and when I asked her what she meant by those words, you heard her: she told me that every day she is afraid all of them in her family will have no more food to eat, will begin starving to death — and now she is pregnant again."

We talked at further length, my medical friend and I; then, we returned to my conversation with a woman still in her thirties, tired and sickly, and without a doubt worried that she might soon die. Such apprehensions came to the surface, again, as she told me of her travails, the strains on and threats to her health that accompanied her

128

many, many pregnancies. Moreover, her children were born at home, delivered by kin or neighbors or, twice, by one of the nuns. It was to her, actually, that I would pose that same question put to me by the mother, a question I never did answer on the day it was asked, though my doctor friend took the liberty of giving his earnest, heartfelt reply: no — and he went further, saying that he couldn't believe that God wanted any women like her, already so overburdened, to keep bringing children into this world. The nun was interested in my friend's remarks (she knew and admired him: he gave a lot of his time to unpaid work with the poor), and to my surprise, she wasn't ready to dispute his position directly: "I see what he means. I understand him — what he says. I won't tell you I don't get discouraged, too — and when I do [feel that way], I get confused."

Now, silence, and she crosses herself. I feel in the presence of holiness: she works so hard, so long, on behalf of others terribly hurt, vulnerable, wretched even, in the hope of being of some help. I also feel all too smug and intrusive — the outsider doing a research project, whose values don't get tested as that nun's do: every day of her life committed to women like the one I'd just visited. Still, I want to say something that has been welling up; talk about the need for something — I want to talk about the need for education about birth control among the *favelado* parents I've gotten to know and, of course, millions of others like them in Brazil and elsewhere.

I start in; I speak of the particular woman whose life we have been considering. I deliver a not unusual or surprising secular homily — and the nun nods as she hears it translated. At the end, I am told that she sees what I mean, that she appreciates my line of reasoning — and yes, there are times when she quite agrees with me. I sit back in the slightly unstable chair I have been occupying, and almost fall to the floor, but rescue myself. She tells me I should go sit across the room, in a more comfortable and spacious chair. No, I protest, I am where I am. She smiles, teases me, tells me that I am advocating "change" for others, but am nonetheless holding on to my own position, however fragile it be! We laugh, the three of us — and then my doctor friend suggests that I press further, ask the nun what she would think if he and others set up a birth control education program in the *favela*. I do so, a bit shyly out of deference to the nun, but with no lack of enthusiasm. She interrupts our conversation, offers us iced tea, and what she calls "a sweet." I begin to wonder whether she has not, that way, told me something — a reluctance on her part to discuss an exceedingly vexing matter. I am prepared to change the subject, but she quickly returns to it after she has shown us a generous kind of hospitality, her own cookies, which the many hungry children love, constantly seek. "I am not a theologian," she begins — then a wry smile, meant to acknowledge her realization that her disavowal was unnecessary. "All I try to do," she resumes, "is be of assistance to these people here. They suffer a lot, and at night, when I lie in my comfortable bed here, with my stomach full, and the roof solid, so no rain is pouring over me, and the floors and walls solid, so no rats are running through — it is then that I know how lucky I am, and how unlucky all those people you have met are, and it is then, I have to admit, that they will continue to be [unlucky], all their days."

A pause — I notice that she takes a deep swallow of her tea, and then this, the hard part (I'd later understand): "I pray to our Lord about all this. I am not an evangelical [a Protestant], but I do, sometimes in my mind — I confess — separate Jesus from our blessed [Catholic] church. The church is run by men [her doctor friend smiles at that moment, and she blushes, acknowledges his big smile with a thin one of her own], and men make mistakes, even men devoted to God and His chosen church. Our church has admitted mistakes in the past and (who knows?) it may admit more in the future. Maybe one day it will worry about these women [she points to the flimsy shacks up the hill] the way you both want — worry about women in poor health, near starvation, having child after child after child: all those hungry, malnourished little ones. I walk at night, sometimes, and look at [the statue of] Jesus [so well known, on a hill dominating the city and harbor of Rio de Janeiro] and I ask Him: What do You think? What should we do? I ask Him: how about Anna — who died the other evening, giving birth to her tenth child, all of them barely scraping by, in awful health; eating scraps of food, and pushing one another aside when they come here for their [daily] glasses of milk and cookies. I think I hear him crying and crying for Anna's children, the way she did when she was with us! I am not one, you see, to wave a finger at other Annas still alive, and tell them, with so little for themselves, to give us [the church] more and more, the more souls the better! No, sir." A second's hesitation, and then the two words repeated in a rising voice: "No, sir."

She resumes, now speaking more quietly, though more slowly, too, for obvious emphasis: "I will tell you what I think the church has been trying to say to us all these years — and maybe it hasn't done a good job [of conveying its message]: we have to learn to be bigger than ourselves; we have to try to go beyond our comforts, our pleasures. It is so easy and tempting to wrap ourselves in our desires — and defend ourselves [as we do so] for being compassionate toward these *favelados!* To connect our sexual life to children, to the gift of life to the world — that is a noble idea, a high ideal. To ask people to sacrifice on behalf of the next generation, to deny themselves some pleasures and conveniences so that another child and another child come here [on Earth] to live — that is also a noble idea, a high ideal. A lot of people — I believe it, I observe it — want to control our 'population': it is a principle, an abstraction, they are upholding. In their own lives — they care mightily [hugely] for themselves, and they don't want 'a lot of children' because they don't want to exert themselves in that direction, only in other directions, for [toward] themselves. Is not selfishness, plenty of selfishness, a part of this story — as well as ignorance, and maybe (all right, I will admit it) 'our' mistake [that of the church]?"

She crosses herself. She looks out the window, toward that statue of Jesus, His arms outstretched high and wide. I follow her lead — and I notice my medical colleague is doing likewise. Condoms and other birth control devices cross my mind — their important value for so many; but I think, too, of the egoism we all bear, and how cleverly we conceal it from ourselves, banish it from sight as we take after others with our righteousness that slips all too readily into self-righteousness. It certainly is easier, I can't help but thinking, there and then, to be "for" birth control (the more of it, the better) than to locate oneself, one's life, in the place chosen by that nun, or in other places, actually, like it at home — ghetto neighborhoods, for instance. It is easier, as well, to urge birth control as a high-minded principle than to take a candid look at the way much of our culture (our movies, our television programs) portrays sexual life, with its possibility of reproductive life: a collective narcissism, an unapologetic hedonism — for all of which I doubt that nun would want to summon the descriptive phrase she kept using, "noble ideas, high ideals." Still, all of that apart, she aches in her heart for the women whose lives she attends — and she certainly aches (she eventually made it quite clear to us two doctors) for a church that is very much hers, for a church whose stated doctrine (some of it, with respect to birth control) she finds herself trying to set aside in her mind as she does her daily work.

January 1995

On Sex Education for the Young

ABOUT FIVE YEARS AGO my wife, Jane, a high school teacher of English, and I were visited by two friends of ours, the parents of a nine-year-old boy and a fourteen-year-old girl. Both the mother and father were more than a little upset by what was happening in the elementary school their son attended and in the high school in which their daughter had just begun classes. The boy was coming home with vivid accounts of human sexuality, including its variations, if not (as many would have it) peculiarities or aberrations. The teenaged girl was attending classes in which various kinds of contraceptive devices or procedures were being discussed — and along with her classmates, she had learned that condoms were available in a machine located in the school, a so-called public health initiative. The parents were both upset — and, frankly, a little ashamed to be upset. They were anxious to indicate, right off, that they were not "uptight," were not "prudes," had no claim to being "puritans" — and, of course, we knew them to be thoughtful, sensible people, he a lawyer, she an old friend of my wife's and a one-time teaching colleague of hers.

As we talked, I began to realize that their comments about themselves, so uncharacteristic in the sense that these were not a pair of egoists, were clearly meant to fend off criticism, either already sent their way, or soon to arrive, so they might fear. In that regard, I can still hear both of them telling me what they together had experienced at the hands (the mouth) of someone called the high school psychologist, who in addressing a group of parents with reservations about the "sex education curriculum" had referred to its opponents as somehow "resistant" to what he called "emotional insight" — and by implication, not as "progressive" and "enlightened" as these parents clearly considered themselves to be.

Not that I hadn't experienced before, and first-hand, what they had been going through — Lord, as I sat with them, I was flooded with memories of similar meetings with other parents, and with a few of those so-called experts who teach "sex education" courses in our nation's schools. I guess I was somewhat protected by my occupation — a child psychiatrist and a pediatrician. I'm supposed to know some things about children, but, in fact, years ago I kept hearing about AIDS and teenage pregnancy as if my own elementary school children, my teenage children, were in imminent danger of both — unless, of course, they absorbed thoroughly the lessons being offered them, again, in the name of "sex education," in the name, too, of "a progressive, public health-oriented curriculum," another mouthful of words spoken, I noticed, with no felt embarrassment that the limits of modesty were in any danger of being tested.

Today, as I recall that past, I wonder at our willingness to be so willing to let so-called experts working for particular school systems claim and assert such authority over us — tell us that they know best what our children ought to be taught with respect to something called "sex education." Today I also realize that the second time around, so to speak, my wife and I were far more prepared to challenge such "expertise" — did so, actually by sharing our experiences with our friends who had come to us for advice. In that regard we were frank to tell of both our bemusement and indignation — sexuality vigorously described, but sexuality also taken for granted as enacted, sexuality assumed as something high schoolers (even junior high schoolers) simply "do" — hence the constant talk of being "prepared," of learning how to prevent a pregnancy. Yes, "abstinence" was mentioned — but only as a passing nod to a distant, quaint past.

In fact, on several occasions, while serving on medical panels or in the course of speaking before various groups of parents or youths, I have tried to make the case for "abstinence," as indeed it had been made for me by my parents, though without resort to that particular word. So doing, I have summoned not religious precepts, but psychiatric and psychoanalytic experience — what I have learned, actually, from my patients as well as (many years ago) my teachers, or, as they often get called in child psychiatry, my "supervisors," the men and women who try to help along hospital residents so they will gradually feel able to sustain the inevitable frustrations and mysteries (and, yes, provocations) that go with the work they have chosen. Again and again I have shared with those colleagues or parents or youths these words spoken to me by Anna Freud, the founder, it can be said, of child psychoanalysis: "Children and adolescents, both, need to have acquired control — the ability to say no to the instinctual life, which presses upon them (upon all of us), and which can overwhelm anyone who hasn't learned 'the virtue of nay-saying.'" At that point, I interrupted Miss Freud to comment on the phrase she had just used — hardly the usual psychoanalytic language. She immediately sensed the curiosity behind my aesthetic response, "That's a nice way of putting it." She allowed herself a thin smile, and proceeded in this manner (I've edited her remarks): "I heard that ['the virtue of nay-saying'] from an elderly schoolteacher. We have become friends. She keeps telling me that psychoanalysis has had a bad influence on our 'culture' [in England], even though it may be helpful to our patients. I keep answering her in no uncertain terms; I tell her no, no, no: It is not us [psychoanalysts] — we are not the ones who advocate 'license,' as she puts it. We are on her side: we know — *do we!* — the risks, the great risks that go with a weakened conscience, a weakened capacity to tame the 'drives,' the instincts, a weakened will to do so, whether due to a person's upbringing (no effective lessons at the hands of parents who want that [outcome] to occur, and are ready to work for it) or due to a society, a world that stirs those instincts, encourages their expression, no matter the cost to all of us."

A pause, for some water. I'm thinking that she hasn't given me the context for that schoolteacher's use of the phrase under discussion — and then she resumes as if she has only stopped to read my mind: "My [teacher] friend talks of 'the virtue of nay-saying,' and I tell her yes, yes, indeed — for children, for adolescents, for all of us. I tell her that young school children have to learn how to obey rules as well as explore the world — I try to explain [to her] that I'm no 'romantic' who thinks children are inherently 'good' or 'creative' if only 'left to be themselves,' as some used to say, when we were starting a nursery in Vienna during the 1920s. And I try to explain that as children get older, they need to gain control over their sexual urges — or they [the urges] will, pretty soon, own them! Of course, there can be the 'craziness' of too much control, and my father's generation saw, experienced that in some people: so much 'repression' that the individual becomes weird, overwhelmed by inhibitions that spread, as we put it, into 'all spheres,' that is, affect the everyday life of the person, apart from the sexual life. But these days, we see the opposite, all too often young people who haven't been given the encouragement (haven't been taught) to rein in their impulses, to build a 'psychological distance' between what they think (or think they want) and what they (right away) try to find for themselves — and who cares about the consequences! We [in psychoanalysis] have always been on the side of thoughtfulness, you could call it — the gradually developing capacity of young people to sort things out emotionally, figure out how they want to behave, and with whom: All that takes a long time — and is what adolescence, all of it, turns out to be for. So, I'm with the 'nay-sayers,' with the virtue of 'deferred gratification' as some of us in psychoanalysis have called it."

I push a bit; I use the word "abstinence"; I say that some folks in "the States" urge it, especially so in view of a rapidly rising illegitimacy rate (a phrase, even then, in 1970, thoroughly outdated, if not suspect!). Miss Freud nods — says wryly that "abstinence is, of course, a traditional kind of sexuality," and then clarifies tersely: "The capacity for sustained [sexual] abstinence precedes the capacity for a genuine [sexual] choice — otherwise there is what my father called the 'polymorphous perversity' of childhood fantasy life, updated to adolescence and beyond — promiscuity and more promiscuity, impulsivity and all its consequences."

We continued in that vein, and as we did, I was reminded, yet again, how *conservative* Freudian thought really is, in one sense of the word "conservative" — a realization that anarchy awaits us, if we haven't learned a range of personal constraints, and a realization, too, that the *family* is the most important, the most influential agent for the enunciation and consolidation of those restraints. Indeed, as any teacher knows (the huge significance of those "preschool years"), without the family as such an agent, a child becomes less than human, meaning driven by urges that go uncontrolled, hence expressed to the detriment of anyone and everyone around, including (always) the child himself or herself.

Against such an accumulated background of clinical knowledge and experience, a century in duration, one wonders why, in the name of contemporary psychiatry or psychoanalysis, "abstinence" would be all that controversial — or, too, an emphasis on the importance of the family as a major and proper educative (moral) influence on young people with respect to their sexuality. There is no question, in that regard, that particular families fail — and the result is all too obvious these days: children who are ruled by impulse and, yes, children who beget children. But by the time such "children" appear on the social scene, as it were, many important years have gone by, and I truly wonder whether "sex education" courses will be the remedy for the years of moral and psychological abdication that have preceded what now gets recognized as troublesome behavior, indeed.

March 1995

– 34 –

Pride

ALL THE TIME, as a child, I heard my mother mention "the sin of pride," though she wasn't inclined to do so with anger, wasn't inclined to point her finger, chastise me; rather, she would be the wry, ironic observer and teacher, ready to summon, say, Ecclesiastes ("vanity of vanities, all is vanity") in order to give herself, never mind me, a bit of perspective on things. How well, for instance, I remember her response to an especially good report card I once brought home. I wasn't such a good student at the time (fifth grade). I was, in fact, a noisy brat who hung out with two other boys just like me — a bothersome threesome to our teacher, who would call us "fresh," tell us to mind our manners, threaten us with "demerits" and trips to the principal's office, where we were roundly rebuked, sent back with warnings that our parents would be notified, that we would miss "athletics," our favorite "subject," and instead be asked to write one hundred times avowals such as "I will obey the teacher from now on." Still, in the clutch, I knew to shut up and try to behave myself, lest the teacher make good her promise to call my parents in for a "conference" — sometimes a child, thereafter, would be told to miss school for a few days. Now, for once, I'd parted company with all of that, turned into a momentary scholar of sorts, even secured a high grade in "conduct," attesting to a spell of apparent obedience, respect for rules and regulation. Now I had evidence in hand, those letters "A" and "B" that had me, without reservation, on something called the "honor roll." The teacher herself had sent a note home, meant to accompany the report card — an expression on her part of satisfaction, appreciation, even celebration. I had "quieted down," my parents were told; I had taken a long first step on the way to being "good."

To this day I recall my delight as I went home quickly with that report card and that letter — none of the usual dawdling, the diversionary tactics that could drive my mother (especially) and even my ever so reserved, even detached father to distraction: Where *is* he, and what is he doing now that will, soon enough, get him (and, by extension, us) into some kind of trouble? I still remember, also, the satisfaction, the obvious pleasure my parents took in the card I handed them, and the teacher's letter. My father allowed himself a thin smile, a wink: his wordless version of strong approval. My mother, far more talkative (a mixed blessing, I often felt) showered me with her appreciative gratitude. She "knew" I'd "pull through"! (Whence, I wondered, such knowledge on her part, when it certainly had eluded me?) She had "prayed" for this "turn." (Is that what God has to hear, millions and millions of such entreaties — and how does He ever have the time to listen, never mind respond?) She had spoken to her sister about this matter of a son's rebelliousness, and she, a schoolteacher herself, then living in Sioux City, Iowa, had counseled "patience," had urged my folks to let me "grow up," as assuredly I would. (But I had heard them criticize so-called grown-ups for the very qualities they found all too present in me — a naughty disobedience, a rebellious streak). Still, these perceived qualms or doubts on my part — a child questioning his parents, even as they worried long and hard about his inclination, at school, to question (to defy) adult authority — had at last given way to a swell of self-satisfaction, and, with it, good will, as my parents remarked upon (or in Dad's case, indicated) their relief, their approval.

Suddenly, though, a shift in the weather. Suddenly I feel chilly — if not totally taken by surprise. Now, I am hearing my beloved and warm-hearted and so often quite affectionate mom singing a different tune. Now, I hear this — and I swear, I know the message, word for word, from memory, not the workings (obviously!) of a tape recorder, though (Lord knows) the lack of mechanical validation presents a serious challenge to what can be accepted as "objective," as opposed to "subjective." (How about the "objectivity of subjectivity," I once heard Erik H. Erikson muse, ask a few of us with some barely subdued annoyance as he contemplated something called "oral history," with its glorification of a machine called the tape recorder — as if it doesn't also shape what we say, engender self-consciousness, curb truths as well as enable their expression, all in the name of "progress" with respect to, and in contrast with, the tradition of the memoir, the essayist at work with his or her remembered past). Now, I am sitting at the table, and across from me my mother speaks, her voice noticeably lowered, her look grave: "Bobby, we must always worry about pride." She is ready to go further, to explicate, but she knows she has sent forth a signal that will worry her husband, my dad — that will, actually, make him quite irritated. He registers that emotion, yet again, silently: He frowns at her, casts me a look of obvious sympathy, and then the sound: He has picked up the newspaper, as if thereby shielding himself from what he knows will come, a kind of "overwrought Bible-talk," he once called it, when he had succumbed to (for him) a vast loquacity. Mother has given him his "say," and now she has more of hers: "You see, we are tempted by pride at moments like this." A pause, while I wonder at her choice of pronouns; I haven't noticed any such inclination — though by then, I can anticipate what is to come, her insistence on precisely that point, and sure enough, I'm not disappointed: "That is how God works — He judges us not only by our accomplishments, but by how we bear them. And that is how the devil works — he tempts us with pride, and we become quite pleased with ourselves, *too* pleased with ourselves."

She's gone as far as she wants to go — too far for Dad. He puts his paper down noisily, but won't settle for that break with silence. He is simmering with a kind of down-to-earth, commonsense outrage that I had learned, already, to appreciate mightily — his scientist's earthiness against Mom's religious flights of fancy (and righteous admonishment). Finally, his words, all the more precious for their relative scarcity: "For heaven's sake [the irony!], why are we [*we!*] making so much of this!" My mom lowers her head — but not in fear or surrender, both Dad and I know. She is praying for us! How to beat *that,* I would a few years down the line begin to wonder! Dad goes for the final plunge to victory: "You know, there must be a kind of pride in warning people — in warning yourself — of pride!"

That does it — the argument is fully engaged by both of them: Mom agrees with that last, psychologically astute comment, but reveals her own theological and psychological (and adversarial) skills, by remarking on the pride of the person who warns others of their obscure and not so obscure forms of pride. Dad counters that she and he can keep going back and forth in that way — to what effect, though? Mom tries to free both of them, all of us, from an overly focused subject-matter: "Phil, I'm just warning us about the danger of smugness." He rejects the overture, however: "Sandy [her given name was Sandra], don't you see that you are letting that Bible go to your head — it's pushing us into this intense discussion, as if it's a question of Life and Death, Heaven and Hell, all because Bobby came home pleased as punch with his good grades, and so are you and so am I, and I think that should be the end of it." She says yes — but also no: "All right, I agree. I *am* pleased as punch! But I still think I should tell these children — I still think you and I should worry — that success can be a real challenge to us; that the greatest success is a humility that you have to fight for, every day, and especially on days like this, when the sun is shining brightly on you." He retreats, in an instructive acknowledgment which I hope I'll never forget: "Yes, things can go to our heads, I agree."

In retrospect, I realize that my dad never did go for my mom's biblically informed psychology; rather, he settled for a secular kind that did, however, meet hers part of the way. In retrospect, too, I thank the Almighty Lord for my mom's provoking, at times unnerving, insistence upon "pride" as the great moral and psychological measuring rod. In New Orleans, when I visited the psychoanalyst I was seeing in his Prytania Street office, five days a week, that side of my mother often came up for examination. Indeed, the doctor who sat behind me on the occasion of the many years of a "training analysis" often wondered what the mere child I was could possibly make of the kind of discussion I've just set down. Wasn't I "angry," for instance, or at least "confused" that my mother implicitly would chastise me — when all I'd done was try to do a good job at school? Oh, yes, I assented; but then I'd hasten to point out plenty of smugness and self-importance in us, the big-shot doctors who make up membership (or aspiring membership) in psychoanalytic institutes, not to mention medical schools or other graduate schools, or colleges, and on and on downward, even to elementary schools, where (I've noticed since doing voluntary teaching in them) some boys and girls try to lord it over others, tease them, scorn them, call them "dumb," define them as lower intellectually, among other ways — and so, I am left, late in life, with a grateful remembrance of my mom's tough, demanding psychological awareness that never for a moment, it seemed, forsook its connection to the Hebrew Bible, to the Christian Bible, both.

April 1995

35

Envy

W HEN FREUD listened to his first patients, he observed their substantial difficulty in coming to terms with their sexual thoughts and impulses — to the point that, he began to realize, this aspect of their lives was hidden even from them, never mind others who might want to attend them, be of help to them. So it was that the unconscious, thoroughly familiar to novelists and poets and playwrights over the centuries, took on new life as a construct in a neuropsychiatrist's metapsychology — one, however, derived not from the reveries of a theorist, but from his daily clinical effort to understand his patients. Today, of course, sexuality is a virtual mainstay of our bourgeois, capitalist culture, a commodity, even — sold, as it were, on the covers of magazines, in the advertisements for a host of products and, increasingly, in the advertisements by individuals on behalf of themselves that appear in the respectable press (journals, newspapers), never mind the scandal tabloids.

Those of us who are psychiatrists, psychoanalysts, no longer have to wait long, probe persistently, in order to learn about what Freud called Eros, as it lives in our particular patients. These days, the men and women, even the children who come to see us are ready, even eager, to share thoughts, fantasies, impulses that bespeak of — well, in a way, their citizenship. Put differently, they are late twentieth-century Americans who have watched the talk shows, with their chief staple, confessional sex, gone to the movies, picked up periodicals, the daily paper, glimpsed billboards, raced through the best-selling pulp fiction, and thereby learned what is not only acceptable, but desirable — to the point that, yes, I once heard a monogamous man in his thirties wonder what was wrong with him: he found himself attracted *only* to his wife, and he was appalled by what he saw on television and at the movies. Was he some odd variant of a prude, a puritan? Was he "repressed," abnormally so? His colleagues in the law firm to which he belonged were all the time horsing around, making mention of this or that sex scene they'd thoroughly enjoyed seeing on television or taking in as they leafed through one or another magazine. They also had a constant supply of jokes to share, all sexual in nature. Why, he kept asking himself, as they gabbed and guffawed, did he feel left out, even disgusted?

I knew, upon hearing that kind of self-addressed inquiry, to suggest that we table the matter — move on: try to figure out why *else* those colleagues might bother him, apart from their constantly articulated sexuality. I kept asking this fine, sensitive upstanding man about his working life, rather than his sexual life, which was for him and his wife quite fulfilling. Even as he worried that he had some "hidden psychological problem," because of the animus he felt toward his fellow lawyers at the firm, I kept trying to learn about those lawyers, their achievements and attainments, and most of all their daily activities and responsibilities as attorneys who belonged to a big-shot enterprise of sorts, one well-connected to a host of businesses and well-to-do individuals.

Gradually I began to realize that those colleagues bothered this sensitive, thoughtful patient of mine in ways other than he quite realized — the modern unconscious exerting itself, all right, but not, ironically, in the service of the sexual repression he speculated to be at work. He had come to see me because he felt restless, at times quite anxious, and on occasion, a spell of insomnia visited him, apparently out of nowhere: all seemed well, yet he tossed his way, awake, through the whole night. Eager to get to the bottom of things, he virtually embraced his "asceticism" (he once called it) as a symptom of sorts — sexual inhibition as an obvious sign of mental and emotional abnormality! But the more I heard him talk of all that — always, it seemed, in connection with his "law partners" — the more I wondered (to myself, at first, and later aloud, in conversation with him) whether those men with whom he had his morning coffee, his lunches and after-work drinks, didn't pose another kind of concern, or maybe even, threat to him. He had gone to a small, Midwestern college of Lutheran denomination, had done reasonably well there, but had been unsure of his future direction right through the four years he spent there. Upon graduation he joined the Peace Corps, spent two years in Sri Lanka, returned home still at a loss as to how (and where) he wanted to spend the rest of his life. "On a lark," he told me, he took the G.R.E., the Graduate Record Exam, and the L.S.A.T., the Law School Admission Test, and did brilliantly on both, much to his surprise. He had never before contemplated a career in law, but now did so — and the long and short of it: he was accepted at several fancy Ivy League schools, one of which he attended. He did very well at the place (our present president also went there), and the rest was a predictable history: first-rate summer jobs in "top-notch" firms, a valued clerkship with a federal judge, invitations galore to join various groups of lawyers, a decision to "go for the top," join one of them, the settled, quite comfortable suburban life that followed. His wife, he let me know, once, in a casual aside, had been a legal secretary for several years: "She didn't go to college, the way all of their wives did [those of his buddies at work]."

It was then, upon hearing such news, which the teller felt to be quite aside the point of his visits to talk with me, that I began to approach what I was beginning to understand as the heart of the matter — a knowing, nagging sense of vulnerability that this wonderfully bright, able, dedicated, and accomplished man (and husband and father and lawyer) felt when in the company of those professional associates, those peers of his. True, he had come far, but in his mind, they were always "on another plane." When I asked about the characteristics of that high plane he kept mentioning, where those men dwelled, he was good at listing variables (family background, that of their wives, fancy colleges attended, cases won, places visited on vacations), but not forthcoming about how all that registered in his heart — or as the banal phrase goes in our time, "how he felt about it." One day, feeling myself challenged by a psychological boil of sorts that begged puncturing, I began to talk (a long stubborn silence had taken place) about some thoughts that sometimes crossed my mind, the rivalries, the resentments, the envies that informed those thoughts, gave them their content and energy, both. When I was through (and thereupon worried, given a continuation of the silence, that I'd made a mistake, mouthing off so long), I was about ready to end our time together a little early, talk about when we might meet again, when suddenly it was my eyes, not my ears that were clinically alerted to something: a handkerchief taken out of a pocket, a few tears wiped away, legs crossed and uncrossed, and crossed again.

How hard it was for that decent and honorable person to know about, never mind talk about such matters! How quick he had been, long before he and I had arrived at our time of psychological candor, to concentrate on sexuality as a defining aspect of others, and by its relative absence in daily chit-chat, its presence in him as well. How deeply ashamed of himself he felt as he began to speak of envy — he'd prefer, any day, he would eventually tell me, to uncover some sexual impulse that he'd massively kept under wraps! As we aired such personal moments in our lives, such attitudes toward ourselves and others (a lack of this or that in ourselves, the mighty presence of this or that in various others) we both were acknowledging envy as no small part of our day-to-day existence. One afternoon, right off, my lawyer-friend (I felt him to be, my "patient" he is called by us, these days) wondered aloud at great length about envy — how common is it, and is it "wrong (oh, excuse me) is it abnormal," and if so, how does one get rid of it?

A long story, that one — how one regards envy, his and mine and that of others who also walk on this earth, and take note of their brothers and sisters, their friends and neighbors, not to mention people who live here or there, have this or that advantage or privilege or competence or acquisition or talent or gift of nature or chance or circumstance to their credit. I would eventually say, in the course of our exchanges, that it is my suspicion that even Freud, like the two of us, may have found it easier to explore and discuss his sexuality, not to mention that of others, than the envy he may have felt now and then; that envy comes naturally to us, since we are all limited in our distinctive ways, and so others, limited in *their* ways, can seem so strong, so lucky, so blessed; that we are bombarded so heavily in this secular world with invitations, suggestions, possibilities, promises, that we are bound to feel inadequate to their weighty presence, as we see it given life in others, hence our wish to be them, our shame at abandoning ourselves that way, our anger that such has come to pass; that envy is part of our humanity, something not to be banished (not by will, obviously, but not by clever psychological interpretations, either); and that, finally and ironically, envy (like other sins) can help us toward grace. (Can there be grace without sin?) If envy brings the pain of knowing what we lack, envy also can set in motion the reflection that, in turn, can prompt us to ask who we (as opposed to others) are, and what we really do want out of life—envy, again, a potential aspect of our redemption.

May 1995

36

Covetousness

FOR WE WHO LIVE in today's America I fear covetousness is a daily hazard of life — to the point that it may be regarded as less a danger than a necessity: without it, we might lose our determination to achieve so that we can *get, have, own,* those verbs that describe the energy that fuels our economic system. I write this after reading some essays written by college students of mine — candid efforts at self-scrutiny of their past, in which they quite poignantly discuss tensions in their minds and hearts: the desire to do well, so to speak, to act on their own behalf, as against their desire to do good, to work on behalf of others. Over and over these young, intelligent, talented youths are frank to acknowledge their wish to live a certain kind of life, to have things, acquire them, enjoy them. Naturally, they are thinking of (they mention) a home, cars, the possessions that so many of us either take for granted or yearn to acquire. But they go on to be more introspective, more confessional, actually — they tell not only of their ordinary needs as Americans who will, most likely, be lawyers, doctors, business people, engineers, and teachers (members of that great inclusive amalgam known as the American middle class), but also of their wants. "I worry," one of them acknowledges, "that I'll always be desiring something else, something new, and that [therefore] I'll put my idealism on the back burner, because I've *got* to have this something." He goes even further, admits that much of what he may so passionately crave, come his future successful life, will be sought in response to others, what they happen to have: "I must admit that even now when I see friends get something new, like a car or some clothes, I get excited, and not just for them. I want what they have!"

This was not St. Augustine writing. The student isn't a churchgoer; he is of vaguely Protestant background — with "organized religion," by his own telling, distinctly a thing of his family's past. Yet, he experiences some discomfort as he contemplates the above described inclination, already evident in his late adolescent dormitory life. He wonders, as a matter of fact, whether he has a "problem" in that regard — a not unexpected resort to psychology as the arbiter of one's behavior. When I meet with him, talk with him about his paper, I pick up on that, ask what he means. He repeats out loud what he has written — his sense that perhaps he is "too greedy." I ask for his quantitative criteria — how are we to define that phrase? That is the point, I am informed — his inability to figure the matter out, decide whether he is "just a normal person," with various material appetites, or a person who won't rest easy while his eyes have found something that belongs to someone else, and that he very much wishes to be his own.

I am surprised, talking to him, at the trouble I have in being of any concrete help to him. I hear myself speaking in what my wife often would call the "relative mode" — the way I was trained, it so happens, to think: Well, let's see, if you're basically doing all right in this life, and not letting these worries or ideas or "problems" get you down, get in your way, then you're within that wonderful world, that heavenly world, known as "the normal." If you have fallen outside such a domain, then you don't, of course, judge (in the sense of find fault): you try to understand, to make things clear. So I was doing — and in consequence, I became reassuring: Look, we all struggle with such thoughts, even preoccupations (let's call them), so the point is to be aware of such a truth, and get on with life (in this instance, get on with, among other wishes, the urge to get, to keep getting, and especially, to get what others have gotten).

Later, in my car, listening to the music of Bach, the religious music of Bach, I caught myself wondering what teachers like me might have thought, centuries ago, about someone's professed covetousness, were it an established presence in a young and quite idealistic life. As children, my brother and I were admonished against a kind of inner state of mind once called covetousness, but more as a matter of psychological and moral principle than spiritual principle. We ought to be, we heard, masters of our own (emotional) fate — wish for what we have learned to consider worthwhile, useful, and in keeping with the values we had obtained in the course of our family's life. To "succumb" (the word often used) to others, to wish for things because others have them, to want things because others want them, is to lose one's independence, one's own authority. Of course, mental traits can also be objects of desire — *coveted* qualities, present in others, hence very much sought. There, too, we were taught the importance of restraint and, naturally, self-respect: Learn to accept who and what you are, and then you won't be eyeing your neighbors, friends, relatives for this or that, whether the yearning is for a quality of mind or body or for something of material nature in the world beyond one's self.

I must say that a particular patient of mine, whom I treated many years ago, and whom I still remember ever so well, gave me some second thoughts on this matter of covetousness, though it was not that she (a nurse) was at a remove from the various inclinations that go under that name. Nor did she come to see me because she was having "difficulties" with the more avaricious side of her personality (and who exactly is without such a side?). No, she was in trouble with her boyfriend, and our discussions were therefore as prosaic, maybe, as those that take place on any afternoon television soap series. But she did, in passing, mention the way she was turned on by what some people she knew owned, and showed they owned, and when I shrugged that off, observed casually that "we all" have such moments, she announced her agreement — but wondered at my apparent lack of concern, and, yes, lack of anxiety. *Well* — I quickly wanted to know why in the world I ought to be made "anxious" by such a quality of mine. Wasn't it "normal," "natural" for all of us to have these "secret wishes," the fixations or hankerings or yens that are prompted by what is available to others, possessed by them, hence very much objects of our own appetites?

She was not intent on arguing with me descriptively or, to get hifalutin, phenomenologically. Without question, she assented, to be covetous is to be human — but her way of looking at what it meant to be human, I began to learn, diverged from mine. She told me of her intense religious background: her mother a Catholic, her dad raised as a Presbyterian, but not a regular churchgoer (and not a convert to Catholicism, though he agreed for her to be raised in "the Mother Church," a wry double-entendre he often summoned). She told me, also, that she was brought up to make distinctions between good and bad, right and wrong — clear distinctions, and ones that had to do with everyday matters, not only those ordained by law or even society. It is *wrong,* she insisted, to be covetous. To be *what*? I asked. To be "covetous." I remember asking her why she was using that word, a rhetorical escalation, I thought. Weren't we just talking about the common and universal tendency to have a whim or two that is stimulated by what we see out there in the world, in store windows, on counters and in showrooms, and, not least, in the homes and garages of our fellow citizens, maybe even brothers and sisters?

She heard me loud and clear. She heard me, in particular, use that word "universal." Yes, that was the correct word — no argument there. But there was something missing in all this discussion, something she couldn't, wouldn't let pass, hence, this terse comment: "Sin is universal." At that I perked up and, I have to admit, became mystified, got worried. *Sin* — what in the world did *that* have to do with what we were trying to comprehend in this office! Now my mind started down its predictable road — this young woman certainly was capable of giving herself a rather bad time, and thereby was making herself feel anxious, apprehensive, worthless. Wasn't she needlessly embracing a kind of admonishing self-arraignment, at least by implication? Why turn the psychologically quotidian into the morally, the spiritually reprehensible? So I would, in time, observe — and she would certainly contemplate what I said. But she would not eventually consent to my way of seeing (and putting) things; and in time, I would begin to wonder myself, wonder where this all ends — this willingness to stay the hand of a judgment based on transcendent faith in favor of a bemused toleration in the name of human understanding. She was holding on tenaciously (maybe it could be said with *proper* desperation) to certain convictions of what is *wrong*, however prevalent, and I was trying (ever so subtly, I suppose I have to add with some smugness) to persuade her that what is ever so prevalent is — oh, just *that*, and no more, so long as (the great liberal *caveat*) no one is thereby hurt — herself as a sinner. That kind of knowledge, as it is put by any ilk, does not appear in the textbooks we study!

June 1995

37

Sloth

IN SUNDAY SCHOOL, listening to enumerations of sin — the kinds thereof, their significance in God's scheme of things — my brother and I always perked up at the mention of sloth: a great word, one that evoked, of course, some exceedingly slow-moving creature that surely must know how to get the best out of this life without too much exertion. Pressed by our parents to do our chores, to work hard at school, to find ways to give unto others as we would want given to ourselves (some of those pieties even pasted on the refrigerator, from time to time, confronting us as we tried to indulge in a snack), we wondered whether sloth might be the grandest state of all — just to lie about, and indeed to become lay-abouts!

I remember discussing this matter with my dad — and his reasons for disagreement with us were clearly, decisively stated: We live in a society that requires every possible effort from every one of its citizens. He was all for that in his own life — industriousness, a dedication to various duties and responsibilities. He not only worked hard, he expected others to do so — not only us, his children, but anyone anywhere. He voted Republican. He had a profound distrust of government — it is something that has to be carefully watched, lest it curb the initiative of citizens. As for those citizens who seemed headed nowhere, whose lives are hard-pressed and marginal, he refused to see them as beyond...well, their own possible redemption, if only they would "work hard," be "resourceful," "refuse to take life lying down." I remember those phrases even now, though I fear a recitation of them makes my dad sound hard-hearted, callous. In fact, he had his own way of showing respect to the poor: They needed no condescension from the rest of us, no "depending" upon this or that program or agency; they needed, in a way, *themselves* — an ethic of personal sustenance, of energy committed to action. He was forever, in that regard, pointing out the "want ads" in the papers — the opportunities that awaited "anyone." My mother took sharp and constant issue with that line of reasoning, with that idealized work ethic (the notion that anyone who "really" wanted a job could find one). She voted Democratic. She was forever reminding us how cruel and unfair life can be for some people who are down on their luck, not because they don't want to work, haven't tried to find work, but because (for instance) no

work is available to *them,* because of who they are. For Dad, ingenu-
ity and determination would ultimately prevail: for Mom, this world
can make a mockery of those traits, turn people into disillusioned,
embittered souls, because they have tried and tried to no avail.

I now realize how much those two parents of mine had in common, despite their opposing political and social views, their apparent
disagreement with respect to the relationship between individual psychology and the society to which a particular person belongs. Both
my mother and father took for granted the importance of hard, hard
work, of personal initiative constantly put on the line. We ought to
be, they both insisted, diligent, productive, energetic, conscientious,
busy, tireless. We ought not be lazy, lethargic, idle — slothful. Later, in
college, when I would read Max Weber's *The Protestant Ethic and the
Spirit of Capitalism,* I would realize how well my folks had adapted to
the demands of that ethic, and consequently how much it informed
their lives, their manner of living, and, too, the values they handed on
to their children.

But if they agreed on the vice of sloth in everyday secular life, they
certainly disagreed on the applicability of such a word to the spiritual
life. Dad wanted everyone to be conscientious (as he surely was), but
if someone turned out to be a crook, a delinquent, that person was
bad, and ought to be severely punished, *period.* He had no great interest in the psychology of the criminal, nor did he think of such a
person's possible wrong-doing as forgivable as a consequence of his
or her social, economic, or racial background. Mother, on the other
hand, was worried about *why* people turned out bad, went awry or
amok, and she constantly wondered how such people might be "re-
deemed," a word my dad was not at all inclined to use. Still, her idea
of how such redemption took place was not completely at odds with
that of her husband: by prayers and persuasion, by psychotherapy —
forces from the outside brought to bear on an errant soul, even as Dad
wanted the force of the law to do likewise.

In college I would become a student of an original-minded and
thoughtful teacher, Perry Miller — his field of study was American
Protestantism in its early incarnation: the Puritan divines of the sev-
enteenth and eighteenth centuries. He scoured their words, sermons,
essays, poems, and he examined their assumptions, their way of seeing
the world, not to mention the God Whom they so fervently addressed,
sought, summoned in judgment on themselves, on others. It was in
one of Miller's classes that I remember the "sin of sloth" being mentioned — the first time since those childhood moments in Sunday
School. The word made me smile — it is an uncommon one, these

twentieth-century days, and I could only remember the pleasure my
brother and I had savoring it — a lust of sorts we had (even as we
doubted, already, the likelihood of fulfillment, given our family background): days and days become years given to doing nothing, relaxing
under some sun with some breeze flowing gently over us! But for
mother (and for Christianity, we all should begin to realize) sloth had
little to do with that kind of self-indulgence. Sloth, Professor Miller
told us emphatically, is not to be confused with "ordinary laziness."
Oh, yes, I recall thinking — sloth is, then, extraordinary laziness. But,
of course, our teacher wanted us to take a leap into another world,
as it were. "Sloth," he told us, is a "spiritual laziness." All right, now
I knew: that argument our mother had so often made to us, that we
keep saying our prayers, keep invoking the Lord in our daily effort
to be "good," to do His bidding. But Miller wouldn't quite let the
matter rest there. He nodded to my mother (maybe, all mothers) by
saying, yes, sloth did have to do with a disinclination to take the
Lord seriously through prayer, church attendance, compliance with
His commandments. Still, sloth has "many lives," he insisted — one of
which might well be, ironically, a "Christian complacency" which took
that very form — an eagerness to get down on one's knees at home,
in a pew, to pay heed to biblical mandates. Sloth is kin to smugness,
he insisted (hence to pride, that sin of sins). Sloth is acceding to the
apparent in a religious tradition, the conventional, the readily accessible, and thereby letting the matter (that of one's soul's obligations)
rest there.

Of course, we were reading under this professor's tutelage those
fierce Puritans, but also others, such as Kierkegaard and Pascal and Simone Weil, not to mention St. Augustine and St. John of the Cross —
and gradually, through that reading, never mind the professor's reading of the reading, we began to see what sloth really is by its absence
in those spiritual figures or, maybe, by its presence as made evident by
the struggle they may have waged, lest a spiritual laziness with regard
to soulful contemplation take over their lives.

All too often I find spiritual sloth far more inviting than the secular sort. That is, I have been conditioned to work hard at my various
jobs, and I suspect, if it is at all possible, I will do so until the last
breath. But I can quite comfortably slip into a church, go through
certain motions, as it were, and depart quite relaxed and pleased with
myself: one more duty done, one more (again, the irony!) habit or
responsibility in this life acknowledged. As for those fevered "writers"
Miller assigned — what *was* their "problem"! Why not simply "accept"
a given religious tradition, enact its rituals, then "trust in the Lord"!

Maybe such an attitude is, indeed, "all" that is necessary, though I suspect more is asked of us — that such "trust in the Lord" not become an excuse for spiritual complacency. Sloth, I would eventually hear the passionate Professor Miller declare, is one of the slier sins, not always as evident as some of the others: lust, anger, gluttony. Sloth, I fear, creeps up on us ever so vigilantly industrious ones. We take church in vigorous stride the way we do so much else — far be it from us to overlook any task in this busy life we lead. The private urgency and soul-searching, with its inevitable moments of doubt, of agony, even — that is foreign to many of us, for whom sloth also seems foreign, and so it goes in this constantly paradoxical life.

July–August 1995

38

Anger

W HEN I WAS STUDYING PSYCHIATRY, and especially psychoanalysis, I read and heard a great deal about "aggression,"
which Freud would eventually give the status of a "drive" — a seemingly inevitable part of our nature. He had for years been all taken
up with "libido," his way of referring to the sexual interests and energy which each of us, in one way or another, gets to feel at work in
our minds (not to mention our bodies). The more he listened to his
patients and, maybe, the better he understood himself and, certainly,
the more he took notice of the tragedies of war that descended on
the so-called civilized continent of Europe in the first decades of this
century, the more he had second thoughts about his theory of instinctual life — the singularity of the erotic, no matter its disguises. In the
1920s he was clearly ready to posit an aggressive side to our mental
makeup — and he was not talking about something occasional or acquired by virtue of troublesome experiences, but rather a universally
present aspect of all of our psychological lives. In a metapsychological
leap (a speculation really, because we are not in the realm of empirical
natural science, where an assertion can be rigorously tested and proved
true or misleading or false) he spoke of a "death instinct," by which,
grandly (he was not without conceptual ambition), he meant not only
the inevitable limitations of our mortality, but something that has to
do with our daily struggles with one another as human beings, something present in children and youths, never mind older people — an
aspect of our being, as surely as sexuality (whether openly expressed
or kept under wraps) is part of who we are, what we think and desire.

In my clinical psychoanalytic work, Freud's ideas on sexuality were,
of course, constantly being summoned, by me or by the supervisors
of my work, to whom I constantly reported: those case presentations and discussions which helped us rookies slowly become more
sure-footed. But I was puzzled by that drive called "aggression" —
Freud even dubbed it "Thanatos" at one point, an escalation that enabled him to rival his beloved Greek thinkers and writers: Eros as
against Thanatos, a confrontation worthy of an Aeschylus, a Sopho-
cles! I found it considerably harder to pin down, to comprehend
"aggression." So often the anger, the ire, the rage of my patients
was prompted by difficulties I came to regard as broadly sexual in

nature — the frustrations and disappointments in the various attach-
ments they sought, or sought without success to maintain. Sexual
rage is, of course, no new (twentieth-century) discovery: nor sexual
jealousy, nor sexual assault — "aggression" as an expression of desire
and its vicissitudes, its aberrances and worse. Still, I had one supervi-
sor who was accessible enough, unassuming enough, for me to dare
talk with him "in general" — to pose questions that clearly showed
me to be ignorant, naive, all too awkward and imprecise in the way
I looked at not only my patients, but the everyday life around me.
Once, I put this question to Dr. Ludwig: "I wonder about this 'drive'
called 'aggression' or 'thanatos' — how to recognize it in my patients."
He smiled and replied more or less like this: "I think you could take
a look, first, at yourself, or at me, at anyone nearby, and you'll see
those everyday moments of pettiness and crankiness, of irritation and
anger, that are, so often, irreducible — that is, they are not a substi-
tute for something else, a cover for another 'problem,' or 'impulse'
(meaning 'libido'), but rather, they tell you and me that no matter how
'normal' or 'well-adjusted' we are, no matter how lucky and fortunate
our [psychological, sociological, cultural, racial] fate has been, we're
inevitably going to have our darker moments, times when we're sour,
inadequately responsive, distant, doubtful, displeased with someone
or something, put-out, out of sorts, you use whatever word you want.
Life for everyone is frustrating at some point — and, besides, we can't
always feel 'satisfied,' even when we *are*, when our lives, by and large,
are satisfying."

He went on to tell me more, to use more technical language (a
descent!), but he was clearly moving (as Freud did) from the world
of psychopathology to the everyday one in which we all live. He was
talking about our capacity to want and want, to be frustrated, then
disappointed, then enraged; he was talking about our inclination to
bite off (speaking of aggression!) more than we can chew, our tendency to knock down others, rather than look squarely at ourselves.
He was talking, that is, about our conscience, *its* energy, as well as our
"drives." Aggression, he was reminding me, may be an exceedingly
elusive *concept* (with respect to its origins and nature), but it is surely
a quite evident, and indeed pervasive, part of our daily lives. We get
angry at various moments, whether we reveal our feelings openly to
others or not, and that anger can be a part of our nature, an aspect of
our problems, a response to a particular moment's stress, or all of the
above, or perhaps a passing moment in what some theologians call
our "finiteness."

I don't think anger, per se, is necessarily a sin — I think of Jeremiah's anger, Isaiah's, and of course, that of Jesus in the temple and elsewhere in the course of his brief, dangerous, frustrating, demanding ministry. I believe that the anger that is one of the "seven deadly sins" is of another kind, not righteousness willingly espoused, shared, but a meanness out of proportion to the merits of the case. Maybe such a comment is easier said than tested by application to everyday life: but I do recall times in my life when I have become angry because I am — well, a mere mortal, who slips and falls with some regularity on this pilgrimage called a life. I realize now that Dr. Ludwig, in his own way, was trying to tell me as much over three decades ago — he was saying that anger (and its modulations, from irritability and arrogance to ire and wrath) has to do, again, not only with mental illness or neurosis, but with our ordinary, day-to-day nature as it gets exerted in (and tested by) conventional experience, never mind the exceptional moments of crisis we are inclined to highlight these days, accustomed as we are to an interest in the abnormal, the psychopathological.

We can, then, be "down" without being "depressed" (or on our way to depression): we can be irritated or ungenerous or unkind or moodily brusque, or unforthcoming or outright angry, not because, again, we are "sick," or headed in that direction, or not because we are "sublimating" energy that has its origin in some other corner of our mental life, but because we can't ever keep up with our wishes, and besides, we are not made perfect, meaning without moments of displeasure, dissatisfaction. Anger, in a way, is one of our more obvious and direct qualities or capabilities — it is often hard to conceal, it rises and craves expression, though many of us have learned to hide it with some success (maybe more of it with respect to our own self-recognition than the recognition of others). I had a friend, actually, who extolled anger, called it "clean" — by which he meant not only righteousness, but the bluntly open irritation that he regarded as a kind of honorable candor about oneself, shared with others. In contrast, he loathed (some anger there!) those who are always "cool, calm, collected," as the saying goes, almost "perversely even-tempered," he would say. He believed that anger was a gift of the Lord (he was a lawyer, not a man of the cloth), ours to do with as we will; and he believed, with Dr. Ludwig, that a demonstration of anger tells us a lot, sometimes, about the conscience of an individual — how he or she regards himself, herself, therefore (there*after*), how others are regarded. For him, then, a certain kind of anger is simply a self-judgment revealed: "I'm annoyed at something or someone because I've been taught to make distinctions, come to conclusions, moral ones as well as aesthetic or psychological ones — and so, *here goes!*" On the other hand, he well knew, anger can express craven desires, needy impulses — indeed, anger can be a vehicle for the other limitations we possess, the sins we bear, a means by which we indicate our covetousness, say, our gluttony, our pride, our sloth.

Interestingly, many in my profession spend long hours with patients helping them uncover anger not acknowledged, even felt — only to hope, with our patients, that once understood, their anger will dissipate. But, of course, such an outcome is not the end of it: *some* anger departs, leaving them restored to their normal capacity to assert themselves, not rarely at the expense of others. Here is where anger becomes not only an unsurprising part of our humanity, but sinful — our critical selves, our annoyed or irritable or momentarily cranky selves, directing outward that "aggression" Freud and his followers mention. In a sense, then, anger craves an object. Covetousness and gluttony crave things; anger craves people, though it can be disguised and directed at the abstract, at ideas or institutions or customs. I think the theologians of centuries past knew in their bones the psychology Freud eventually came to comprehend and enunciate — that we dare inflict on others the consequences of our own doubts, uncertainties, apprehensions, worries, as they inevitably confront us from time to time, and so doing, so *being* (the creature of anger is the creature of awareness, the creature of language) we all too gratuitously and all too often express ourselves, express our sinful possibilities, express our wrath. Inevitably inadequate at one or another moment, we seek company: Those who receive our barbs become thereby our (also flawed) companions — anger as an expression of that loneliness or aloneness (or both) that philosophers have remarked upon as they contemplate the nature of our vulnerability and, as well, our recognition of it. Feeling forsaken or at a loss briefly or longer in our spirits, we strive to link areas in this odd and melancholy way with others, living up to the age-old aphorism that misery loves company: anger as our urgent, desperate cry in the wilderness.

September 1995

39

Lust

IN OUR TIME lust is far from a secret or hidden part of ourselves;
rather, it is an everyday and evident companion, ever ready to connect with us — urged on us in advertisements, on talk shows, in the
movies and on television: sexuality and sensuality and desire — the last
for sex, of course, but also for all that has been sexualized, and that is
a whole lot (our clothes, our cars, our food, for starters). But by lust I
mean, here, no ordinary impulse or wish, no commonplace fantasy or
daydream that has to do with a person, usually, or a place or a thing.
The issue is intensity, fixity — how much of one's life is given over to
a particular concern. These days, the word "obsessional" gets used — a
constancy, a tenacity of thought, of passion, to the point that the rest
of our thinking life, and maybe our doing life, gets diminished.

Sin, in general, has to do with violation — a transgression that puts
one at a remove, morally and spiritually, from God, as He is revealed
to us, step by step, in the Bible, and afterward through the religious
life that has been an important part of our churchgoing history. It is
not easy, in these last years of the twentieth century, to talk about
sin with the college students I teach, or with many doctors, psychiatrists. If I talk about sex, about obsessions, I am heard. If I talk,
even, about the violation that an obsession can cause in someone,
I'll also be heard, though such violation is not the kind I just mentioned a few sentences back — rather, the reference has to do with
"impaired psychological function," with "diminished psychic energy"
for other aspects of a life so heavily burdened by one or another fixa-
tion or fetish or, to use today's pleasant vernacular, hung-up. Yet in our
own secular manner, sometimes awkwardly and ponderously, courtesy
of the technical language of psychology and psychiatry, sometimes
more vividly, arrestingly, as in "hang-up," we seem to know what
the saints, the church fathers, the theologians, the ordinary people of
faith have known all along, that the assertion of any appetite is not
be confused with the domination of a life by that same appetite. In
our own way, too, we make our judgments — though of course (and
alas) without resort to any divine order, any mention of God, of sin.
We summon the language of the social sciences, usually, words far
from objective or merely descriptive; rather, we make normative use
of phrases, such as "primitive defenses, "acting out," or "borderline

behavior, "impulsive character structure," "dysfunctional"—a manner of condemnation, or maybe a way for us to express our moral alarm, our very human worry and misgivings, without of course venturing into religious territory.

Yet those words and phrases often don't work for us, even for us psychiatrists, and those who are all too eager to listen to us. We become aware of someone whose lusts have brought obvious ruin to others and we want more than the cool, slippery language of psychology or sociology to be spoken—we crave an outright judgment, though we may not be sure what particular moral code to call upon as a help in doing so. No wonder the late Karl Menninger asked wryly and plaintively, urgently and bravely, in a title he gave to one of his last books: "Whatever Became of Sin?" He was, thereby, reminding us that somehow a stand has to be taken with respect to certain kinds of human behavior — no small challenge to the moral and cultural relativists among us, for whom a *yes* is anyone's prerogative, and a *no* is well, just that, only that. For Menninger *no* has to be grounded in something more than an individual's decision—in laws, one quickly adds, though laws can be readily changed, challenged, overruled. Sin, in contest, has to do with divine laws — and here was a well-known psychiatrist, from the American heartland of Kansas, wondering with some regret, some yearning, about the disappearance of sin as a credible notion for many of us so-called educated ones. Since Dr. Menninger's death (in 1990) things have only become worse. Lusts now are a mainstay of our talk shows — publicly discussed with no apparent embarrassment, let alone shame. Indeed, the ones who tell us of their various lusts, as they get expressed (and expressed and expressed), are applauded, admired, or referred to some so-called therapist, who may even be employed by the television show that has presented the lustful one to an audience of presumably entranced, rather than horrified or scandalized, viewers (and the payoff, the raison d'être of the whole business: Those viewers will soon enough be lusting after, then purchasing whatever is being advertised in between the declarations of craziness and perversity which now, one suspects, fail to raise an eyebrow, even, in millions of us).

Lord forbid that those talk shows be regarded as sinful, that those who appear on them, not to mention the men or women, the circus trainers, who run them ("talk show hosts") be regarded as sinners. I sometimes wonder what Dr. Menninger, whom I was privileged to know, would make of all that — the frantic search for more and more bizarre kinds of passion and lust which are fed us (in movies, on daily television soaps, as well as the talk shows) as a matter of course: Here you are, folks, here is something to nod at, to find "interesting," that dreary word, so carefully free of even hint of judgment. As Dostoyevsky, among others, kept reminding us, and especially in the Grand Inquisitor scene of *The Brothers Karamazov,* when people regard God as dead, anything and everything soon enough becomes permissible (protected by this or that amendment); becomes called, in tic-like incantation, "interesting," or is merely frowned upon, called worthy of psychiatric attention. "I have noticed in recent years," Anna Freud once remarked, "that the Super-Ego [the conscience] that my father took for granted is no longer the great power and authority in our patients that it used to be." She was remembering the old days, when giant consciences did indeed drive some people to considerable distraction. Now, such consciences have become less and less influential, as we hem and haw with ourselves, never mind our children, as to what is off-base, wide of the mark, and why — ever so fearful (God forbid!) of calling something *wrong,* unequivocally, and further, worthy of vigorous, explicit public condemnation.

What kind of conduct, if any, is to be considered beyond the pale, and why? Are any taboos defensible, even possible, these days, when incest, when every imaginable kind of sexuality, is the stuff of daytime television — granted, thereby, access to everyone's home? In a third-grade classroom where I have taught as a volunteer in recent years, I have heard eight-year-old boys and girls talk about incest casually — an off-hand response, on their part, to what they heard on Oprah or Geraldo. Those youngsters laugh and tease one another as they do so — and I am grateful, I realize, for the slightest evidence of nervousness, of embarrassment. But none of these children is shocked, outraged — or surprised and perplexed. It is as if they have grown up to expect intense, insistent, unrelenting desire — desire that won't take no for an answer — to be around any and every corner, and that's that. For them, in a ghetto, even the desire to kill is something one accepts as a daily event. The rest of us stop there, maybe only there, so far. We abhor "violence," want more and more police and prisons to protect us from it. Yet, most violence takes place not on the street, but within our homes — is inflicted by one person in a family upon another, and is in some way connected to lust, to the jealousies and envies and rivalries, to the roar and rage of a frustrated or disappointed or threatened or abandoned love. Then there are our driving habits, speaking of violence: the fast cars we crave, the high speeds we seek, the murderous consequences of a lust to overcome time and space at anyone's expense, a lust that smacks of the highest order of hubris, one the ancient Greeks, surely, would regard with far greater alarm than that of sexual prurience.

Lust enacted is obviously a letting go of restraint, of self-control — or maybe, in our time, it is a letting out, publicly, a display of what is humanly possible in the absence of the social and cultural restraints that can become familial ones in millions of homes. Freud wrote of "polymorphous perversity," the rampant impulsivity that children possess — soon enough, he observed, brought under wraps in what gets called a boy's, a girl's "socialization": tender love mixed with firm moments of prohibition, the latter increasingly explained as the child increasingly can comprehend, but in no way weakened, undermined. Now, many of us say we are not sure what is right and what is wrong; that we can see how others might advocate or practice what we don't happen to find (again!) "interesting," desirable; that the French aphorism *tout comprendre, tout pardonner* very much holds, aided and abetted by modern social science; that God is dead, or is someone's private notion, and certainly has no place in our schools, our public places, only on our currency; that teachers and doctors and lawyers ought to be "value-free" or "neutral" as they do their work, since of course each person has *his* or *her* values; that if there is a common ground for values, it is to be determined by someone's polls, and certainly not from on high (by custom, never mind legally or spiritually). So it goes, and here we are, to draw upon the ancient Greeks again, in a world where "whirl is king," the moral whirl for which we congratulate ourselves with the attribution of "modern knowledge": lust is everyone's to have, to speak of, to realize expressively — the whole universe our living prey, and damn the consequences (for surely there are no sinners to be damned).

October 1995

40

Gluttony

THESE DAYS in the privileged precincts of America, gluttony is an all too evident aspect of our existence — the overweight ones as victims, the determinedly thin ones as prideful winners in a constant war against temptation. I doubt Adam Smith and other early apologists for capitalism ever imagined how central to its survival a hyped-up consumerism would one day become — the endlessly clever and manipulative messages that tell us to want more and more, hence by implication, to live, always, on the very edge of dissatisfaction. Every day, in countless shopping malls across the land, millions of us assemble in an almost desperate effort to acquire things, as if our very worth as human beings is at stake. Young people in droves use those same malls as hang-outs, places to assemble, to pass the time of day, places where they can gawk and themselves be regarded, and trysting places, too — in movies and restaurants and in the nearby armies of cars, themselves a memorial to a progression of sorts: from a helpful convenience to an economic and social necessity, not to mention a psychological instrument that lends itself to all sorts of symbolic expressions, all sorts of idiosyncratic needs, aspirations.

For many years I never did understand why such a desire to get, to have, to buy and buy, to eat up, to wear then set aside in favor of tomorrow's garb, to drive *this* car — why all that hungry inclination to possess, to own (and show to others) amounts to a serious sin. Gluttony and greed struck me as serious, present-day vices, but not especially evil in a spiritual sense. But during my Catholic Worker days (when I had the opportunity to help out at a "hospitality house" and talk at some considerable length with Dorothy Day), I began to learn otherwise — learn from her, and others close to her, not the virtues of asceticism (a misconception in the minds of some: that she and Peter Maurin were committed ideologically to a kind of Catholic Puritanism), but the distinct danger of a materialism that gets out of hand, becomes outright gluttony, hence sin. Here is Dorothy Day to help us, me, in 1968, to understand the progression I have just mentioned — a response, on her part, to my inquiry as to her attitude toward possessions: "I'm not the one to judge others — I have enough to do trying to keep myself in line [with respect to moral matters]. But I know — from personal experience, that's how I know — that

160

anything, just about anything can turn into a big trap for us: we want it, we want it, we get it, we want more, and more, and more — and we're not [thereby] only greedy, we're 'sinful.'"

She paused long enough for me to tell her that I didn't quite follow her move (for me, then, a leap) from greed to sin, unless we were embracing a kind of self-denial, self-abrogation that, itself, so I was intent on arguing, could become quite sinful — a manifestation of pride. Soon enough, I'd hear this: "I've never been interested in saying no to people — to myself: no to good food, and no to nice clothes, and no to travel. I've loved all that in the past, and I still do, even if I live differently now [than was the case during her twenties, when she was, by her own description, a Greenwich Village bohemian of sorts]. I happen to enjoy myself here [at the Catholic Worker hospitality house on the lower east side of New York City]. I mean, these days fill me up — I like talking with our guests [the poor whom she served a daily lunch], and I like being part of a community. You may think I'm an advocate of austerity, but that's because I conceal my gluttony!"

Her *gluttony!* I laughed — and looked for her wry, ironic smile, so familiar to me by then. But she was dead serious, I soon realized. I didn't have to speak in order to elicit the following disquisition of sorts: "You think I'm fooling! You haven't seen me in a book store! You haven't seen me when someone wants to borrow one of the books I love and tell people to read. When push comes to shove, when someone takes my words to heart, and asks me for a novel of Dickens or Tolstoy or Dostoyevsky — right there on my shelf, and not being read by me now and in the foreseeable future — I'm likely to freeze. Oh, I don't say what's on my mind; I try to be nice, and often I'll lend the book, but I'm sure to ask that it be returned soon, and to tell you the truth, I'm almost counting the days, the hours, until that book is safely back here!

"You may consider all this trivial, but I don't — because I see in myself not only the wish for more and more books, and the wish to hold on to them for dear life, but the meaning of this: I get so taken up with something, I lose all sense of [moral, spiritual] perspective — and that's what gluttony meant, I think, to the church fathers — you behave as if your life depends on eating this or getting that, rather than on God's judgment of how you're living this life He's given you!"

There was much more explanatory and self-critical comment; and I began to understand what she was getting at. Gluttony for her was not a matter of being challenged secularly: appetite control in the interest of longevity. Nor was gluttony a violation of a Puritan ethic — the notion that less is better, by virtue of John Calvin or some environmental guru. Gluttony, for her, was a universal possibility, something that can arise in the poor (or those like her who essentially choose poverty) as well as the well-to-do: a hunger for something, a possessiveness about something, that becomes distracting, indeed—a means by which one loses sight of God, amidst one's frantic eyeing of one or another object or option. Even the vernacular expression of being a "glutton for punishment" has an interesting implication to it that Dorothy Day would surely recognize as not beyond her personal recognition: we can take on so very much hardship in this world, prove ourselves (proudly) virtual martyrs, and all the while overlook the *why*, the supposed purpose of such a sacrificial effort. A lived series of burdens become, themselves, a collective acquisition of a kind.

Gluttony, in a sense, is one of the more devious sins — it is meant to be a diversion, and it readily succeeds to the point that we may recognize the nature of the deed (the eating, the collecting, the amassing, the buying and buying, spending and spending), but we overlook the larger significance of the particular preoccupation as it gets lived out. Put differently, gluttony shows us materially or emotionally driven, but we are all too apt to overlook the spiritual consequences — and maybe, as well, the spiritual cause. "I don't have the time to go to church," I heard once from a patient — and then, an explanation: "I could make the time, I know, but I don't see eye to eye with the pope these days." Not a rare comment, and one I did not at the time choose to challenge. Instead, I listened as he moved directly on to what he *did* have the time to do — go to auctions in search of stamp collections and a certain kind of "country antique": chairs, tables, lamps, all of which (save the stamps) he stored, ostensibly for his children, grandchildren. I had no interest in judging, even interpreting his actions and interests — we had other things, pressing hard on him, to discuss. But I thought I'd heard something important, had been unselfconsciously taught something, yet again, by this person, a thoughtful and sensitive man who had a way of dropping provocative asides as he told of his life, its vicissitudes as well as its relative good fortune.

Unwilling to immerse himself in religious issues which vexed him and, maybe, threatened a comfortable adjustment to a contemporary, late twentieth-century American set of values, he chose another road: that of catalogues, then shops, then bidding wars. He and his wife would chide themselves occasionally, laugh derisively at their "greedy ways," but were not at all inclined to understand them — and by that last observation, I don't fault them in the psychiatric sense. It is tempting, of course, for all of us to do just that — look for the covert emotional sources of just about anything we do. But there, too, we can become gluttons — anxious to accumulate ideas, interpretations, theories, explanations. The issue is essentially ethical, if not spiritual — in the words of David Riesman, not a theologian, but an ever so shrewd, knowing observer of our end-of-the-century (end-of-the-millennium!) habits, preferences: "affluence for what?" That "what" is rhetorical of course, meant to turn our heads; to prompt a moment's pause — so that we might wonder *what* it is that we want out of life — *what* it is that we truly believe, *what* our purpose is in this time we're given here. In three carefully chosen words, a social essayist was suggesting that affluence (and the gluttony that can so inspire us to get money, then use it to satisfy dozens of tastes, if not sate ourselves) can go thoroughly unexamined by us, to our collective and personal detriment, both. No longer hungry in our bellies, literally, we are hungry in our souls — and sometimes mistake that hunger for a "psychological problem," when it is a larger, more "existential" one that both Dorothy Day and David Riesman had in mind, I think, when they took a look at all of us as we take on the moral perils that go with life in this rich country of ours.

November 1995

41

Moral Smugness

To DENOUNCE SIN is, of course, to risk it in no small way — the meaning of that well-known biblical injunction that challenges the sinless one to throw the first stone. Tone or attitude matter enormously: how we regard our errant neighbors — with an understanding that takes account of our own limitations and worse, or with a righteousness that has turned to self-righteousness. No question, that word "understanding" can pose its own difficulties — the kind that refuses all judgments, as in the French aphorism, *tout comprendre, tout pardonner,* mentioned in an earlier column: Hitler, say, as victim of child abuse, as he seems to have been, at the hands of his violent, alcoholic stepfather, and that is that. Maybe the foregoing instance poses no trouble for all of us — Hitler was a monster, we agree, and to devil with the childhood problems that may ultimately have given impetus or shape to his murderous hate. Still, I suspect that many of us have struggled hard with the temptation, in the name of modern "enlightenment," to extend the limits of our forgiving, our understanding, even as we are also constantly inclined to notice the foibles and faults of our neighbors and friends, while giving ourselves, at a minimum, every benefit of the doubt.

All the time, at faculty meetings, at clinical conferences, or when I'm talking with students, or simply in the course of an ordinary day, attending my chores, I find myself stumbling into one or the other of those two postures — I'll be quick to pounce on someone, write him or her off morally in no uncertain terms, or I'll bend over backward to try to figure out what it is that may have prompted so-and-so to behave as he or she did, thereby avoiding for myself a tough, critical response to a given deed. Either way, I have to admit (on those occasions when I stop and think about things in a half-way honest manner) that I'm in great jeopardy. Often, when I'm quick to criticize someone, I'm apt thereby to distance myself all too decisively from that person: *he* is full of himself, *she* is a pretender, *they* are hypocrites — all qualities of mind that, of course, are beyond me! On the other hand, I have to acknowledge, that a determination on my part to hold off with respect to judgment can prompt a similar psychological turn of events. I insist that I am not one to get involved in *this,* to have a critical say about *that:* the high and mighty stance of someone who fancies himself above and beyond the sweat and blood of a moral struggle — that "neutrality" we clinicians seek and, yes, regard with a pride that not rarely slips into smugness. Others may be unable to be "objective," may let their passions take control of their scrutinizing intelligence, may quickly succumb to sentiment; but we are "trained," are "professional," have gone through hurdles, passed tests, been certified, and now are entitled to link ourselves to that word "science" in all its implications: seers of human understanding who don't, won't succumb to the rashness of reproach, who will, rather, stand on the high ground of diagnosis, clarification, and interpretation, the truth our accumulated knowledge enables us to offer, to pronounce.

I remember so well learning how to take that latter stance, one I did not regard as a moral one but, rather, a necessary therapeutic one. *Someone* has to stand apart, be detached and open-minded, in pursuit of what *was*, what *is*, no matter the obstacles put in the way by people who are obviously troubled, wrought up, maybe even out of their minds. It never, alas, occurred to us, or those teaching us, that such a dichotomy or polarity (even if it were true, a big "if") put us in considerable jeopardy: the vocational hazards that go with regarding oneself and being regarded as somehow above the human fray. This coveted omniscience, this effort at dispassion, valuable to a degree, can soon enough provoke a soaring egoism — a conceit. We know so very much, we tell ourselves, and are immune to so very much. Others flail blindly, have their outbursts and worse, whereas we notice carefully, figure out constantly, and at the right moment, and only then, make our observations, spoken with a mix of authority and cool that an entire culture has learned to emulate, imitate (and thank God, parody). Yet, in our heart of hearts we know well what we share with those others called "patients"; we know the turbulence of our own souls, the worries and hurts and missteps of our lives, even if we so often insist on not acknowledging what we share with our fellow human beings — or if we do confess to a bit of difficulty in a psychiatric, a psychoanalytic encounter, the patient or analysand is once more set upon, faulted: his or her troubles prompt troubles for us ("countertransference"). To be sure, we sometimes acknowledge our own share of difficulties — but in our professional and public presentation of ourselves and, I suspect, all too often in our private sense of who we are (the former can surely give shape to the latter), we are often loath to put our own emotional cards on the table: here I am, a fellow sufferer, and thereby (actually) one who might be able to fathom what puzzles and pains others, even (being needy myself) join in a kind of collaborative healing.

Nothing doing — the above is not a suitable, an acceptable notion of medical or psychiatric care, so many of us discover in the course of pursuing a postgraduate education. Instead, we learn to consider ourselves more and more knowledgeable, but we also, at a certain point, seem to jump ship, as it were — inhabit this new and special world that gives us an all too unquestioned hold over others who look at us as uncritically as we look at ourselves, a moral disaster for us, and no small disaster for our patients, who often enough have already suffered long and hard at the hands of people who have patronized them, failed to level with them, treated them with an inscrutable reserve that gets interpreted as rebuke and scorn.

I am not arguing here for a constant confessional outpouring on the part of us who practice medicine or psychiatry. Obviously, we *all* need *some* distance from one another; and obviously, those who work all the time with hurt and anxious people are especially entitled to a certain remove from the otherwise enveloping emotional hurly-burly of their patients' stories as they get told, let us face it, with an intensity and perplexity that already threatens to drown them, and might well catch their would-be rescuer in the same undertow. Still, we who swim toward others, who are flailing in a sea of discontent, in hopes of bringing them ashore, need not believe we do so by walking on water. If we have become reasonably adequate, reliable lifeguards, it is because we ourselves have had plenty of cause to fear drowning. To forget that aspect of ourselves is to forsake our very humanity — and that is what moral smugness more than risks: we become pitiably self-assured with respect to our various virtues and capabilities, and soon we are floating above all others, courtesy of the hot air we have pumped into ourselves. All the more dangerous, of course, that others conspire with us in that direction: the gullibility of so many, today, with respect to various secular "experts," and the particular kind of gullibility (and adoration) that get going in various medical and psychiatric encounters: true, an expression of a quite normal human situation, namely, the needs, the vulnerabilities, the felt jeopardy patients bring to those doctors' offices.

Sometimes I think that a good part of psychiatric work has to do with challenging the isolation which patients have learned to construct for themselves as their most determined sanctuary — that sense of being utterly different, of being unworthy in some defining way, hence best kept, by ones' own will, crucially (and self-critically) at a distance from others. We doctors try to undermine such an attitude; we explain its origins as we ourselves learn of them. So often, though, our patients remain unconvinced — perhaps because they still have cause to wonder whether their misery, now increasingly comprehended, is really shared by others. Here the doctor has a great chance to take on that self-imposed withdrawal by working toward a certain common ground with his or her patients: it is a *we* that is present in this room, not only by virtue of that all too commonly mentioned and discussed "relationship," but out of our shared humanity — the doctor as one who has also known suffering, who also struggles with demons. The point, again, is not an orgy of self-revelation — enough to send the poor patient into quick recoil, if not permanent flight. (I need *this?!*) Rather, it is our general attitude that matters, and that all the time gets conveyed to our patients, often wordlessly (those glances or gestures that tell so much about what we think, who we are). We can let our guard down enough, that is, to signal a comradeship in the land of affliction and failure, or we can keep our guard up high, and so doing, so being, become ourselves the saddest victims of all, cornered by a clinical hauteur that ultimately finishes us off morally and psychologically, both.

December 1995

42

The First and the Last

I T IS AN OLD and not uncommon story — the smart person, well-educated, too, who is morally dumb. Hitler and Stalin both had no trouble recruiting an assortment of prominent intellectuals to their cause and, as well, all sorts of professional men — doctors, lawyers, professors, and schoolteachers, even the clergy. Still, many of us who have staked everything, it seems, on the grades we get in various schools, colleges, postgraduate training programs, have little reason to undermine our own authority (in our own eyes, never mind those of others) by reminding ourselves too insistently how compatible a high academic record can be with smugness, hypocrisy, even collusion with out-and-out (political, social) evil.

When I was living in Louisiana, in the early 1960s, getting to know the black children who initiated school desegregation there, I also spent a lot of time with their parents and grandparents — the latter, in certain homes, very important figures, indeed. In one such home I got to know a late middle-aged, courtly man who had worked for many years in a well-known Garden District home, then as a black assistant to the white waiters in a New Orleans club frequented by business-men, lawyers, doctors, professors, architects, "all the fine people doing all the fine work," as that man (then fifty-five) told me. Once, proudly, he let me know this: "They all been to college"; then he added, "a lot of them went beyond." I seemed a bit puzzled, so he explained to me that many of those men had gone to professional schools and were, thereby, "as educated as you can get." His respect for such folk was evident — his awe, even, of them: "The tops of the white people, that's who they are."

He had occasion to listen to such leading individuals speak, to ob-serve how they behaved with one another. Often he was enormously impressed by the conversation he overheard: talk of deals, huge deals, deals entailing millions and millions of dollars; talk of breakthroughs in research, in grants elicited from foundations or individuals, in the ranking of this or that school; talk of cases won or lost in courts, of cases healed, cured in hospitals, clinics; talk of political victories, ex-pected and unexpected; talk of children admitted to schools hither and yon, of children's plans to go here, there, everywhere; talk of the past, of places seen, people met, of memories that linger, and talk of the future, of what is expected or assumed and, sometimes, feared. All of that stuck with him, crossed his mind, in bits and pieces, as he went about his work, of course, but also as he lived his personal life in a neighborhood not far distant, as the crow flies, but an obvious ocean away, as he knew, and knew to say in his ever tactful manner: "I had to smile when I heard the President [Kennedy] say we're going to get to the moon one of these days soon — I thought, I've got a better chance of getting up there than I do of living where these folks I wait on live, or getting in the club where I work, other than to do what I do. I could even get one of those high degrees some of them have; I could have lots of big ones [fifty or one hundred dollar bills, say] in my pocket, and it'd all mean nothing."

That word "nothing" stopped him cold. He seemed to be musing on it, hence a prolonged silence, which prompted in me a search for a subject matter to put into words. But his evident seriousness discouraged my interest in light talk, and so I sat there, waiting. Eventually, a smile on his face, he had more to say: "I hear so much because those folks don't think I'm anyone; they think I'm no one — so it don't make one iota of difference, if my ears pick up the words coming out of their mouths! Someone who's nothing can hear anything; that's what my mamma told me when I got my job, and I told her all I was learning, filling up glasses with ice water and making sure if someone slipped a match book in his pocket, I was there with another one — and she sure knew the score! I'll be standing there, close as can be to them — it's usually two who come and eat together; and one will call the other 'my luncheon friend,' that's what I've heard; and they'll lean forward, as though it's a big secret, but they don't lower their voices, because it's only me that's within distance of hearing, and I sure enough don't count. 'You make Mr. Charlie think you count, and you're going to drop from zero to way below zero' — my Uncle Fred and his advice to us kids, growing up!

"I hear them speaking of stocks to buy and stocks to sell. (Of course, I don't know a thing about stocks.) I hear them speaking of people to call, and they'll help with this and they'll help with that. They say all kinds of things: the wife is drinking on the side; one of the kids has got himself into trouble at the [private] school, and he was warned, he's got to 'clean up his act'; there's a 'beautiful woman,' and she's working as a secretary, or she's a student (it depends on who's talking!) and it's a big temptation, Lord it is — 'to make the move or not'! I think if I was there with a machine like you have [a nod to the tape recorder], I'll tell you something, they'd still not pay me much mind! You know why, you want to [know why]? They'd think it doesn't matter, what I hear, because no one will ever listen to me saying anything I hear — because I can't understand them, and the people I be spending my time with, they're no more than me, so they're down to zero, as well."

Nevertheless, he understood all he heard, and while listening, smiled to himself, cringed, felt his blood surging to his head, bit his lips, and needless to say, held his tongue, looked away, lived out as best he could his nothingness. At times, though, he wanted to smile at someone, slap him on the back, tell him he was sure doing fine, and even applaud: "I'll hear one of those gentlemen say he's worried about 'the colored,' and 'they seem to want everything, these days,' and 'you give them an inch and the next thing, a mile is gone' — and I feel like smiling and winking and whispering, 'Hey, Mister Charlie, don't you worry, because you're way on top, and us folks, we are way on bottom, so no worry, no sweat! You just go enjoy yourself with that new girlfriend, and if you need some excuse or some alibi, you let me know, and I can figure out something. Like you said: 'Those colored folks, they're only good for mischief these days,' and ain't that the big truth!"

He isn't even allowing himself (or the two of us) the leeway of a slight, ironic smile. He is staring at the *Times-Picayune,* with its picture of "continued racial tension," meaning mob action, in front of the school where his daughter is a student with only two other black children. He is not staring, I decide; he is glaring, glowering; he is evidently tired of being goody-goody in front of all those Mister Charlies (me included, I nervously conclude). Suddenly, a fantasy: he is waiting on a table, the water pitcher in his hand, and he hears yet another mean-spirited, dismissive comment, another wise-crack, another sly or openly vulgar slur, directed at his people, and this time he spills the water not into the empty glasses, but upon the empty heads, and thereupon walks out — my mind at work. But from him I hear this: "It's not easy, trying to be nice to people who don't pay you no mind, none whatsoever. I can lose all my patience — but I don't show it. I can't unless I prefer no money to my weekly check. I feel my teeth clamping down. I'll grind them a little — and I force a smile on my face. I'll be thinking of the money I see when I take my check to be cashed [for a stiff price at a neighborhood grocery store]. Those dollar bills work their magic on me — and so does the Bible. In church, the minister reads to us what Jesus said, and He seems to be paying attention to us, He sure does. Once, hearing Jesus' words, I thought: they'd never let Him go into that club where I work, never. Afterward [as they left church], I told my wife what I'd thought, and you know what she said? She said, He came here to throw all those tables in the club upside down, like He did when He went into that church [synagogue] and got upset, seeing what went on there! That's what she said — and she reminded me of what the minister had read that morning: that the last will be first and the first will be last — those words of His. That's dynamite, you know: it turns everything upside down! I'll be remembering that come tomorrow and the next day, when I'm filling their glasses, and I hear them be loading up on themselves, saying how great things are going, and how great they are. They sure do brag, and they sure do think highly, highly of themselves, and they sure do think they're way up there, and they are, they're the first, all right; that means they'll end up being the last, that's what I keep telling myself — what Jesus came here to tell us, them included, but why should they pay Him a lot of attention, when they've got themselves to remember, all the time remember!"

So it went back then, so it still goes: those both loaded and "loaded up on themselves," going about their big-shot, big-deal, important ways, as happens among "the first" — attended by others, the unnoticed ones, the nobodies who have nothing, who are "the last" (with the least to their name) among us. But the past and the present, we were once told in a prophetic moment nineteen plus centuries ago, will yield to an altogether different, indeed, a contrary future, one exceedingly hard for us, here and now, to imagine, given the limits of our moral consciousness.

January–February 1996

43

The Power and the Glory

THOSE WORDS *"thine* is the kingdom, the power and the glory" are not meant to be the easily recited piety so many of us find ourselves uttering — words and more words tossed toward the mystery of time and space, of infinity, that separates us from God's being and knowledge. Indeed, I suspect, many of us have to contend with that first word "thine" — we know to insist upon it, to stress it when speaking it, perhaps to italicize it when writing it, but we also know the issue is ironic as well as rhetorical: for long stretches of our daily life we are fully convinced that "the power and the glory" surely are to be found in one or another aspect of this secular, materialist world, which is ours for the grasping, some hope and, yes, pray. The same holds for Graham Greene's lowly, bedeviled, pursued "whiskey priest" in the most memorable and morally challenging of his novels, *The Power and the Glory* — we meet him, initially, as one with a keen eye for wine and women, and no interest in standing up for principle at the risk of suffering death. Still, he most certainly is a humble, haunted, and hunted priest — and interestingly, he is given no name. He is very much like Ralph Ellison's protagonist in *Invisible Man* — both men are invisible to others; both are on pilgrimages; both are witnesses to a world of conceit and deceit; both are able to see, gradually, the blindness of others — and yes, their own blindness, which slowly begins to lift as a consequence of a series of experiences with those others. Of course, Ellison has faith in an enlightenment that progressively takes place when human beings by design or accident or luck stumble into one another and become teachers. His story's hero may still be in hiding from the world (and himself), a contemporary version of Dostoyevsky's "underground man," but more and more light descends on this man's darkness — a bold symbolism for Ellison to use: a man whose skin is black paradoxically gets enlightened by virtue of the shadowy, dingy white world whose corruptions and phoniness he keeps meeting on his trek from the country to the city, from America's South to its North.

Similarly, Greene's priest is constantly on the move; he is pursued by a 1930's Mexican version of institutionalized hate — though, of course, in a novel such an abstraction becomes the stuff of particular human experience. Greene's priest is trying to escape those who would capture and kill him in the name of a revolution's "progress" and "purity" — yet another fiercely self-righteous and unforgiving ideological insistence on the part of man the rationalist and the reformer. Rather too readily, the reader links arms with this hounded priest, wants him to escape his relentless persecutors. Indeed, for a while Greene gives us one of his detective stories, a "criminal" on the lam, the police after him. Yet, the lieutenant who heads the search can't even recognize the object of his hunt when the man is right in front of him — a writer's show of cleverness, but in this case a writer's effort, also, to move beyond a conventional crime story to a larger, more ambitious examination of human benightedness: the illusions and worse of those who persecute others, but also the self-deceptions of those who are potential victims. For a good part of the novel, after all, the priest is as much a stranger to himself as he is beyond the recognition of those out to capture him.

In a sense, *The Power and the Glory,* for a while, tempts the reader to become a moral accomplice of the fugitive priest, to cheer him on. He is, we remind ourselves, a holy man, no matter his obvious flaws, and the saga of his past mistakes, errors, sins, as they are chronicled. Yet, Greene denies us the priest's escape — because, in fact, the priest becomes less and less interested in such an outcome. As he turns his back on freedom, we are left to wonder what is happening to him, yes, of course, but by implication we are confronted by our own assumptions and rock-bottom values. The priest's growing indifference to the power of his would-be captors, his willingness to take huge personal risks on behalf of his "office" as a man of God means that this novel, at a certain point, disappoints its readers, eager for a successful flight, for a conventional victory of right over might. Instead, the hero is caught and killed — as was Jesus, of course.

We are, in this novel, once again confronted with the mystery of Christianity, whose God-become-man ended up, to repeat, a convicted criminal, given the extreme punishment of the death sentence. Greene's priest is as scorned as Jesus was and, needless to say, carried in himself an aspect of his Maker (the capacity for spiritual inwardness) that was not only invisible to the lieutenant and his cohorts, but to the priest himself and those who were on his side, in the sense that they gave him shelter, or were not quick to suspect him. Yet, this unattractive, lowly, flawed man, betrayed by the mestizo, another nameless, faceless member of what we have learned to sum up as the "lumpen-proletariat," becomes, gradually, an instrument of God's grace. He has, to be sure, been that all along — his vocation as a priest. But Greene pursues this priest, as it were — to the point that the lieutenant's wish to find him becomes a secondary aspect of the novel. The priest's search within, his eventual ability to look at himself, acknowledge his vocation, his purpose here on this earth, becomes the story's real search — and most instructively, it is in jail where that moral and spiritual transformation takes place.

Not that the priest has been "recognized" and apprehended; he is in jail as a common thief of sorts, a "stranger," an outsider, a "low-life." His captors don't recognize the big deal prisoner they've inadvertently caught; he is a "small fry" — and so being, we have to keep reminding ourselves, is just what his God, Jesus, was for those who had arrested Him: one more annoyance, to be dealt with harshly, hence that crucifixion scene, with a common thief on either side of the man from Nazareth. It is in such a state of confinement (the opposite of the physical liberation, for which we had been hoping) that a man becomes open-hearted, a priest reveals himself to others, even as he comes to some peace with himself, an inner liberation.

All through this novel a master of mystery and intrigue in the service of the traditional hunt-and-chase narrative turns his attention, and eventually ours as well, to another kind of mystery: that of Christ's topsy-turvy spiritual lessons as He taught them, and even more unnerving, lived them. Those with a lot may well end up with little. Those who seem to have nothing may have everything that truly matters. The apparent can be terribly deceiving, the real truth of things found in the most unexpected of places. The whiskey priest's journey toward his vocation (the priest as a penitent in search of forgiveness) is meant to nudge us, at the least, toward a moment or two of apprehension, perhaps a necessary precondition to a bit of self-scrutiny of our own.

In the end Greene gives us the survival of the priesthood, not the priest, an institution's survival, for all its inevitable failings, rather than that of an individual. But this is not a novel of Catholic triumphalism. Rather, we encounter a priest who is vulnerable, threatened, in jeopardy, as it went for those early Christians for whom "the power and the glory" meant not buildings, and cash on hand, or money in the bank, or applause at the hands of big-shot politicians and their compliant mercenaries or bedazzled supporters, but rather, the energy that comes out of a faith that was tested all the time, threatened and condemned — the huge irony, yet again: what is popular and accepted and celebrated may be shallow, no matter its apparent authority, whereas what is seemingly eccentric or beyond the pale may be nothing less than God's voice whispered in the ears of some ever so ordinary people who thereby become, as Dorothy Day once put it, "fools for Christ."

Speaking of Dorothy Day, I remember well a long afternoon's talk with her about that novel of Graham Greene's, one of her favorites. I was at the time full of praise for the fictional priest — his anonymous, persecuted, impoverished life seemed so unequivocally honorable, and yes, truly Christian, a contrast surely meant to challenge those of us who have so very much and profess our loyalty to this or that church so loudly. She was less overwhelmed, I began to notice, with the virtues of the priest, at least as they are chronicled in well over half the book. She kept remarking upon his flight, not only from the oppressive, vengeful state, but from himself — the desperate effort to elude a scrutinizing conscience. She regarded the novel as a brilliant reminder of how hard it is "to profess Christ and live like Him," a phrase I still can hear her using. We twentieth-century readers, I began to realize, courtesy of her comments, applaud the priest on his trek for a very good reason. We hope that he (and the rest of us with him) will slip by all the fearfully demanding, hardly bearable circumstances that have befallen the priesthood (and would-be believers) at any given time and place in the church's history. Such an attitude on our part tells us a lot about ourselves — the gift a great novel possesses: its character portrayal become a mirror to the reader.

In several senses, then, *The Power and the Glory* is a novel of revelation. The priest, finally, tells others exactly who he is (because he has, at last, come to full terms with what he believes, ought to uphold), and now that we have met him and cheered him on during his journey, we stand naked, too — the choice he has made has become ours: whether or not in the name of one's faith, to risk the ultimate punishment a secular society can mete out, its condescension, its disregard or dismissal. (You believe *that*? You *really* believe that?) It is a test, Dorothy Day kept reminding herself, that no one in the church, priest or ordinary parishioner, can simply assume he or she will pass with flying colors.

March 1996

44

The Heart of the Matter

I FIRST READ Graham Greene's *The Heart of the Matter* in 1948, when it came out. I was eighteen at the time, a college sophomore enrolled in a course taught by Perry Miller, titled "Classics of the Christian Tradition." Miller was a passionate student of New England Puritanism, but also was interested in contemporary novelists who dared concern themselves with spiritual matters. He did not put Graham Greene or François Mauriac on our reading list, but he strongly urged both of them on us, and many of us obliged, especially with regard to the above-mentioned novel. I can still remember myself struggling with Henry Scobie, the colonial functionary of Greene's story — a quite ordinary, if somewhat scrupulous and introspective man when one first meets him. The Second World War rages in Europe, but Scobie is living in one of the English colonies on the western coast of Africa. There he has staked his all on the ladder of the imperial bureaucracy, only to learn that he is not to be promoted. Meanwhile, his wife, Louise, wants to live the comfortable life of the imperial caretakers who, then, had the responsibility and privilege of ruling vast stretches of land and people across the world. Scobie borrows money from Yusef, a Syrian black marketer, so that he can enable his wife to live a better life, materially — and in no time, things go downhill morally, to the point that an apparently honorable, decent man is being blackmailed, is smuggling diamonds, is involved in an adulterous relationship with a widow who has been rescued from a torpedoed boat. Soon enough, he is under suspicion and closely followed by a government agent, who has begun to document the errant ways of a man only months before utterly at a remove from such reason for moral humiliation, never mind legal jeopardy. Overcome by despair, deeply ashamed of himself, utterly determined to call himself to account, Scobie takes his life — and if he leaves behind his perplexed, frightened wife, his hurt, melancholy mistress, his coolly impersonal, pitiably self-important fellow bureaucrats, he also walks away from the reader with an abrupt, provocative finality that prompts a responsive continuation of the introspection that has informed the novel from the very start.

Suicide is, of course, an awesomely momentous event, both psychologically and spiritually. "The unconscious is timeless," Anna Freud once pointed out — and by that she meant, among other things, that deep down within ourselves, death is unimaginable, unthinkable, notwithstanding the everyday evidence that everyone dies. To terminate one's own life in a way, is to become godlike: to go against what seems to be nature's mandate of survival, to challenge the tenacious hold on this existence that even the most vulnerable and troubled people ordinarily aren't willing to relinquish. Put differently, suicide is a kind of ultimate willfulness — and here psychology connects with theology. Those who believe God has given us life, know full well that it is for Him to end it. Those who don't believe in God have no such reason, clearly, to abstain from taking their lives; and yet, millions of avowed agnostics, atheists, have never come near doing so — in a sense, then, affirming a commitment to self-preservation that persists to the last breath. No wonder, then, many of my psychiatric colleagues want to call all suicides "sick": men and women who, finally, were overcome by an illness — though a good number of people who ultimately end their lives by their own hands show no evidence to anyone that they are in any psychological (or physical) trouble, and by far the majority of those who are struggling with serious illness (with respect to the body or the mind) don't come near contemplating suicide with any seriousness.

What, then, does Graham Greene have in mind for us to consider when he has Scobie, once a sincere, thoughtful man of Catholic faith, abruptly end his life as a response to his marital infidelity, his illegal commercial dealings? I suppose we can become allegorical, regard Scobie as a representative of a smug, corrupt, exploitative colonial world — its mainstay, actually: the small-time official who does the daily dirty work. Such a world the author knew first-hand — he himself lived in Britain's western African territory during the Second World War; and such a world he surely knew, even then, was on its last leg. Indeed, much of this novel exposes the dreary, moral stupidity of that very world — exposes the so-called normal life that, arguably, is sicker than any sickness doctors know to diagnose: an arrogant egotism of race, first, then class that gives a grimly concrete meaning to the sin of sins, pride. Not long into his story, Greene has us squirming amidst the details of such a life: the lunches and dinners, the cocktail hours, the pretenses, the gossip, the constant effort to fit in or show off or come out first in this or that bit of silliness — a landscape of phoniness and deception that no one wants to question, only bleed, day by day, for all its worth. Step by step, though, Scobie leaves that terrain. He is denied a promotion — a rebuke, a refusal. Thereupon, he becomes an outsider, a stranger, with all the consequent vulnerability, to be sure, but also with the heightened awareness of an observer whose broken ties have enabled a far more acute comprehension of what is, what ought to be. Scobie's "fall" enables his (and our) enlightenment. The dirty business below the surface of an Empire's "majesty" surfaces, much to everyone's chagrin: that of Scobie, needless to say, but also the chagrin of the other characters in the story and, not least, the chagrin of the reader, who is meant to learn something very important, to take it to heart, as the title more than implies.

Boldly, a novelist with strong religious interests, if not loyalties (at the time Greene was still a Catholic churchgoer) dares wonder whether suicide isn't somehow, sometimes an expression of religious experience, even if of a kind gone awry. Scobie, after all, is not crazy, not a clinical "case," unsuccessfully, futilely treated. Nor is he yet another of this century's existentialist anti-heroes — as in the writing of Camus, Sartre, who were both in their post–World War II ascendancy among the secular, Western intelligentsia around the time Greene dared publish this novel, with its sincerely then desperately self-scrutinizing Catholic layman whose distinguishing characteristic (in the exploitative, ultimately materialistic circle of colonialist henchmen) is, ironically, his capacity for a troubling, unnerving interior life, that of a Catholic communicant. It is precisely this conscience, this religious sensibility, this instrument of divine judgment, killed with the rest of Scobie by his act of self-destruction, that we readers are asked to consider — how to regard what happens to it: the failure of an agency of God's justice, or another kind of failure, namely, someone's frantic effort to escape that conscience, that justice.

If Scobie were Dostoyevskyan in temperament — wildly, toughly willing to make a mockery of conventional norms and values, even those of a church inevitably undermined by the flaws of its adherents — then we might readily embrace him as a prophet of sorts, willing to stand up to a living death (bourgeois, colonial normalcy) in the most assertive manner possible: I will walk away for good. But Scobie is quietly tormented, never given the moral authority Dostoyevsky dramatically (and Tolstoy, quietly) gives to certain figures in his novels. Scobie appears to be a victim of bad luck — an almost passive accomplice to an overwhelming evil hungrily in search of expression. All the way, he drags his feet, tries to hold on to a Catholic faith which, as he understands it, gives him no access to forgiveness. A man who becomes at a remove from conventional society now parts company with conventional religion. All he need have done (a lot, admittedly) was go confess his sins to a priest — but instead, he harbors those sins, tries to conceal them from everyone, even as an investigator trails him, learns more and more. God, however, knows everything, knows all the pain caused by all the missteps, knows all the mistakes, all the efforts to patch up a sinking, solitary lifeboat; and Scobie can't forget that omniscience of God's. This God may well be the Protestant one Greene knew before his conversion — a God unmediated by the Catholic Church's instrument of forgiveness: a confession earnestly meant. But this God, surely, is not unlike the One whom many of the saints regarded with "fear and trembling," as the phrase goes: hence their not uncommon inclination to self-laceration (literally and symbolically).

Perhaps we are meant to regard Scobie as a failed saint — tormented by a candid moral awareness that won't let go of him, honest enough to fathom the extent of the suffering for which he is responsible, yet unable, finally, to endure the distance from others required of a sinner who has, through repentance, become holy. Scobie took exact measure of a duplicitous world, never mind his own duplicities — and so doing, squarely faced down sinfulness (the great achievement of all the saints). But he could go no further — could not envision God's grace, the acceptance of which, no question, involves for many a tumultuous, extended struggle all its own. He had, in a way, reached the last mile of one road; and with another road not within the grasp of his moral imagination, not an aspect of his felt spiritual destiny, a self-imposed end to it all seemed sadly fitting — a soul's earthly impasse, its situation of limbo, given a terrible, final acknowledgment.

April 1996

– 45 –

The Bluest Eye

B LIND, our racist possibilities are crippled. To be sure, the ears can be of help, give us clues of who is what, comes from where; but sight matters most, especially these days, when schools are available to all, a big boost to a growing aural homogeneity. A student of mine told me a story a couple of years ago—he had a job answering the phone at the private school he attended, on scholarship. So doing, he got into occasional conversations with parents and others, trying to reach particular students. In certain instances he got to know individuals, struck up continuing conversations with them. Several times it came out that he was (he "came out" as) black, much to the surprise of his telephone friends. The issue of race, then, is sight: what we do with the neurophysiology that connects the optic nerve to the frontal cortex of the brain—hence, Ralph Ellison's *Invisible Man,* and a substantial furtherance of its powerful theme in Toni Morrison's *The Bluest Eye,* both first novels, both set, temporally, in the America that immediately preceded the civil rights era, the years when we as a nation didn't want to look closely at so very much. Again and again, Ellison's anonymous hero reminds us that his invisibility bespeaks our blindness; and Morrison directly picks up on that same theme—her Pecola Breedlove, all of eleven years old, will yearn for eyes other than those she has, in the hope, thereby, that a world hitherto uninterested in noticing her with any favor will now pay respectful, kindly heed.

Ellison's protagonist is a young man whose naiveté contrasts with the continual corruption, trickery, and mischief he encounters within the world of his own people, and that of the whites whom he encounters on his journey from a southern college that is a thinly disguised Tuskegee to the north of Manhattan, Harlem. Morrison's story centers on a Ohio girl, who already knows too much about life — the novel tells us, essentially, that a child can witness only so much pain and misery and meanness: eventually, she shuts off all recognition, takes herself to another world. In that regard, Morrison tempts us mightily, we who summon psychology with quick reflexes. Her mere child (so we view a Pecola by our "developmental" standards) knows firsthand a textbook of psycho-pathology and sociology—knows her father's violent, raging desperation, her mother's hurt, scared vulnerability. These are people at the very edge of things in a Midwestern industrial city—the trek north, as with Ellison's "invisible man," come to naught. Morrison moves us through the seasons of a year in the life of that family, starting with the autumn, a time when death begins to take place in the natural world, even as Pecola's world will soon enough begin to fall apart. Page by page we learn of a family's hard-pressed life, but there is verve and pluck and toughness and shrewdness in those people, as well. The Morrison we would later know, the great singer of *Jazz* and *Song of Solomon* and *Sula* and *Beloved*, is already rehearsing and refining a powerfully lyrical, summoning voice that, no matter its subject matter, challenges its audience to more than the responsive self-indulgence of pity, the cheapest sentiment around, and the most deceptive, because it is a cover for anger, contempt.

In the novel's time, in the span of that single year, madness gives a girl raped by her father, pregnant with their baby, a hallucinatory, alternative vision of things: her imagined blue eyes a desperately reparative effort to locate a more secure and gracious world which she, in turn, will judge worthy—with herself, thereby, at last (as its inhabitant) capable of self-respect. Morrison published *The Bluest Eye* in 1970, when the civil rights struggle in the South had given way to an unprecedented national challenge to our foreign policy. Her Pecola Breedlove is a child of a desolate, unforgiving urban poverty, and if we are tempted to patronize this girl, all too quickly become woman, with our pity, we are forewarned by the first page, which offers a passage that parodies a Dick and Jane reader for children of comfortable, white suburbia: "Here is the house. It is green and white. It has a red door. It is very pretty. Here is the family. Mother, Father, Dick and Jane live in the green-and-white house. They are very happy."

We are given that brief picture-perfect story three times, a clarion-call warning in the night: first as such a description would appear in a book for children, then as a narrative without punctuation, and finally, as a jumble of tightly packed words that merge—a gibberish that is a madness all its own: the deceits of a pretentious world laid bare. We learn, right off, that this is a book about color (the black and white of race) and about the colors that have gotten connected to the subject, such as the blue of eyes that is also the blue of a clear, sunny day's sky, where heaven is purportedly to be found, and the green of a flowering, luxuriant landscape, not to mention the cash some have in abundance, thereby enabling purchase of those fine ("green and white") homes. For the Breedloves, in contrast, there is only the darkest, threadbare (black) living that takes place in a home as physically exposed, even flimsy, as it is emotionally vulnerable.

All through the narrative the author scatters the Dick-and-Jane caricature, lest we forget her essential point: that thoughtlessness, truculent self-regard, indifference to others, have a way of spreading, undeterred by the social and racial barriers we sometimes think to be so solidly protective; that madness begets madness — the crazy vanity of a "lucky" or "beautiful" blue becomes the crazy obsession with a blue that is thought to be saving, redemptive. If we white readers concentrate on Pecola's demise in such a way that we don't look inward, catch a glimpse of our own deranged values and ideals, so often symbolically connected to various colors, then our blue-eyed blindness is a match for Pecola's frightening, telling journey into make-believe.

Rape is the devastating theme that runs through this powerfully stark novel. A child is raped by her father, but we are not to dwell only on this familial version of cruel violence. The father, we learn, as a youth was caught making love (his first sexual encounter) by three white men, out hunting, and they compelled him, now become their prey, to continue his activity under the glare of their powerful, poking flash-lights — once more a scene of commanding eyes staring at defenseless others in such a way that they are denied their humanity: an animal show in the woods. What others standing over us see, we learn to see: the oldest story of everyone's childhood, and a tale that Pecola the child, her father (Cholly), each in certain respects wounded, have to tell us, yet again.

In *The Bluest Eye* a black writer makes a debut as a sharply knowing, unflinching psychological realist, who refuses the temptations of sentimentality — the kind that covertly gloats in the victimization of race or class by resort to an unearned, a gratuitous compassion. Throughout her now glorious writing career Toni Morrison has shown a brilliant command of the symbolic connections the various colors get going in our mind, black and white especially. The blue eyes for which Pecola yearns tell of her personal embrace of a larger (cultural) craziness, tell of the way our children learn to find hope in the weirdest and most improbable places, a consequence of the hopelessness of their daily lives. Pecola's mother, Pauline, or Polly, is a maid who works in that white, that blue-eyed world. By the time she comes home her daughter is, inevitably, an afterthought to a long day of effort on behalf of one or another white boss. No wonder an imaginative child attempts a "leap of faith," a jump into the "wild blue yonder": *their* eyes must glimpse a happiness otherwise unavailable, so why not conjure up a conviction that has a part of me now a part of them. If such a maneuver is psychotic (that is, utterly at variance with "reality" — the word bandied around all the time by psychiatrists to judge and

distinguish patients: their degree of "contact" with the so-called social "environment") then the Dick-and-Jane world, offered to children
of "all sorts and conditions" (as the phrase goes) is no less bizarre,
wildly absurd, loony, as we are meant to realize, right off, before we
meet Pecola and her parents, through her friend Claudia MacTeer, a
nine-year-old neighbor.

It is this psychosis of the powerful that Pecola's creator wants us,
finally, to attend — the egoism that has our view of things, regarded
through our (blue) eyes, as a moral arbiter of all that transpires in a
given time and place, the America we inhabit today. Pecola, as a consequence, is, indeed, hallucinatory, she who has appropriated those blue
eyes, along with voices that she, and no one else, hears; but across
the color-line, and the class-line, too, the delusions that Dick and Jane
learn are quite something else: "normal development," as the psychology textbooks put it — hence the historical willingness of publishers
to send out stories such as the one Morrison gives us at the beginning
of this disturbing novel and intersperses at points in its midst. Pecola's
father is as brutish with her as a blue-eyed world has been with him,
and the girl tries to jump ship, as it were, put herself in *their* — well,
eyes, rather than shoes. So doing, she loses herself — but perhaps she
has already sensed (an intuitive, inarticulate calculation) that all seems
lost, wherever she looks, hence that last-ditch reason (a mind's desperate decision) to try getting another (visionary) handle on things.

May 1996

46

Endo's *Silence*

THIRTY YEARS AGO (in 1966) the Japanese novelist Shusaku Endo published *Silence,* a novel meant to tell of history, deal with missionaries in seventeenth-century Japan, when their efforts were subject to fierce repression, through a story that concretely examines nothing less than the nature of faith, of loyalty under extreme duress to Jesus and His church and, therefore of martyrdom. The novel's central character is a Portuguese Jesuit, Sebastian Rodrigues, and what we read is an account of this young missionary priest's experiences in Japan, where he has gone in order to learn the whereabouts, the fate, of another Jesuit, Christovao Ferreira, who is reported to have apostatized after a long career in Asia, much to the disbelief of his fellow Jesuits in Rome and elsewhere. Father Rodrigues and another Jesuit, Francisco Garrpe, eventually get to Japan (the year is 1638), and the heart of the novel is a letter written by Father Rodrigues (it is declared a part of Catholic missionary history) which chronicles the extreme suffering of persecuted believers, not to mention the spiritual tests and trials put to the man whose words are a record, obviously, an account of a story, but something else, too — a challenge to us: what does Jesus ask of us, expect from us, in our daily lives?

Endo's disarmingly direct and poignant narration masks a complex moral discussion that many of us, perhaps, will prefer not to join. Indeed, Endo more than implies that the church itself was not easily inclined to look into the matter of Father Ferreira's apostasy — Father Rodrigues had to wait and wait for an approval for his proposed mission of inquiry — and in fact, the book hints at a possible explanation for such a reluctance: Father Ferreira's apostasy is probed, all right, by Father Rodrigues, and by the time we readers learn about what happened, we are more than a bit stunned. It is interesting, in this regard, how *Silence* has been reviewed: critic after critic, extolling the book, refuses to divulge its climactic moment — when Father Rodrigues, caught by the church's persecutors, is confronted with their demand, that he defile a holy image of Christ, and thereby add his apostasy to that of the one whose actions he has come to investigate. One reviewer doesn't want to "betray" the plot for his reviewers; another declares that "it would be unfair to reveal the decision" that

Rodrigues, in the end, makes — having been told that if he tramples on the *fumie*, which is an icon expressly fashioned for such a gesture, others in the midst of terrible torture will be spared. Yet, I wonder whether all of us aren't so profoundly troubled by the novel's posed religious dilemma and choice that we ourselves become part of the "silence" to which this book's title alludes. That title, Endo tells us, has to do with the felt silence many apprehend from the Lord's side of things amidst the unspeakable horrors that human beings inflict on one another — horrors that we of this century have especially known, as Elie Wiesel, for example, reminds us in his autobiographical *Night*, with its description of the Nazi murderousness he experienced in the early 1940s. In the face of such monstrous evil, of seventeenth-century Japan, of twentieth-century Europe, where is God's voice?

From the more comfortable precincts of Christianity, untested by what Wiesel went through, or Father Ferreira (the spectacle of torture and murder as immediate aspects of everyday life), it is possible to be smart, learned, utterly loyal to a spiritual, a theological tradition — and insist that a reference to God's so-called silence indicates a grave misunderstanding of who God is and, of course, who we are. Yes, God is "silent" — our freedom, including the freedom to be evil, is what constitutes the heart of our being, the biggest gift possible: the freedom to obey God's commandments, His expressed and revealed truths, but also the freedom to ignore them, defy them, or put differently, calling upon Endo's imagery, the capacity or willingness to hear God's "voice," as it has been given articulation over time, or the choice of a chosen heedlessness, deafness on our part. For Rodrigues, for others who have surely come after him, such abstract knowledge has had to contend with — well, life, in all its sometimes terrifying moral confrontations, and it is just such a concrete, vivid, particular moment that a novelist's vocation allows him or her to grant, as Endo does here.

Endo is a quietly engaging writer with no interest in large-scale or dogmatic moral argument, with its unfortunate risk of bombast and self-righteousness. He lets us meet this modest, perplexed, yet obviously determined "vessel of God," as the expression goes — a priest in the long and noble, if at times ill-fated and tragic history of Jesuit evangelization. We meet, too, those he gets to know when, at last, a secret intruder, he sneaks into Japan, makes contact with a segment of its beleaguered, hounded community of Christian believers. Soon enough, this visitor, himself in hiding, realizes how much danger and jeopardy these ordinary people must endure almost every moment of their lives — *their* martyrdom an aspect of a humble faith, lived daily, that isn't given the notoriety, the celebrity of sainthood. With the help of a guide, Kichijiro, our protagonist has come to meet these people, and it is precisely this man (he will remind the reader of the mestizo who follows Graham Greene's "whiskey priest" in *The Power and the Glory*) who, Judas-like, will betray Rodrigues — all of that action a prelude to this story's enormously challenging showdown with his Japanese captors.

Rodrigues has been haunted by Jesus, by the sight of Him in his mind, by His teachings. Now this unassuming, gentle man, who has wanted to know what happened to another Jesuit, will learn the answer, all right: Father Ferreira apostatized so that others, held hostage and brutally treated, might be spared. Betrayed, captured, arraigned, a morally awake, soulful Father Rodrigues, for whom Jesus is a constant, intimate presence, now weighs the choice before him, wonders what to do. He can refuse to tread on the *fumie*, refuse to utter the demanded blasphemous utterances, thereby guarantee his slow, miserable demise, and thereby become yet another Christian martyr; or he can continue his intense, moment-to-moment conversations with his Lord, which have preceded this terrible time and, presumably, will continue until his last breath, and so doing, with agony of mind, contrition of heart, go through the motions of submission, apparently apostatize, so that others be spared torture and death (others who — the stunning irony of it — are themselves anguished, afflicted Christians on the constant brink of their own obscure martyrdom).

I suspect many readers, like me, expected Endo to provide the former outcome for his character, offer Father Rodrigues an earthly departure of torture, to be followed by a tested believer's ascension to the highest place in our esteem: one who stood fast, under excruciating circumstances, for his faith. But the Jesuit whose spiritual sincerity has been apparent to us all along, surprises us, startles us, agitates and confounds us and, maybe, disappoints and dismays us — he goes through the required motions, apostatizes. Why? With what rationale? Are we to pronounce him a coward? What train of thought, what tangle of emotions have brought him to this awesome (we are tempted to say, awful) decision? The author tells us a lot about his own sense of who Jesus is through this shocking, narrative turn — a trajectory of martyrdom become a tale of apostasy. For Endo's Father Rodrigues, Jesus is a devotedly compassionate and understanding companion who has scant interest in spelling out, without resort to context, the exact terms of how we should behave under every single, imaginable set of circumstances. Rather, this version of Jesus has Him skeptical of a martyrdom that is enabled — again, the jolting, grip-

ping, shattering irony — by the martyrdom of others. Instead, Endo
has us consider this: even the martyr can be, by dint of his or her humanity, held in the sway of pride, caught in its intoxicating undertow:
the martyr as yielding to St. Paul's "letter," rather than "the spirit." For
this Jesuit who refused martyrdom, as did his predecessor, Father Ferreira, the point was to mock those who wanted him to mock Jesus, to
parody their efforts to parody Jesus, to swallow this variant of pride,
the potential martyr's, in order that others, good and decent and spiritually noble men and women, for all their "ordinariness," be spared
further suffering.

To be sure, the priest can be charged with weakness, with a fatal loss of nerve, if not of faith — by which of us, though, by
this or that comfortable burgher of the late twentieth century, for
whom dedication to Jesus means an hour or so in a church building
on weekends? If today's psychology (speaking of icons) casts doubt
on Father Rodrigues, calls him an anxious, frightened man, driven
to self-serving (self-saving) rationalizations, he was at least spared
that torture. Rather, he weighs the terrible decision before him with
Christ's life in mind — how He responded to whom on His short-
lived pilgrimage in Galilee and Jerusalem and their environs: Jesus the
man of great, embracing, affectionate compassion, who confronted,
always, religious and moral literalism and, by implication, Jesus the
One who might even smile wanly at the spectacle of torturers being
stymied by a priest's knowing, brave, risky leap of faith! The guise
(and guile) of an enacted apostasy, become a gesture of devotion, of
faith! With such a choice Endo's man of God quells theological arguments, psychological analysis, brings a kind of silence to us, who are
dumbfounded and, surely, stirred to wonder, once more, about the
riddles, mysteries, provocations of faith.

June 1996

47

Endo's *Deep River*

W ITH THE EPIGRAPH to his latest novel the Japanese Catholic writer Shusaku Endo not only signals his story's intention, but by implication dismisses those critics who have made much of his relatively unusual situation as a Christian intellectual (he was baptized at the age of eleven and educated by priests) who has lived in a nation that is far from the West, and for a long time successfully resisted its ever-probing cultural (not to mention economic and political) assertiveness. Endo calls upon a "Negro spiritual" for that epigraph, and indeed, for his book's title: "Deep river, Lord: I want to cross over into campground." His story, he is suggesting, will tell of a universal vulnerability, and the yearning that goes with it — the desire for a redemptive journey, a passage into more promising, secure terrain. The river in this instance is the Ganges, for Hindus a sacred setting of awesome significance, a way-station toward new kinds of life to be assumed, rather than a spot that marks the end of things, but for modern Japanese as well as Americans, reared on antisepsis and biotechnology, a place of absurdity if not danger — funeral pyres everywhere and, too, bodies of human beings, of household pets, floating downstream.

Before he brings his characters to that scene, Endo explores their contemporary, bourgeois, cosmopolitan lives; does so almost clinically (they are called "cases"). These are all troubled, restless people, no matter their privileged situation. Each of them has known disappointment, loss, psychological and moral jeopardy. Even as bodies float on the Ganges, these four men and a woman are perplexed, uneasy, pursued by various demons of a past life — adrift in their own ways. Isobe is a middle-aged businessman whose wife has died of cancer. Until she took sick he was cool, detached, all too self-absorbed — making money, climbing higher on this or that (social, economic) ladder. He and his wife had learned to stay together, but keep their substantial distance. With her death, more than the expectable sadness overcame Isobe. A rigid emotional control, a determined practicality that had little use for playfulness or imaginative speculation, were challenged by a moment of overwhelming fatefulness, which, in this instance, seemed to make a mockery of all the carefully tended rituals and habits, if not compulsions, that had constituted a life and, maybe, were meant to preclude any hard, searching look into its meaning or purpose. Taking aim at an agnosticism rooted in science and its powerfully pervasive enlightenment, which these days is proving to be transnational, transcultural, Endo puts his finger on Isobe's spiritual pulse this way: "Because he lacked any religious conviction, like most Japanese, death to him meant the extinction of everything" (p. 22).

Before she died, Isobe's wife, Keiko, is haunted by disturbing dreams and becomes persuaded (hope against hope) that death is not, after all, final: "I'll be reborn somewhere in this world" (p. 17). She asks her husband to try to find her — thereby, of course, to remain loyal to her, remember her in a decisive rather than cursory or occasional manner. When she dies and is cremated, a Buddhist priest, in ceremonial attendance, explains his religion's assumptions: "When an individual dies, their spirit goes into a state of limbo. Limbo means that they have not been reincarnated, and they wander uneasily about this world of men. Then, after several days, they slip into the conjoined bodies of a man and a woman and are reborn as a new existence" (p. 19). Such a deduction is, of course, no more easily accepted by Isobe and millions like him in Japan than it would be among most Westerners.

This overall atmosphere of skeptical materialism pervades the thinking of the others who figure in Endo's evocation of late twentieth-century Japanese life. Mitsuko is an attractive divorcee, highly intelligent, relentlessly cynical, forbiddingly calculating — and yet, unbeknownst to herself, desperately vulnerable. She left a marriage ideal in secular terms — her husband another of Endo's (of our) prosperous burghers. Now she does volunteer work in a hospital (she took care of Isobe's dying wife) and is haunted by memories of a relationship she had as a college student with Otsu, another "case" — a young man who would ultimately enlist as a seminarian in a Catholic order. Mitsuko became Otsu's temptress, a derisively callous one at times. But she was also increasingly intrigued by, then taken with this exquisitely innocent and generous person, so much her opposite. Together they discussed religion, and their chosen name for God, Onion, becomes a symbolic theme that threads its way through the narrative: the many layers of faith, the humility that it asks of the believer, the connection between belief and tragedy — all of that conveyed through the ordinary, lowly onion, that one can peel and peel, though with tears. Onion addressed by those two youths eventually becomes Onion pursued with great passion, Otsu within the Christian tradition, Mitsuko within the confines of a willful and manipulative self-centeredness that today's psychiatrists would find unsurprising — and very hard to challenge clinically.

To fill out his cast of characters, all save Otsu headed by plane on
one of those sadly banal travel excursions meant to distract people already, it can be said, more distracted (ironically) than they ever might
realize, Endo offers Numanda, a writer and naturalist who could put
his heart into the construction of storybooks for children, and converse passionately with birds—while holding himself aloof from his
own wife and, it seems, all other fellow humans; and Kiguchi, a veteran of the Highway of Death in Burma, where cannibalism was
rampant—a terrible finale to Japan's ill-fated early 1940's effort to
conquer the Asian mainland.

These individuals, in their sum, make up their creator's take on
modern man—as in Jung's "modern man in search of a soul." (Endo
has studied psychoanalysis with interest and, especially, its Jungian
variant.) Each of these "cases" (again, save Otsu) has tried to live a
conventional, reasonably successful, secular life—and has failed to do
so not in a dramatic way (an ostentatious turn to an "alternative life
style," a collapse into madness), but with the muffled cry of a vague
apprehension that bespeaks of a despair that isn't even known, never
mind acknowledged. Under such circumstances these are curiously restrained protagonists, a seemingly unpromising crew for a novel that is
traditional enough to offer as its glue a specific plot: a trip to a strange
land; a tour guide who is a religious teacher of sorts; some minor
but instructive, even emblematic characters (a young honeymooning
couple, the husband a greedily prying photographer, the wife callow
and spoiled, who give their creator a chance to comment on the self-
indulgent fatuousness of a certain kind of Japanese — and not only
Japanese—youth). Yet, Endo is a master of the interior monologue,
and thereby he builds, "case" by "case," chapter by chapter, a devastating critique of a world that has "everything," but lacks moral
substance and seems headed nowhere.

Even as his characters confront in India along the Ganges and elsewhere the great mysteries of Hinduism and Buddhism, including their
notion of the migratory life of the soul, Endo himself gives once
more a new life to some of his earlier characters, his longstanding
metaphysical passions. Mitsuko has appeared in previous Endo fic-
tions, and here, as before, he explicitly connects her to one of his
mentors, François Mauriac; she is a version of the latter's Thérèse
Desqueyroux, whose sinful preoccupations and behavior, whose capacity for evil, were of no small and continuing interest to him. Endo
himself was educated in France, and here, as in others of his stories, he takes, for a spell, a Japanese protagonist to a Europe (Lyons)
that is for him quite familiar, even congenial territory. In fact, his

Otsu, the failed seminarian, so easy prey, when young, to Mitsuko, and later an obsession of hers, is very much a character out of another French novelist's literary and religious imagination — the curé in Georges Bernanos's *Diary of a Country Priest*. That curé, too, seems to be a bumbling innocent, no match for the savvy, the guile of various high and mighty folk, especially certain church bureaucrats, who can't for the life of them comprehend him, his nature and his manner of being. This is the Judeo-Christian story, endlessly retold — by the prophet Isaiah, for instance, by the writers of the four gospels, and by a succession of novelists (Dostoyevsky and Tolstoy and Dickens), and given by Bernanos the expository life of a rural French parish in the early years of this century: Christ foretold, Christ remembered, Christ evoked.

The unnerving, chosen marginality of the man Jesus, his topsy-turvy embrace of the weak, the "despised and the scorned," as against the big shots of church and state alike, has sent shudders down the backs of all sorts of people long after his death — among them, presumably, plenty of bishops and the functionaries who do their important bidding. This is the dilemma Catholic novelists (as opposed to apologists) of whatever national or racial background have had to confront: the spiritual truth that emerged from an informal community of humble Jews, peasants and fishermen, inspired by a radical teacher and healer, who was rather quickly hounded down, as against the later historical truth of a tight-knit, powerful organization which has been, supposedly for his sake, in the thick of things for all these centuries, and which has often enough more than stumbled. What the Catholic theologian Romano Guardini said ("The church is the Cross on which Christ was crucified.") Shusaku Endo has known to give us in novel after novel — in his brilliantly original *Silence* (which takes on that subtlest, maybe most pernicious version of pride, Christian smugness) and now, twenty-five years later, in this most recent tale, wherein Otsu, like his savior, dies young and badly misunderstood not by yet another of history's mobs, but a fictional one.

All through *Deep River* Otsu's pilgrimage haunts Mitsuko, his secular antagonist, and through her, the other characters in this beautifully wrought, lyrically suggestive story, so charged by the moral energy of its maker — who (like Thomas Merton at the time of his accidental death in Asia) wants to bring a Catholic sensibility to the shores of Hinduism and Buddhism, both. Not that this is a novel of easy or gratuitous grace. Doubt, Shusaku Endo has always known, is very much an aspect of faith. In the last pages, his sardonic, shrewd, embittered heroine glimpses "the sorrows of this deep river of humanity"

(p. 211), realizes herself to be a part of it, a momentary step away from the tenacious pride that has prompted her to be so standoffish — though soon enough, we know, she (like many of us) will be aiming again for her solitary, privileged perch above it all: the defiance of the egoistic observer. If Christianity gives us the lonely individual challenged by a God who entered history, Buddhism gives us people who are ready to surrender, finally, a measure of their human and spiritual particularity, and who, with acceptance, join their fellow creatures as part of the great tide of humanity — and Endo manages to give us both of these streams of faith, brings them together into a flow that is, indeed, deep: a soulful gift to a world he keeps rendering as unrelievedly parched.

48

Edward Hopper

W HEN A FULL cultural history of twentieth-century America
is written — no doubt at the start of the third millennium —
Edward Hopper will surely command a great deal of attention. Arguably, he will rank as our country's leading artist of that century —
one whose canvases became part of a public consciousness, part of
"a whole climate of opinion," in W. H. Auden's words, meant to describe the assimilation of another gifted person's work (that of Freud)
into a broad kind of social awareness. Not that Hopper had an easy
time of it from the start. Like Freud, he had to endure years of
outright rejection, insistent disfavor. Like Freud he had stamina, stubbornness going for him — a refusal to be deterred by the judgment of
those who had power. In Austria Freud had to persist in the face of
fierce opposition from the university world; in America Hopper en-
dured dismissal and condescension from any number of art critics and
museum curators who were far more taken with, say, abstract expressionist artists than with his kind of American realism. Both men, it
can be said, triumphed through the appeal their work had for a growing army of readers, viewers, rather than through the favor of the
intellectual custodians of their respective professions (those who run
departments of psychiatry, those who choose paintings for display,
write about them).

For many years Gail Levin has devoted her considerable and
thoughtful energy to the study of Hopper's work and life both. She
has written essays on his life, and presented his work to us in volume
after volume — his career as an illustrator, an engraver, an artist whose
paintings gradually engaged with the moral and social imagination of
so many of us. She is, actually, the one who has given us the defin-
itive presentation of Hopper's art, the *Catalogue Raisonné,* and now
she is his most ambitious biographer — with the important help of
his artist wife, Josephine Nivison Hopper, "Jo" to Hopper, and the
one depicted in some of his drawings and paintings. Indeed, it is hard
to imagine this long, thorough, revealing, and quite provocative book
without the constant voice of Jo, whose daily diary entries inform
page after page — a running chronicle of a great artist's life, but also
of an exceedingly tempestuous marriage, which lasted and worked, no
matter its strenuous strains.

Hopper was born in Nyack, New York, to a family of modest circumstances. The name is of Dutch origin, even as all his life he looked up to Rembrandt — and both were wizards with "light," able to use it as an instrument of compelling character analysis. Hopper never attended college — yet another American autodidact. He read broadly, deeply; studied with artists in New York; went to Europe as a young man, but thereafter shunned those transatlantic trips so appealing to artists (and others of relative privilege). For a while — for decades, actually — he was a salesman of sorts; he went from magazine to magazine, with his portfolio, in search of assignments as an illustrator. He did so, of course, to make a living — but he never gave up the desire to paint, to be an artist at the beck and call of his own spirit, rather than that of commerce. Even as he did pictures aimed at selling products or helping readers become visually involved with the stories they were reading, he repaired in his heart to his studio, where (on the canvases that awaited him daily, for half a century) he struggled with forms and shapes, with pigments, with light and shadows, and not least, with ideas, which he chose to tether to a representational reality.

Today any description of, response to his paintings (especially the best-known among them, such as *Nighthawks, Early Sunday Morning, Office at Night, Summer Evening, Gas, Solitude, Hotel Lobby, Chop Suey, New York Movie, Sunlight in a Cafeteria*) has to contend with the heavy weight of a criticism that draws on "existentialism," or on the dreary banalities generated by a secular preoccupation with psychology and sociology. Yet, there was a time, well before the influence of Camus and Sartre had reached our shores, and well before the social sciences loomed so large on our campuses and beyond, when an obscure painter was merely taking keen, persistent note of how we get along in this hugely materialist, industrial society. Without saying a word, he gave us what he had witnessed, what he, a genius, could singularly convey. Even now, time spent with his pictures can bring fresh meaning to tired words such as "alienation," "loneliness"; even now, his talent as a painter rescues his work, and us, the beholders of it, from a generation of socially and psychologically labored interpretation. His powerfully suggestive inwardness, his reflective breadth and depth, his disciplined craftsmanship, his restless, sharply knowing interest in a nation, its people, their ways with one another — all of that still offers him a certain immunity from the killing possibilities of cultural attention, whereby someone is "summed up," and soon enough abandoned for the next, then the next objects of fashionable interest. Hopper lingers, survives even critical acclaim. Himself taciturn, a master at rendering the inarticulate, the yearnings and worries we have learned to hide from ourselves, never mind others, he brings us mood and revelation with a pointed intensity that makes a mockery of contemporary psychological, sociological (or religious) language — and *there* the magic of art: to bring us, in the words of Henry James (whose novels he loved) "the manners, the manners" in such a way that we are left free to muse and wonder and make connections on our own.

This lucid, almost hovering biography (season after season set down for us) is worthy of its subject, his approach to art. We are denied, here, the temptations of an art criticism all too fluidly, abstractly sure of itself; denied, too (a miracle, these days), an overwrought, intrusive psychology, ready at the quick, to classify, label, demonize reductively: the mannerisms of the clinic trotted out, so that Hopper, the one whose paintbrush enables us to stop and see things in a different light (his "light" become our enlightenment) becomes yet another candidate for someone's "interpretations" (or these days, pills).

Wisely, generously, this biographer (as restrained in her medium as Hopper was in his) lets Jo's day-to-day struggles with her mighty, inscrutable, tenaciously determined husband get presented by her — a continuing, detailed narrative by a protagonist, and at times, an antagonist. For over four decades these two artists lived together, loved and inspired one another, and, not least, locked horns. Theirs was the mystery of an attachment that lasted, no matter its serious flaws, vicissitudes; an attachment fired, shaped by a shared immersion in a particular profession. Jo's words give an account of the exceptional capability of a particular artist, who could wrest so much from the world around him. All the while, she observed him, the artist observer, and described what she saw feverishly, painstakingly in a torrent of declarations, exclamations, abbreviations, asides. Hers is a diarist's chronicle that proceeds at a fast clip, now summoned by a biographer able and willing to provide us a context for all those dark nights of a steadfast marriage's soul: Jo as Edward's ally, his model, his nagging scold, as watchful of him as he was of everyone else.

"Before the problem of the creative artist analysis must, alas, lay down its arms," Freud volunteered in a self-addressed warning, an unusual moment of resignation (speaking of a biographer's restraint — he was writing about Dostoyevksy). Gail Levin has given us, with obvious erudition and admiration, Hopper the "creative artist" and Hopper the reclusive, cranky, brilliantly thoughtful, impossibly egoistic, highly industrious man, no less limited in mind and heart than the rest of us, if quite distinct from us all in one respect that counts ever so much. A constant wanderer across our American scene (by foot, by train, by automobile), he took our close measure, documented the headlong, sprawling, anxious nature of our early and middle years of this American century; bequeathed us, in his pictures, a landscape of our edgy, worried, assertive selves at home, on the road, at work. In this engaging, instructive biography, we meet him and his wife, Jo, learn of their emotionally intense time together, follow their careers, and, no small feat on the part of their biographer, are left with respect for these two, respect for what they separately and jointly accomplished — a tribute to them and the one who hands them over to us.

49

Uniforms

WE HAVE BEEN HEARING a good deal, of late, about the value of uniforms as a means of encouraging young people to be more disciplined, law-abiding. The rationale goes like this: children and young people need a sense of order; need firm rules with respect to how they ought to look, behave; need to feel themselves very much part of particular institutions whose educational and ethical principles are meant to strengthen our various communities and, by extension, our nation — and uniforms help address that necessary psychological and moral aspect of child-rearing. Not that clothes in and of themselves possess magical transformative powers. A child (or adult) bent on being rowdy, mean, hurtful, criminal can do so wearing a coat and tie, and shoes polished to a sparkle, whereas youngsters who appear to certain fastidious and formal adults as slobs and worse (their pants uncreased and wrinkled, their shirts sloppily worn) can be conscientious, decent, considerate, kindly — respectful of others, if not respectful of the notion some of us have as to how they ought to be attired. Moreover, for some young people, such casual, laid-back garb is itself a uniform — to appear relaxed and "cool" is felt to be a mandatory manner of self-presentation.

For years, actually, I have heard the word "uniform" used by certain Harvard college students of mine, who have arrived in Cambridge from small towns in the South or the Midwest, and aren't familiar with a kind of constraint that is imposed by indirection: "I went to a Catholic school in Minnesota, and we were told we didn't all have to wear the same kind of blouse and skirt and socks and shoes, the way it used to be — but, you know, we did have to wear some kind of blouse and skirt: I mean, no jeans and no T-shirts. So, when I came here I wasn't as uptight as some people I met here [during the first days of orientation] who came from schools where there really were uniforms and everyone had to wear them, be dressed the same. But it doesn't take long to discover that there's a 'uniform' here too — and if you don't wear it, you'll pay a price. I mean [I had, obviously, asked] here, if you wear a skirt and blouse to class, you can feel out of it: too formal. Here, the scruffier the better, that's what you learn right off, boy or girl! There's a way to dress when you go to class, just as there was when I was in high school, only the clothes are different — and

Lord help you at breakfast if you come into the dining room looking neat and tidy, and your hair is combed and you're wearing a dress (a dress!) and some jewelry, a bracelet or a necklace: people will think you're on your way to a job interview, or something has *happened* — you have to go to a hospital, or a funeral, or church, something unusual! You'll hear, 'Is everything all right?' Now, I hear myself thinking those words — if I get the urge to wear clothes that are just the slightest bit 'formal,' the way I used to all the time! If I told my roommates or others in the [freshman] dorm what I've just said, they'd think I was odd — making a case out of nothing, one guy put it when I got into a discussion with him about all this, and made the mistake of pointing out that all the boys here wear khakis or jeans, and sneakers, the dirtier the better, and open shirts, work shirts, a lot of them, as if we're in a logging camp out West!"

She was exaggerating a little, but her essential point was quite well taken — that in a setting where studied informality rules supreme, and where individualism is highly touted, there are, nevertheless, certain standards with respect to the desirable, the decidedly unattractive, so that a dress code certainly asserts itself, however informally, unofficially: a uniform of sorts, as the young man she mentioned did indeed agree to call it, a range of what is regarded as suitable, and what is unusual, worth observing closely, even paying the notice of a comment, a question. Nor is such a college environment all that unusual, with respect to a relative consistency of attire that is, surely, more apparent to the outsider. We all tend to fall in line, accommodate the world (of work, of study, of travel and relaxation, of prayer) we have chosen, for varying lengths of time, to join. We take notice of others, ascertain a given norm, with respect to what is (and is not) worn, and make the necessary choices for our wardrobe, our use — or we don't do so, thereby, of course, for one reason or another of our own, setting ourselves apart, even as others promptly do the same in the way they regard us.

All of the above is unsurprising: the stuff of our daily unselfconscious living, yet, an aspect of our existence that ought to be remembered when a topic such as "uniforms" is brought up for public consideration — a necessary context. Still, these days, when the subject of "uniforms" comes up, it is meant to help us consider how to work more effectively in our schools with young people who are in trouble, who aren't doing well in school, who may be drop-outs and already up to no good — well on their way to delinquency, criminality. To ask such individuals (to demand of them when they are under the jurisdiction of a court) that they adhere to a certain dress code is to put them on due and proper notice: a certain kind of behavior is expected, and no ifs, ands, buts — the uniform as an exterior instance of what has to take place within: obedience, self-restraint, a loyalty to institutional authority. True, to repeat, clothes don't make us decent, cooperative, respectful human beings, in and of themselves — but they are an aspect of the way we present ourselves to others, and they are also daily reminders to us of the world to which we belong, and by extension, the values and customs and requirements of that world. To tell a child, a young man or woman, that he or she has to "shape up" in a certain way, dress in a certain manner, speak a certain language (and not another kind!) is to indicate a determination that a particular community's jurisdiction, its sovereignty will be asserted, maintained, upheld, from moment to moment.

I hear all the time, of course, that in our fancy private schools and colleges such an institutional insistence with regard to dress has been, by and large, abandoned in the name of a modern individualism, a lack of pretentiousness, a respect for our variousness, a refusal of "authoritarianism," of the "repressiveness" of yore. To be sure, clothes can be a badge, an instrument of fearful, blind submission, of snobbish, cliquish affiliation, of gratuitous and relentless and unthinking indoctrination. On the other hand, as mentioned earlier, even the most vigorously iconoclastic, even those righteously enamored of a social or political or educational privatism that resists compliance with any number of conventions or habits, will not easily escape their own, ironic nod (and more) to social cohesion — one uniform replacing another, ties and skirts abandoned in a compulsory stampede for jeans or sweatpants, or for undershirts become all there is above the waist.

Many of the youngsters I have met, taught in ghetto schools, many of the youngsters I've known who are in trouble at first-rate suburban or private school, have enormous need for "control": they haven't learned to subordinate their impulses to the needs of others; they are self-absorbed to their own detriment, never mind the harm that such a tenaciously reflexic egoism can cause to others in a classroom, on a team, a playground, anywhere in a neighborhood. Such boys and girls, such youths can often be desperately in search of the very commitment to an (educational, religious, civic) community they seem flagrantly to refuse, scorn. Indeed, their only hope may be the moment when a school or judge acts on behalf of a rehabilitative or corrective program that draws the line, insists that a uniform be a step (a mere step, but nonetheless, a significant first move) toward integration into a world outside any given self, a world in which others count, are respected, a world of obedience and self-control, as well as self-regard and self-assertion (the nature of the mix is all-important).

In a sense then all clothes are, as Freud, not to mention Shakespeare, reminded us, symbolic — we send signals, thereby, as to who we are, what we hold dear, with whom we wish to connect, affiliate ourselves. Moreover, it works both ways: we receive messages with respect to our appearance from the nation, the culture, the various institutions or communities to which we belong (or to which we are *told* we must join, such as the schools) — as anyone will realize upon visiting a foreign land, a different continent, but also while here at home, where what we wear can tell a lot about our hopes, inclinations, dispositions, aspirations, loyalties, and, too, our fears and worries, and worse. Small wonder, then, that uniforms worn by young people adrift, wayward in various ways, can bring a promise of direction, can offer a community with a shared purpose certain values and ideals, all of which, literally, are worn on the sleeves of its members. Of course, the heart of the matter is a person's interior moral life, but some of us badly need to be reminded, again and again, that there are others out there to whom, so to speak, we belong, and of whom we have to think with consideration and respect. We do, indeed, dress for those others, not only for ourselves — and for all of us that daily gesture has meaning, even as for some of us such a gesture may mark the beginning of a life that itself has, finally, come to possess some meaning.

July–August 1996

50

The Need for No

CHILDREN REQUIRE DISCIPLINE, limits we all know — and yet we all struggle, as parents, as teachers, to figure out when and how to assert our authority. I well remember an experience I had four years ago as a volunteer fourth-grade teacher in an inner-city elementary school. For weeks the children before me whispered constantly and got up as they pleased to leave the room. I tried harder and harder to engage their interest — all the while telling myself that these were boys and girls from impoverished homes, who required particular understanding from someone like me, lucky all along in life to have had a fairly comfortable time of it.

One morning, however, the limits of my patience were stretched too far. Suddenly, I lost my cool; I abandoned my rational efforts at persuasion in favor of — well, an outburst. I picked up the blackboard pointer, slammed it down on the desk, shouted a loud *no* at the entire class, and then told them off. I said I was through putting up with their rudeness and that if they didn't shape up, I simply wouldn't come back. When I finished talking I noticed something: an almost eerie silence that, in fact, lasted — thereby challenging me to respond. I now spoke in a more subdued tone, but was still upset, and I wanted the children to hear why. My explanation was followed by another spell of silence — and I doubt I'll ever forget a girl's comment that broke the ice: "Let's start out all over again."

In truth, *I* was the one who needed to do so. I knew in the abstract that children ought not be allowed to get away with being spiteful, callous, defiant. Weeks earlier, I should have acted on that knowledge, let those children hear me say no, loud and clear, even as all of our children, of whatever background, need to learn what is permissible and what is decidedly not.

Unfortunately, all too many of us have come to believe that children ought to be spared "no's," that in some way they will be hurt ("traumatized") by being made aware, firmly, that certain words, deeds are utterly impermissible, that limits exist and will be consistently upheld. Indeed, the recent Jessica Dubroff incident surely offered us an extreme example of what can happen when a child's wishes are allowed unrestricted leeway (and, maybe, given the sanction of adults). Why is a seven-year-old child, still with plenty to learn about flying, allowed to pilot an airplane? Would a seven-year-old be given a horse to ride on her own before she had become a capable rider?

To be sure; "no" can become abused — a chorus of refusals that indicates parental callousness or worse. But "no," judiciously used can also be a sign of caring concern — a parent on the lookout for the child's safety and need for self-control (the latter, after all, has to be taught). I suppose some of us feel "guilty" when we say "no," worry we are "hurting" our children — a sign, maybe, that we aren't spending enough time with them, because anyone who does put in those hours with a young boy or girl will learn how urgently he or she needs the help of older people in learning what is desirable, what is not only undesirable, but dangerous.

Children have to learn, even before they start school, that boundaries go with life, that impulses must contend with rules, for everyone's sake. All the time, of course, children *do* learn to stay away from moving automobiles, lest they be hit. They learn that they mustn't grab things in a store. They learn "please," "thank you," and table manners. They learn to hear others out, rather than intrude because something happens to have crossed their mind. Such learning, however, is not a mysterious gift from on high — it requires constant teaching on our part as parents or surrogate parents (at home, at school). The best way for us to do so is to make clear to our children, as I guess I finally did in that classroom, that we really mean what we say when we are setting restrictions.

For example, before eating, a child ought to wash his or her hands, an elementary exercise in "public health." The parent can set the example — and if necessary, makes clear that no one comes to the table unwashed. Similarly, with a sensible (but minimal) dress code.

Freud's daughter, Anna, the distinguished child psychoanalyst, once observed that children who become truculent "haven't really been given the *attention* that the imposition of discipline requires from parents and teachers." She meant by "attention" a consistency of attitude that is conveyed as need requires, with affectionate firmness. A child then experiences love not only as hugs and kisses, but as constant reminders and corrections — even an occasional outburst or loss of temper. No one *recommends* such "fits" on our adult part, yet in retrospect I realize that for those desperate children in that fourth-grade class, my "fit" was, really, a gesture of concern — of concern not only for myself as a teacher in jeopardy, but for a group of youngsters in dire straits. Those children were at the mercy of their worse side, which had yet to be toughly countered by me with a firm statement of what would no longer be allowed and why.

Of course, today we often worry about being *too* strict. Guilt may assail us because our own lives don't allow enough time for our children. Yet, the worst thing that we can do to our children is to leave them at the mercy of their impulses — then we will, indeed, have something to regret. A parent's moral authority is, actually, a gift to a child. A child not taught "no" can become a slob, can become endlessly demanding, spoiled.

Children are likely to be more understanding of us — the nature of our life and its demands — than we may realize. We do them (and ourselves) no good by worrying about whether we have earned the right to assert authority over them in those daily ways that constitute a big part of any young family's life. I *do* remember, actually, holding my tongue quite consciously as a beginning teacher of that fourth-grade class — I felt so privileged, compared to those children, and I worried that if I really "cracked down" on them, I'd be adding one more insult to lives already heavily burdened. In fact, ironically, I was contributing to those burdens through a failure to exert a missing moral leadership. Such leadership is, of course, our responsibility as adults, and must be exerted to help our children grow ethically. They copy us, imitate our moral acts.

So it goes, too, in our more fortunate world — we need to know to say no, because children have a great need for no as well as yes, for a frown now and then, as the occasion demands, as well as a smile: a parent at the table, for instance, insisting on a reasonable civility, a respect for others and, yes, for the food itself.

A firm no can be, actually, a big yes — a sense of purpose and control and direction supplied to a child, who otherwise is left to the mercy of whim and fancy and urge, undeterred by a knowing, solid conscience.

51

Doctors and Death

F OR PHYSICIANS death, naturally and inevitably, is the great protagonist, the enemy ever to be considered, challenged. Every day
doctors struggle with life-threatening illnesses, in an effort to enable
their patients to have more time on this earth, and a better time of
it while here. In the past half-century, with the arrival of antibiotics
as a means of dealing with infectious diseases, chemotherapy as a way
of curbing, at least somewhat, the devouring wildness of cancer, a
host of drugs and surgical procedures, not to mention dietary recommendations, as a response to what for a while seemed like a growing
epidemic of coronary (and hypertensive) heart disease, doctors have
become much stronger, more resilient, knowing, assured, and accomplished warriors, able to stay the hand of death to the point that
the biblical three score and ten is now not an ideal dream, granted
a lucky few, but the reasonable expectation of most of us who live in
late twentieth-century America. Indeed, our *older* elderly (eighty-five
and beyond) increase rapidly, and centenarians are no longer a rare
presence among us.

Still, there has to be an end of this mortal life, and how that conclu-
sion is allowed to take place tells a lot about us. Some people take their
lives into their own hands, do away with themselves, even though
they are in the best of health, physically; we call them suicides, and
a number of us call them "sick," psychiatric "cases." Some people are
foolhardy, take big risks — end up dying way before their natural time
for an end of life; we call them "accident-prone," or adventurous to
a fault, or more portentously, folks who are "driven," who are "acting
out" one or another kind of "self-destructive" impulse. Then there are
those who are quite elderly, who have become ghosts of their former selves, who are in nursing homes, who are hardly aware of the
world around them, or indeed, for all practical purposes, are unaware
of anyone or anything — we think of them as "gone," yet they cling to
life, and if they get, say, pneumonia, they may be brought through it
with antibiotics, or left to die. Similarly with younger people, victims
of horrible accidents, terrible diseases — who survive because modern
medical technology (the respirator, most especially) enables them to
breathe, and further technology, to be fed. Not rarely, the heart beats,

the lungs are made to work, hence the blood gets its oxygen, but the brain is effectively dead.

All of the above is common knowledge — yet the matter of our response to such tragedies is now the subject of heightened controversy. How ought we regard those who take their lives? How ought we regard those who, pregnant, want to end the life they are carrying within themselves? How ought we physicians behave when we have the patients described above in our care — the elderly senile in nursing homes, the victims of illness or other misfortunes who are comatose yet still breathing, even if courtesy of modern machinery? How, for that matter, ought doctors respond to those who are quite alert and talkative, even able to get about, take care of themselves — but are suffering from one or another disease that will soon enough "take" them? More precisely, how ought we respond to patients who are gravely ill, and who want us to help them to die? How ought we respond to the youngest of us, and to their parents — infants born way before their normal time of arrival. Again, machines enable the survival of younger and younger "preemies," as such infants are called, and the doctors attending them have good reason to worry about the fate of those children, even if they do survive — the serious neurophysiological consequences.

I haven't, alas, exhausted even the possible questions, never mind taken up the task of replying to each one of them. We all know of Dr. Kevorkian, and those he has enabled to die, and we know of the Hemlock Society, and its concern that those who want to die have that "right." We know of doctors who without inhibiting moral reservations regularly perform abortions. We know, increasingly, of doctors who "assist" their dying patients — give them not only enough medication for pain, every patient's full due, but medication that enables them to take their own lives, or medication (given by others) that will accelerate death's arrival. In that last regard, the courts have now entered the picture, and voters and state legislatures as well — a growing sentiment that patients dying, and experiencing great limitation, suffering, or even, anticipating such vulnerability, and anxious to make an end of it, be helped along by their physicians, and similarly, those who are beyond such choice (comatose, for example) and who in their "living wills" have stated a desire not to be "rescued" through "heroic measures" from final death when, for all practical purposes (so their doctors and family members are asked to judge), the time has come when they are already "gone."

I struggle with the above matters all the time. I teach medical students, hear them also struggling. Two of my sons are young physicians, and I hear them struggling, and one of my sons is a medical student, and I hear him trying to make sense of all this. Again and again, I come back to Walker Percy's last novel, *The Thanatos Syndrome*, to his reminder and warning in it — that doctors had best be wary, indeed, of the uses to which they can end up being put. Percy had in mind the doctors who worked for Hitler and Stalin, the doctors who became enlisted in so-called "eugenics" programs, in efforts at "euthanasia," in initiatives meant to "sterilize" this kind of person, "rid" us of that kind of person: an attitude toward life (we feel ourselves not only free to end it, prevent it, but righteous in so doing); and, of course, an attitude toward death (it is not something to be resisted, but rather welcomed, even facilitated, all depending on the notion of who is "entitled" to live, or who no longer "desires" to live). For Percy, the ultimate moral and philosophical issue was not only our notion of "them" (those who are to be edged toward death, or, yes, prevented from living), but our sense of who "we" are — the ones who advocate this or that approach or point of view and, most especially, the ones who implement death, the doctors who write prescriptions, pull plugs, do "procedures." We thereby take unto ourselves a moral authority second to none: we fallible human beings now become judges as to who ought to stay among us, who ought to leave — and when, and how. It is, Percy indicated, a matter of the proverbial "slippery slope" — until, horror of horrors, doctors are helping all sorts of ideologues take all kinds of people, all sorts of life, into their own hands.

I will now try to be as forthright and personal as I know how to be, and say this: I believe that we do not "own" our own lives; that life is *given* us, by nature and God, both; that our jobs as physicians is to heal, to try to fight with all our might illness, pain, suffering of body and mind, both. No question, heartbreaking moments come upon us as we try to contend with horribly frightening, terrible turns of fate — the excruciating pain of cancer, the progressive confinement, the paralysis of amyotrophic lateral sclerosis, known as Lou Gehrig's disease, the weird and insidiously humiliating onslaught of multiple sclerosis, and, as already discussed, the melancholy circumstances that can surround either an infant's arrival or an elderly person's impending departure, not to mention a chronically ill person's day-to-day existence, or the victim of an accident as he or she lies on a bed in a hospital: life is so fragile, so thwarted, so impaired, so threatened, so racked by pain, so hard to endure. Still, the issue, finally, is *whose* life, even as the issue, finally, for doctors, is whose life *theirs* is, as well — meaning which set of moral and spiritual principles and laws (if, indeed, *any!*) ought to guide us and, yes, determine the nature and limits of our medical behavior, which (let us not forget) is also our personal behavior.

We live in a society insistent upon (if not obsessed with) "rights." But what of responsibilities, obligations — do we owe any regard to life itself, as something holy, entrusted to us to hold dear, think of as a precious presence, however frail and odd and hurt its nature? A doctor is one who tries to work with such people as human companions of theirs — to do all he or she possibly can do to make things better for them, improve their prospects, their daily comfort. A doctor, to my way of thinking, is not one meant to end life purposely, as a matter of course or routine. I understand that I am now making qualifications, that the definition of the word "purposely" varies among us physicians — but I am talking, here, about a moral attitude, about the moral assumptions of medical practice as it ordinarily takes place. Many of us have been known to withhold heroic measures when a patient is, say, dying of cancer, has become comatose. Many of us, as a matter of fact, quietly use common sense — don't, for instance, go "all out" to keep the heart beating, the lungs working, of someone whose brain has effectively died. But Dr. Kevorkian's behavior is, as the expression goes, "something else again," and the remarks of some who support him have become broadly ideological, have referred to death as if it is an ally, a friend, an "alternative," one keeps hearing — that word a dangerously open-ended one. Death comes to all of us, in its own time, and doctors who start treating it as a colleague of sorts are, I fear, beginning a walk on a road lined with lawyers, judges, bureaucrats — functionaries, all, of the modern, secular state, with its insistent utilitarianism, its grandiose materialism, its unqualified worship of the sovereign self.

What today's doctors desperately need is knowledge of, experience with the great possibilities of hospice care — the way it is now possible to help people die with dignity, even grace. I believe every medical student ought to rotate through a spell of hospice acquaintance — work in one; and similarly with medical residents: an important part of a doctor's knowledge and training. That way, we who learn to struggle against illness will learn how to do so, when, alas, defeat is around the corner: we will learn how to medicate our patients so they are not in pain; and we will learn how to care for them — body and mind, both — so that they have a good chance of going over to the other side, so to speak, with composure, even with a measure of relief and gratitude to those men and women who have helped take away fear and suffering from a final goodbye.

52

Fra Angelico

A T THE DAWN OF HISTORY men and women affirmed their humanity by making pictures — scratches in obscure caves, for instance, which remind us, today, that we are not only doers and talkers, but a creature who sees, hence our need for seers, for visionaries. Indeed, every night we in our dreams construct pictures which may or may not be accompanied by sound (words). Once I heard Anna Freud talk about dreams in a way that has stayed with me when I listen to patients, but also when I go visit a museum or look at a book that offers the work of a particular artist: "Dreams are pictures. We literally 'see things' at night — and often without words. When we wake up, if we remember what we dreamed — *saw* — it is then that we resort to words, to explain what we observed. Yes, some of us have conversations in our dreams (or arguments!), but often the dream is a 'silent movie,' rather than one with a soundtrack, and in any case, it is a series of pictures, which our analysands then explain to us, later, with language. I notice that when I ask a patient what he *saw*, what she was *picturing* [in a dream], I'm often greeted by surprise, confusion. If I ask to be *told* about a dream — that is what is expected. Words are the arbiter, you see, of that middle-of-the-night movie our brain offers all of us quite regularly!"

An experienced psychoanalyst, in her own way, was remarking upon the cultural subordination of pictures to words, no matter the biological universality of the visual, and no matter its narrative possibilities, which we vastly underestimate, all too often, in favor of talk, and more talk, and not only in the clinical settings Miss Freud had in mind. At another point, actually, Miss Freud allowed herself to go further, speculate in this manner: "Today we see so much — the movies and television keep our eyes quite busy — but I'm not sure people are finding, that way, what they're looking for."

I hastened, immediately, to ask for an amplification, but she was always made uncomfortable by social or ethical commentary, even when prompted by her own ironic and reflective nature. She told me that she didn't want to "overgeneralize," but she did think that people want to be "entertained" visually, true, but also hoped for (looked for) something else: "I think our ancestors used their eyes to find clues for survival — and now, that we live so much more safely than they could ever even imagine, I wonder whether our eyes still don't try to help us figure out how to survive."

I so wanted her to elaborate, but nothing doing. Her eyes twinkled, but her voice was now unforthcoming. I wondered aloud about "moral survival" — our need to figure out visually what is ugly and what is beautiful, what is dangerous and what is useful, helpful, necessary, and, too, who seems friendly, welcoming, and who appears sullen, mean, withholding. She concurred, but we were sidetracked by our need to discuss a particular psychoanalytic concept about which the two of us were to write — talk about the ascendancy of the verbal over the visual!

I thought of that conversation of twenty years ago as I looked, recently, at the work of the fifteenth-century painter (and Dominican monk) known as Fra Angelico — I remembered learning of him, learning from him, back in college and, later, from my wife, Jane, who loved his work. In college, alas, this extraordinarily able and accomplished painter was given relatively little notice — we had others to attend, who came after him by a generation or two (but who shared a city, a part of a century with him): Leonardo da Vinci and Michelangelo, who also graced the fifteenth century and the city of Florence. They were part of the Renaissance; they anticipated "us" in so many ways. Leonardo's scientific curiosity mattered, not to mention his wide-ranging intellectual interests, his subtle psychological awareness (earning him the anointment, eventually, of a major essay by Freud) — in short, his modernity, no matter the five hundred years that separates him from this century. Michelangelo's splendid, brilliant, knowing humanism also mattered — his genius as an artist and sculptor, a man in the tradition of Plato and Dante (he revered both of them), who tried hard and long to render beauty, to reveal the possibilities within us, the splendor of our unique creaturely existence as the apple (so to speak) of God's eye, despite our all too evident and relentless "down" side. For us not especially humble students in a highfalutin seminar offered in a big-shot secular college, Fra Angelico was a gentle soul of obvious religious purity, who had to give way fast to those two giants and others (Raphael, for instance, another Italian painter who was born in the fifteenth century and spent time in Florence). Indeed, Raphael's religious work, as with that of Michelangelo, was held up high in that classroom and others as exemplary, as worth our considered and considerable attention: again, the fabled and important Renaissance, its wondrously gifted artists a reminder of — well, ourselves, all that we are or might be, given enough time, education, encouragement. Put differently, in art history classes we were learning about religious humanism in its variousness, its enormous distinction — not a subject matter that includes, say, Fra Angelico's fresco paintings at the Dominican priory of San Marco in Florence.

No question, Fra Angelico (his paintings were called "angelic" by another Dominican, a poet, and the name stuck to him personally) was no great figure in the Florentine assertion of "man" as a cause for representation, celebration. Rather, a monk chose to bring alive the Christian story on the walls of monasteries, at their altars; but so doing, this monk had his eyes trained on God in all His mysterious presence, rather than on man — the God who for a while became one of us. In the San Marco frescos the story of that arrival from on high unfolds, from the Annunciation to the Crucifixion — a vivid, compelling, awe-struck narration conveyed with tact, dignity, reverence, commanding austerity, delicacy, refinement. This story is told, obviously, in retrospect — and by someone who was within the church. The point, then, is not to see ourselves writ large in Jesus and His disciples, but to reflect upon a story become infinitely more significant than any or all of us, a heavenly story which it is the Catholic Church's solemn and joyous obligation to keep relaying, emphasizing, holding up to us (we who are so quick to forget, as people have known long before contemporary psychoanalysis put its spin on that aspect of our nature).

For Fra Angelico the fresco paintings which adorn San Marco are meant to be part of a rendered sanctity: "the word became flesh," yes — but then that "flesh" returned to God's eternity, hence the reverential, the worshipful spirit of those paintings. Moreover, they were meant not for tourists or the nobility, even the church's nobility; they were meant for a "reformed" order of Dominicans, anxious at all costs to emphasize their scrupulous devotion to a church as easily betrayed at any time as Christ was in His time (and sometimes that betrayal, needless to say, is done in the name of the intellect, of cleverness and sophistication). Fra Angelico's was a hieratic art — paintings both sacerdotal in authorship and intent: an insistence on reminding those fellow Dominicans that they have chosen (hope against hope) to join God's world, not make Him and those who knew Him, attended Him, part of our neighborhood crowd. The frescos are Anna Freud's instructive visual presence — of a kind that is not primarily meant to entertain or impress the viewer, with respect to its beauty, but inspire: pictures as moral companions to monks on a spiritual journey; indeed, pictures as a temporal effort to glimpse a destination none of us gets to know while here.

Fra Angelico, like St. Augustine in his *Confessions*, like Walker Percy in *The Moviegoer* and *The Last Gentleman* and in his essays, knew of that oldest of human contraries, "angelism–bestialism," and his art, living up to the colloquial and laudatory name given him, gives us a breathtaking presentation of the angelic realm: pictures in rooms, in hallways, inhabited by monks busy all the time contemplating a divine order of things, a place beyond time and space, praying for their own eventual arrival there. Once, in *The Mocking of Christ*, this monk-artist becomes uncannily, unnervingly "contemporary," his symbolism right out of our present-day preoccupation with the brazen, the wildly symbolic, the derisive, and, not least, the skeptical — disembodied hands, a shouting, hissing disembodied burgher, a blindfolded Christ: here we are, here we have always been, those of us all too cleverly sure of ourselves. Such a brief appearance of "us" aside, the San Marco frescos gave those monks a wordless dream to ponder — a daily witness to accompany their spiritual trek, their chosen life of earthly pilgrimage.

For my wife, Jane, that "angelic" one was a constantly favored companion — with his prayerful simplicity and directness, his fervent, shining faith, his heavenly angle of vision, his unpretentious search for the sublime (and his corresponding humility, even selflessness, or was it a lack of interest in catering to the endless appetite of our egoism?). She was not wont to analyze her reasons, or even those of Fra Angelico — only inclined to take in his soulful dream with wide-eyed gratitude and, years ago, to press that visionary statement, especially in its San Marco incarnation, on her young husband, so taken with this or that prideful, secular hankering for the authority of the moment over the affairs of the here-and-now.

53

Rembrandt's Old Ones

U NLIKE MANY OTHER seventeenth-century painters or, for that
matter, any number of painters who lived in earlier or later
centuries, Rembrandt stubbornly refused to let rich and powerful
people (in his case, they belonged to a prospering Holland) have complete access to his studio, his skills as a master of portraiture. Indeed,
over half of the subjects he decided to attend were of his own choos-
ing — relatives and friends and neighbors, a number of Jews who
lived near his studio, even blacks, and all in all, a substantial percentage of ordinary people whose appearance or habits or manner
of living, whose *being*, really, he happened to find interesting. Moreover, those he found interesting, he made interesting. The individuals
he offers us summon our attention, show us much about themselves,
or so we conclude — Rembrandt, the careful judge of character, the
faithful witness to it, the wonderfully capable mediator of it: on his
canvases he conveys what he, the moral and psychological observer,
has learned, seen.

Rembrandt van Rijn was born in 1601 to working people; his father was a miller, his mother a baker's daughter. Holland was a mighty
nation then, and its citizens were memorialized in different ways by
Frans Hals, who was born twenty-five years before Rembrandt, and
Jan Vermeer, who was born a quarter of a century after him. For
Hals the people who mattered were the prosperous burghers, whom
he presents in all their fulfilled zest for life: they smile and banter;
they eat and drink and seem to be without major worries — as merry
as their observer makes them. They love to dress up, and we are asked
to take note of those clothes, not to mention other possessions: furni-
ture, tableware, an adorned, lucky, secular life which seems secure for
the foreseeable future. For Vermeer, that life was not only promising,
but thoroughly admirable; his subjects seem less brashly, nervously
affluent — they are the well-to-do who have also become genteel, re-
fined, unashamedly pleased with the "culture" they have learned to
possess, an acquisition all its own, a distinctive one, they seem to
know and indicate, as Vermeer gives them the sustained after-life of
a presence on his canvas: *there*, in all the restrained splendor of their
haute bourgeois daily life.

In contrast, Rembrandt struggled hard to take note of another Holland, another world — his was an art both documentary and introspective. His refusal to become owned by the privileged was a rare act of courage — he thereby resisted a constant temptation for artists over the centuries: paint for those with money, paint pictures that tell of their life, paint *them,* and do so in such a way that they are flattered, given the nearest earthly thing to an honored eternity, the continuing life that a painting on display can provide. In contrast, he found inspiration in his own wife, his son, his kin, and, as mentioned, his fellow citizens. He looked around the neighborhood he inhabited, and he also looked back across the centuries, pictured in his mind the Bible's stories, and set himself the task of connecting them to the people with whom he shared a time, a place.

Put differently, Rembrandt embraced a biblical humanism — he wanted to present the figures who appear in Hebrew Scripture and in the New Testament as the men and women they once were, rather than exalt them visually in such a way that they appear larger-than-life, beyond the reach and understanding of us mortals who have come along later: readers of stories once enacted in various locations of what now is called the Middle East. Rembrandt also remembered what many for various reasons have wanted to forget, that the Bible, *all* of it, is a Jewish narrative — so, if one wants to portray not only Abraham and Isaac and their descendants, on canvas, but Jesus and his fisherman friends, his peasant followers, there is every reason to know Jewish people: their faces are the faces of two of the world's great religions. The Rembrandt who gave us *Jeremiah Lamenting the Destruction of Jerusalem,* or *Christ and the Woman of Samaria,* or *St. Peter,* or *St. Paul in Prison,* or *Christ at Emmaus,* or *The Descent from the Cross,* is the Rembrandt who painted *Portrait of an Old Jew, A Jewish Philosopher, Head of an Old Man, Portrait of an Old Woman, Old Man Praying, Two Negroes* — and yes, who drew *The Rat-Killer, Beggar Receiving Alms, Beggar Woman and Child, Jews on the Street.*

We know of his stunning use of light (so admired and emulated by Edward Hopper in our time); he has that light shine on faces, on the Dutch countryside, on animals or rendered historical scenes, religious moments — and the result is a miraculous illumination that endows a picture with a prophetic power worthy of the heavens: God touching us through His gift of genius to an artist who has become something more, a teacher designated from on high to command, then to instruct our otherwise distracted or wayward eyes. In this case, the artist's life, his values and his preferences, seem utterly worthy of such a divine choice. Amidst a good deal of secular pride — the extravagant self-importance of a rising mercantile class, ever eager to see itself pictured, to repeat, as a purchase on immortality — a painter of great distinction chose to look elsewhere, find in the humble and the hurt, the unpopular if not the exiled, the frail and the obscure, an astonishing and persisting inspiration. At the same time, his own moral energy surely endowed those individuals, those neighborhoods with a dignity and authority hitherto unacknowledged — the painter as one who notices and represents, of course, but also as one who extends sanction: you who are lowly matter a great deal, as in "the last shall be first, and the first, last."

I have always been especially touched by Rembrandt's elderly men and women. Sometimes, when I assign stories about the elderly for my students to read (Tillie Olsen's "Tell Me a Riddle," for instance) I show slides of some of Rembrandt's old ones: his *Head of an Old Man, The Old Man Praying, The Portrait of the Old Jew, The Portrait of an Old Jew in an Armchair* — the great strength of those faces, the character written all over them: a life lived, with all its victories and defeats, and a life soon to end, but, oh, what has been learned! The one who has asked them to sit for him has clearly gained so very much from being with them, letting his eyes feast upon their hard-earned practical wisdom as it informs their features.

I had heard of Rembrandt's "old ones" from a college teacher, Benjamin Rowland, who sang of them, virtually, in his remarks to us in a class as he projected picture after picture of them on a screen — an ode to their justly celebrated being, courtesy of a particular artist. At the time, twenty years old myself, I was interested in mid-century America's blandishments available to students: jazz in particular, and cars that moved fast, fast, and skis that also made for velocity — lean, bent bodies sent speeding down mountains. As I looked at those "old ones" I wondered why this sustained hymn to those worn folks, long gone? If Rembrandt was a "great one," I thought back then, let us keep a vigil by his *Night Watch,* or his series of *Anatomy Lessons,* or his portraits of fancier folk, such as the one we all went to see in the Isabella Stewart Gardner Museum in Boston (*Portrait of a Man and His Wife*). But a teacher's lyrical appreciation of an inexpressibly tender, affecting *Return of the Prodigal Son* got us all unnerved, made us realize (I now know) our own prodigality; made us begin to take notice — and, indeed, twenty years later, while talking with several elderly, Spanish-speaking women in a village of northern New Mexico, my mind raced back to that classroom, to those slides with their magical ability to turn us a bit inward, reflective, in response to the obvious and compelling thoughtfulness of people we were meeting through a visionary artist's efforts and too, the technology that delivered his work of long ago, far away, to us in a seminar room.

When one of those elderly ladies of Truchas, New Mexico, referred to her and her age-mates as "old ones," and amplified with the comment that "we are waiting to be called home by the Lord," I somehow, for some reason, found myself recalling Rembrandt's old men, old women — and when that same lady of Truchas told me that she looked forward to mingling "in God's Kingdom with others allowed to stay here [on earth] a long time," I suddenly imagined her and her husband, both so gentle and wise and kindly, conversing with their counterparts of seventeenth-century Holland, who caught a great painter's eye, and who survive across the centuries for us to behold: the repositories of an enlightenment that decades of human experience provide. Yet, not all of us are able to recognize lived virtue when it presents itself; and so a great artist was also a Dutch moral psychologist, fully aware of whom and what he wanted to bathe in the arresting, haunting light he could cast upon his portraits, his landscapes, his religious stories: heaven's glow sent our way unforgettably.

54

Münch's Look Inward

F OR MANY YEARS in my teaching I have tried to connect the suggestive and visionary power of certain artists with the narrative energy of writers who, for me, are soulmates of those painters. With college students, I link Raymond Carver's stories (their blunt, unaffected American realism) to Edward Hopper's pictures (their similar insistence on offering a glimpse, and more, of how it can go — be — in our homes and offices and streets). Both Carver and Hopper give us the concrete details of twentieth-century life in the United States; yet, both of them cumulatively convey something else — a hint or two about what is happening below the surface of a certain kind of life: the wariness and perplexity, the unrest and apprehension that can eat away at the soul, even as one shoulders with ostensible calm all sorts of daily burdens, tasks.

My first teaching, however, was done with fellow physicians. I taught a seminar for a mix of psychiatric and pediatric residents, with a few interested medical students also in attendance. We read books and articles by Freud, and his daughter Anna, and Erik H. Erikson — the literate giants of the psychoanalytic tradition. At the time I was working closely with Erikson, helping him teach his courses, and working on a biography of him. He had come to psychoanalysis from art — he made woodcuts and drawings as a young man. Once, as he talked of his youth, he made this observation: "Artists don't need to talk — they see, and help others to see." At the time, I was struggling with talk, the dense jargon of the social sciences and, alas, the increasingly impenetrable shoptalk of psychiatry and psychoanalysis — such a contrast with the clear, storytelling prose to be found in the writing of the two Freuds and, of course, Erikson. I decided to amplify the syllabus, respond to the spirit of those three by calling upon an artist whose work I had studied as a college student — the paintings (and lithographs and etchings) of Edvard Münch. As we discussed certain essays, we'd stop and look at one or another picture of Münch's — let his way of seeing things, representing them, become part of our time together: his constant look inward an encouragement for a similar effort on our part.

I know of no other artist who understood what modern psychological introspection, courtesy of Freud and his followers, hastened to tell us. Münch was, in fact, a contemporary of Freud's — the latter was seven years his senior. Both men, as it were, split their time between two centuries, approximately half in the nineteenth, half in the twentieth; and both perused the mind's life as avid, knowing observers, intent on chronicling for others what they had learned through intense self-scrutiny, Freud through his own dreams, never mind those of his patients, and Münch through his interest in moving from Impressionism, with its emphasis on the artist's personal authority as an observer, to what became known as Expressionism — a determination to use that authority not only in the way the outside world of persons, places, things is presented, but in a personal, introspective exploration: the artist's moods, reveries, preoccupations, worries, as a subject matter all its own. Indeed, in the last decade of the nineteenth century, well before Freud had published the account of his own struggle to figure out the workings of the mind (*The Interpretation of Dreams* appeared in 1900) Münch had amassed a major witness of sorts to human subjectivity — a series of lithographs, etchings, paintings that explored the full range of feeling to which men and women are heir. The very titles he gave to his work tell a story — *Melancholy, Anxiety, Jealousy, The Scream, Attachment, Parting, Puberty, The Sick Child, The Dance of Life, Amor and Psyche, The Voice, Chamber of Death:* an attempt to probe the breadth and depth of existence as we humans know it, in the hope of putting before us the yearnings we experience, the fears and doubts and misgivings, the outright chilling dread with which we also not rarely must contend.

In a sense, Münch was a wordless psychologist and theologian — he could render the mind's conflicts, its hopes come to naught, its errors as they spread panic across a face, work their way through a body, humbling it to a hump. He could fathom the heart of our humanity, the questions we keep asking about the meaning of life, and render what he came to understand in picture after picture — men and women struggling to stay alive, to find a place where they feel safe, a person whom they can trust, a world that beckons rather than frightens. He reached out mightily, if again, silently, to his ordinary fellow countrymen, to those who harvest crops, shovel snow, to "workmen on their way home," such efforts a Scandinavian tone-poem of sorts, a symphonic celebration of the many kinds of laboring people who walk our streets, enable our lives through a daily commitment of time, of energy. Painstaking in that regard, Münch never allowed himself to become smitten with himself, as it were — never became yet another gifted person who consorted with the wealthy and, soon enough, took on their sometime arrogance, self-importance. As a matter of fact, he shunned a practice most painters eagerly seek — to sell canvases, once completed, at higher and higher prices. He kept most of his oil paintings, bequeathing them posthumously to the people of his native land — and so, in Oslo his life's harvest is now on permanent display in a special museum dedicated to his work.

"Death defines us," I once heard Reinhold Niebuhr say — the singular awareness we as a creature possess that an end to this earthly life is inevitable. For Münch such an awareness came early: his mother died when he was five; his sister when he was fourteen; his father when the son was twenty-six. Though he himself lived just past eighty, he was (from the start of his career) struggling pictorially with death both literally and figuratively — the effect of sickness on our appearance; the risk of loss that goes with friendship, with love; the contingent and vulnerable side of our daily situation. The people who figure in his paintings and lithographs are often at the seeming mercy of dangers both within and without which they don't know how to comprehend, let alone conquer. They try to withdraw; they writhe or scream; they huddle; they stare in confusion and alarm and foreboding. They are our distraught contemporaries, struggling with all sorts of demons, with anxieties and fears that grip hard, inform daily lives, persist during sleep in dreams that become nightmares.

Münch knew Ibsen, Strindberg; he read and much appreciated Kierkegaard — his fellow Scandinavian seers and mystics, who cut to the barebone of our mortal precariousness and took scant refuge in the materialist consolations many of us have learned to treasure, to revere, and yes, out of an agnostic desperation, to worship extravagantly. No wonder Münch's scenes, urban and countryside, are stripped of the decorative, the pretty, the diversionary. He is searching for a rock-bottom sense of what it means to be alive — to embrace and love, to work with pride, but also to grow old or fall sick, to lose and to leave for good. He could easily paint conventional portraits or natural settings, and he sometimes did — but mostly he defies the "normal," the bounds of social realism, not to be tricky or irregular or defiant, but out of a felt emotional necessity wedded to a gifted artist's craft. He was determined, like Freud, to break barriers and customs, challenge the accepted, the orthodox, take the risks of forthright psychological inquiry, both personal and communal, hence his brooding self-portraits, his unnerving street scenes that give us crowds collectively huddled, afraid; and hence, too, his capacity to endow an animal (*The Galloping Horse*), or a building (*The Red Vine*) with the kind of heightened feeling he can work into his human subjects, who are, it can be said, existentially strung out: at the very edge of things, because all too in touch with what bothers or assails or scares or tempts them.

For my students Edvard Münch has been a marvelously telling teacher. His vivid colors speak of the passions that beckon us and, alas, sometimes won't let go of us. His disembodied faces pop out of nowhere, as in memories that come to us unexpectedly — the return in our random thoughts or our dreams of those we have known, but lost. His symbolic distortions, enlargements, exaggerations speak of our ever-present inclination to invest the world around us with a private significance that often enough eludes even our own comprehension. In a sense, this wordless poet struggled bravely to subdue his own demons by daring to suppose, as Freud did, that they are not, after all, so idiosyncratic or private — that all of us are psychological and spiritual kin, placed here fatefully and, not rarely, unsure how to acquit ourselves, or where, if anyplace, we may be headed down the line. In several instances Münch has his created individuals whirling about with a certain feverishness, or he has his men and women (out of loneliness, or frustrated eagerness, or both) looking on at others caught in such a frenzy — this dance of life, whose drama he wanted so very much to narrate, whose risky unpredictability he knew how to evoke with brilliance, whose lively but mysterious qualities he insisted on investigating, depicting: the grandly accomplished, knowing, but mute psychologist of paintbrush and pigment.

55

Their Eyes Were Watching God

W HEN MY WIFE, Jane, and I were working with the children of migrant farm workers in Southern Florida (the early and middle 1960s) we were wonderfully instructed by a public health nurse, Mary McMahon, who took us to meet a number of families with whom she had become acquainted. Mary knew hundreds of boys and girls whose parents harvested the abundant crops enabled by the rich muck land near the Everglades. She could be seen daily in Bean City, in Pahokee, in Belle Glade, near Lake Okeechobee, giving children their "shots" — vaccines to prevent various illnesses. She observed us talking with those youngsters, with their parents, as well — and she noticed how hard it was, sometimes, for us to understand what we were hearing: two Yankees who had spent their lives in white suburban communities, now trying to learn how hard-working and humble "pickers" (the word commonly used) lived their lives, reared their sons and daughters. Mary was herself Negro (then the favored friendly description) — and a legend among the people, as one of them, a mother of five who was also a champion at "doing" tomatoes and beans, let us know: "She be one of us, but one of you, too — see what I mean? Lord, it's a miracle, meeting someone of her education who be one of us and who has stayed here. They move out — that's what usually happens."

One day, as I sat with my tape recorder, listening for a second time around to a conversation I'd had with that particularly strong-minded and vibrant woman just quoted, Mary noticed my furrowed brow, my body arched noticeably, my ear almost affixed to the machine, and offered once more to be my translator. She'd helped in that way before, and I was preparing to accept, again, her generous assistance, when she suddenly had a change of mind, a new idea: "I believe you ought to go read — go *study* Zora Neale Hurston's book. That way you'll become more familiar with what's being told you."

I had never heard of Zora Neale Hurston, and soon I was hearing about her life, her career as an anthropologist, a folklorist, an essayist, a writer of fiction, short and long, and most especially, her greatest work, *Their Eyes Were Watching God*, which was then, however, out of print. Mary lent us a copy, though; and in no time we were meeting, getting to know the story's heroine, Janie, whose lyrical, blunt,

earthy vernacular language did, indeed, resemble what we were hearing from people, whose background was much like hers — folks who
lived close to the land, who had no schooling to speak of, yet who
(in sudden, unexpected flights of the moral imagination) could take
on with sense and sensitivity questions worthy of philosophers, scholars, artists. It was to such people that Hurston paid close heed; they
are given voice throughout her novel — Janie's search for a "place" in
this life, for a person she could love and respect, takes us close to a
whole world of men and women emotionally fragile, yet as wry and
savvy as they are vulnerable and impoverished. Moreover, Hurston's
characters, for the most part, speak for themselves — their manner of
talking, their choice of words, of images, a challenge and a gift to
the reader, and an opportunity, as well: to cross the confines of race
or class or both in order to immerse oneself in the spoken idiom of
those who are fellow American citizens, though compelled to endure
a singularly hard-pressed fate.

Hurston's novel was published in 1937, in the midst of the Great
Depression — just after James Agee and Walker Evans had returned
from their two-month stint in Hale County, Alabama, on assignment
from *Fortune* to observe the way Southern sharecroppers and tenant
farmers lived. Those two white men, and their white editors, were interested in how *white* agricultural workers were managing — but not
to such an extent that they tried to render their speech, their particular (and defining) way with words. Agee begs our forgiveness for
his intrusiveness as a social observer — and proceeds to use the occasion of his Dixie journey as a writer's (performing) chance: he tells us
what crosses his mind in his own arresting, erudite, inviting voice. An
encounter with Southern, farming families becomes, ultimately, an encounter of the reader's with a brilliantly knowing, provocative author,
and his friend, whose elegantly planned, considered pictures reveal the
exquisite control exerted by an already accomplished artist. Not that
Hurston doesn't also help us along as we move through Janie's life.
The authorial third person is very much a presence at certain times,
but defers constantly to the characters, their talk: a style all its own,
and one that brings the reader closer to a particular world than some
of our best documentary writers could manage.

In a sense, Hurston's novel introduced my wife and me to people
whose lives we were already witnessing, but hadn't even come close
to comprehending. Hurston's Janie is a picaresque heroine on the
existentialist search we tend, unfortunately, to reserve for the well-to-
do, the well-educated, whose language, actually, can sometimes be far
more opaque and frustrating than any to be found in any chapter of

this relatively short but insinuating novel. As one works so hard to come to terms with the dialogue one thereby quits one's own world, develops a different sense of what to expect as forthcoming in the words, the ideas, the narrated memories, the point of view of the various individuals who speak in the story's twenty chapters.

This is a novel eagerly (and correctly) summoned these days by women as very much theirs. Hurston gives voice constantly to the yearnings of Janie for a self-respect not at the mercy of this or that man's moody or demanding egoism — socially and culturally sanctioned by a world's principalities and powers. Still, Janie's introspective musings often make her nothing more or less than a human being and, too, a creature of God's, hence the title: these are people who know to look beyond the travail of this life, even beyond the trials and tragedies visited by an unpredictable nature, not to mention an all too predictable chain of circumstances that we subsume under (to be explained by) those abstract "variables" called "race," "class." In a way, Hurston has her characters leap free of such categorical insistences — this is not a "feminist" novel, a novel of "protest," an Afro-American novel, but rather one that does fine justice to a character's determination to wonder constantly about this life's reasons, its surprises and its uncertainties, its fulfillments and its disappointments, to all of which we are all privy.

To be sure, Janie is "colored," and white people figure in her life as nameless, faceless instruments of force, of danger, of inscrutable will. Nor are we denied a close look at a terrible aspect of American poverty, injustice — hard-working folk who get precious little for all their expended labor. Yet, this is a human scene of great vitality, hence the descriptions of the juke joints, the all-night bars that cater to a bedeviled, though strangely vibrant migrant farm worker population, men and women living for the moment, singing and shouting and laughing and crying, hoping against hope, waiting always for sun up and a long day's working until sundown, then some sleep, maybe, but some moments of furtive or frantic celebration, a liaison with "life" — whereby jazz, the blues, beer, wine, and dancing become a collective testimony: we are down, but don't anyone, please, count us out. I love this paragraph in particular, read it every year to my class: "All night now the jukes clanged and clamored. Pianos living three lifetimes in one. Blues made and used right on the spot. Dancing, fighting, singing, crying, laughing, winning and losing love every hour. Work all day for money. Fight all night for love. The rich black earth clinging to bodies and biting the skin like ants."

The "ants," be it noted, are not a people reduced to an anthill —

the desperate imagery of our twentieth-century effort to understand Nazi and Soviet totalitarianism. These are very much men and women walking upright, on the lookout for constant danger, true, but trying with their eyes, their ears, their minds and hearts, to find purpose and meaning in this life. Moreover, the novel is a story told, shared with a friend — a life's earned wisdom offered one person by another. That is who we are, finally, an author wants us to understand — the creature whose skin pigment, or bankbook, or place of residence does not banish a capacity or hunger for introspection, for figuring out the gifts and hurts which time presents us. Janie looks and looks. Her eyes and "their eyes" of the title seek explanations, a comprehension of this human experience that binds us all together. She looks to others, of course, but she also gazes inward and upward, at life's summoning beauty, at its terrible mischief, as well: trees show their splendor, the earth its munificence, but the skies darken and bring us a hurricane's devastation, and in the end, the loss of her beloved Tea Cake to the madness of rabies, to death. Higher than what we can apprehend is the unseen: our eyes watching for God, ever trying to fathom His ways, the attempt a defining aspect of our humanity — and it is that gift (the capacity and will for such a spiritual inquiry) which Zora Neale Hurston bestows on her Janie and, by extension, on us readers lucky to encounter her on the printed page.

56

Ibsen's *Wild Duck*

A GAIN AND AGAIN in his plays Henrik Ibsen asked his theater-going audiences to contemplate the hypocrisies, the deceptions, the phony pretenses that pass for normal, conventional social life. He was a master satirist or, at his more subdued moments, a clever iro-nist who had a way of cutting to the bone, bringing to our attention the excuses and justifications we summon as a means of getting our own way, at all costs. His genius lay in his seductive ability to make a temporary alliance with those who read or listened to his words — as if he and those who attended him were (for a while) a "we": a con-trast with one or another "them," a lower order of creature morally and psychologically. By the end of an Ibsen play, however, that con-nection is often frayed, if not dissolved: the playwright has intensified his scorn, cast his net wider, made clear his desire that each of us, himself included, confront the various duplicities we spend a lifetime brushing under this or that rug.

Of all his plays, *The Wild Duck* (1881) is the most uncanny in its mix of the tender, the lyrical, the sardonic. Ibsen offers a fiercely un-relenting cultural criticism that doesn't stop short of taking on the social critic in himself: the playwright who condemns and ridicules, but who thereby, not rarely, does his own kind of damage, and at a high cost, indeed, to others. As a matter of fact, that play may be Ibsen's most confessional — the prophetic writer warning his eager followers that they had best look inward as well as outward, figure out whose dire warnings and predictions are worth taking seriously, and for what reasons. We are all gullible (because vulnerable and needy and perplexed) in various ways — and around any corner a pied piper awaits us with an enticing tune which we embrace with a revealing readiness.

Put differently, Ibsen is interested in the blind spots that prompt our personal or collective downfall — and so, in *The Wild Duck* a phys-ical blindness afflicts one of the characters. The play, in a way, tells of the blind leading the blind; it presents a story of late nineteenth-century bourgeois calculation and betrayal — the kind that takes place in living rooms and bedrooms, rather than in the larger arena of politics and commerce. The man who comes to expose that state of affairs, put everything out for inspection, turns out to be the biggest "liar" of all, because he fails to see the terrible damage that a certain kind of aggressive, single-minded candor can inflict. Here, the playwright dares take himself, and us with him, for a walk on the proverbial thin ice he seems determined to find tempting — because instructive. His character, Gregers Werle, has discovered certain truths about his own father and, as well, his own friends. He turns away from his father, takes himself to those friends, and step by step, scene by scene, strips away the misinformation, the illusions which have, it seems, been essential to the everyday survival of everyone in sight. This agent of realism presents himself as an idealist — as in Milton's insistence in *Aereopagitica,* that the "truth" is liberating. But what *is* "truth" — or rather, whose truth, understood by whom, in what way, makes for the kind of freedom Milton presumably had in mind: a more honest and honorable life? By the time Ibsen's play is over a child has committed suicide even as her father has learned that he is probably not her biological parent. The grandfather's maimed wild duck, kept in the attic with other birds and wild animals, haunts the play and its characters — nature's beauty (*its* truth) a hurt, custodial captive to our human folly, our willful intent on tricking ourselves, never mind fooling one another. That "wild duck" is, of course, within us: our lovely and innocent side that occasionally soars, or moves wondrously along the course of our lives — but can be shot down quite abruptly by quite another aspect of ourselves. As a matter of fact, Ibsen's play is meant to tell us that — show how we hurt one another, ruin our gentle and attractively harmless and beguiling selves by surrendering, for one reason or another, to the mean-spirited smugness and, worst of all, the self-centeredness that he is at pains to document, to put before us in ways large and small: the obvious stinginess and arrogance of one character, the less apparent foolishness and selfishness of another.

Worst of all, he seems to be telling us, are those who dupe themselves, never mind others — who wrap themselves in the clothes of asserted virtue and pursue its cause by meddling in the lives of others. There is, sadly, some of today's social and psychological reformer in the play's protagonist, Gregers Werle: he wants others to see, but he doesn't himself see the disastrous consequences of his meliorist zeal — he misses, that is, the hugely manipulative egoism that informs his efforts. Those of us today who are constantly urging people to lay themselves bare, say anything and everything in the interests of scrupulous self-revelation, have much to learn from this play, which was published over fifteen years before Freud's first book appeared. No wonder, he would mention Ibsen's work at some

length in one of his important psychoanalytic essays — the psychological savvy in *The Wild Duck* must have startled the young Viennese
doctor as he contemplated the human mind, even as he would acknowledge a "surrender" on his part to the tumultuously brilliant
novels of Dostoyevsky, with their storehouse of awareness of how
the mind works.

I have called upon Ibsen's plays often in my teaching of undergraduates, medical students. He has a sharp eye out for the kind of
self-importance that is not, alas, rare in academic settings — a conviction that factuality will eventually banish our various personal and
social difficulties. He is too easily embraced as a sharply knowing, progressive observer, whose plays, taken to heart, will liberate us from the
narrowness of this or that old order. True, he was a tough social critic,
who smelled all sorts of stale pretense a mile away and was willing
to say loud and clear what he felt to be true. But he worried about
that posture — its hazards and risks, to the point that his plays can
be unsatisfying for those interested in clear-cut moral (and social and
political) distinctions. At the end of *The Wild Duck* lives have been
destroyed, trust broken, in the name of a relentless righteousness that
has, really, run amok.

Uncannily, a century ago, Ibsen anticipated our psychologically obsessed culture, with its demand that everything be put on the table,
nothing be left unsaid, unacknowledged. God forbid, that we avert
our glance now and then, leave certain matters unexamined. We
are, thereby, "in denial," or suffering from this or that "problem."
Ibsen's pushy idealist wants psychological confrontation because he
believes in its worth, its promise of progress, of enlightenment —
and consequently, people who have learned to accommodate one another, trust one another, are now turned into frightened enemies.
Psychological factuality, interpretations and more interpretations, Ibsen shows us, can do away with a learned, a lived civility, make for
an overwrought self-consciousness that stifles human spontaneity and
prompts a prickly doubt of anyone's motives and reasons, including
one's own.

Ibsen is interested, finally, in the truth of the human heart — his
play *The Wild Duck* warns us that speakers (prophets, observers, and
interpreters of others) had best learn to listen humbly to those being
addressed, if not hectored, lest a ruinous rant, delivered in the jargon
of, say, psychology or politics, turn exhortation or clarification into
manipulation, exploitation. We hear a lot these days about the virtues
of psychological insight, less about the need for perspective and, yes,
discretion, as we talk to one another and about one another. Manners

are not necessarily a cover-up of sorts, a show, a sham, an affectation; rather, they can give us some restraint with one another, so that we take care to be watchful, considerate — hesitant to let our loose tongues become the proverbial bull in the room full of china. We are ever so vulnerable, all of us, in our time to the various speculations of others, put to word — our wild analytic intrusions become a bullet to the wild duck of our hearts and minds. Psychology can become an authoritative kind of cruel gossip, so a Norwegian playwright realized generations ago — and some of us have yet to learn that lesson.